GROWING LEADERS

A Leader-Builder Handbook for:

- **HRD and Training Professionals**
- **Business Executives and Managers**
- **Executive Coaches**

PRICEWATERHOUSE COOPERS

Steve Yearout and Gerry Miles

with Richard Koonce

Foreword by Audrey Weil, *Senior Vice President of America Online*

Linking People,
Learning & Performance

D1315638

Ordering information: Books published by ASTD can be ordered by calling 800.628.2783 or 703.683.8100, or via the Website at www.astd.org.

Library of Congress Catalog Card Number: 2001087841

ISBN: 1-56286-289-8

Contents

Foreword

No More Business as Usual: Why Your Company Must Become a Leader-Builder

People of Earth: A POWERFUL GLOBAL CONVERSATION HAS BEGUN. Through the Internet, people are discovering and inventing new ways to share relevant knowledge with blinding speed. As a direct result, markets are getting smarter—and getting smarter faster than most companies.

> — Rick Levine, Christopher Locke, Doc Searls, and David Weinberger,
> *The Cluetrain Manifesto: The End of Business as Usual* (2000).

We're living in a time when new business realities are putting extraordinary new stress and pressures on leaders. Globalization, e-competition, disruptive new technologies, and rapidly changing business models are all changing the pace and nature of business transactions. In so doing, they are challenging conventional leadership approaches and requiring leaders *at all levels* in companies to operate in brave new ways.

This is happening in virtually all industries, but let me give you an example of how it's affecting mine. In the Internet and e-business worlds, a company cannot afford to take very long today to develop new products or services, or even new policies or processes. The pace of business today won't support it, and customers won't stand for it. They'll simply go elsewhere if you're slow to address their needs or fail to listen to what they're telling you.

At AOL Time Warner and CompuServe, we're acutely aware of this marketplace dynamic. Each member votes with every click of his or her mouse whether to stay with us or to go to another Internet service provider. Moreover, we can get instant feedback from members anytime about whether they like something we're doing. Therefore, we're extremely vigilant about serving our members' unique needs, providing for their specific wants, listening to their individual voices, and continuously reshaping our business to address their requirements.

This emerging new model of doing business—rapid, direct, interactive, continuous—is increasingly the norm (or ideal anyway) in brick-and-mortar businesses and in Internet companies, in places like General Electric, General Motors, and Ford, and in firms like Dell, CompuServe, and AOL Time Warner. At its core, it's about being aligned with your marketplace on a minute-to-minute basis and being in constant "conversation" with that marketplace. Whether you work in banking or chemicals, in aeronautics, hospitality, retail, or pharmaceuticals, this is the model that will increasingly influence how you do business with *your* customers and relate to *your* employees, suppliers, stakeholders, and competitors in the years ahead.

But understand this: The transformation of today's markets into those where the individual consumer or customer is king or queen is putting enormous new pressures on leaders. Globalization is beginning to influence even the smallest of companies; it's forcing all firms to be both "global" and "local" in their operations. Leaders must be able to work both cross-nationally and cross-culturally. As powerful new technologies speed up the pace of business transactions, they are affecting the volatility of stock prices and international markets, sometimes on a minute-to-minute basis. And, as large commercial customers in every industry make ever more complex demands on their suppliers, it's forcing companies to get much better at meeting their customers' needs—and meeting them very quickly.

Not surprisingly, as information and speed increasingly become the currencies of business exchange in all industries, *leadership* today is shifting away from focusing solely on a company's CEO to encompassing whole populations of leaders within an organization who must work closely together every day to meet business goals or to fulfill customer expectations. For that reason, companies are finding they need to take a new, more aggressive, and innovative approach to developing leaders and managing change. Today, for example, leaders in all industries need more robust skills in everything from vision setting and organizational alignment to team building, communications, organizational "energy creation," and change management. This is what it takes to create and sustain agile business enterprises over the long term. Today, doing these things could very well prove critical to *your* company's survival!

Because the need for ever greater speed—in developing new products, exploiting new technologies, penetrating new markets, or serving existing customers—is a reality we all must deal with, the future of all businesses belongs to the swift and brave. Today, any company that fails to heed this is very likely to get killed off by its swifter, braver competitors.

Consider the fate of British-based Barings Bank, which was rendered bankrupt in early 1995 by a rogue trader making electronic stock swaps that caused catastrophic losses in derivatives trading for the bank in Asia. In just two months, the prestigious, 233-year-old Barings, which helped fund the Napoleonic Wars and had as a client the Queen of England, was put out of business when it lost between $1 billion and $4 billion through these electronic transactions, notes Matthew Kiernan in his book, *The Eleven Commandments of 21st Century Management* (1996). It happened because the bank's senior leaders at the time didn't grasp (and the bank's procedures didn't take into account) that in an age when computer keystrokes enable instantaneous capital flows across national borders it had the potential to alter the fortunes of a 200-year-old British institution virtually overnight.

So, what is the moral of this story? Barings Bank was killed because it didn't keep up with the rapid changes affecting its industry and because its leaders didn't anticipate how these changes could ultimately impact their firm. You don't want the same thing to happen to your company. So, how do you avoid it?

I recommend you read *Growing Leaders: A Leader-Builder Handbook for HRD and Training Professionals, Business Executives and Managers, and Executive Coaches* to find out. This powerful new book—a "technical manual" to leadership development and organizational change—provides a road map to help your organization's leaders understand the kinds of leadership issues your organization may be struggling with right now. It also suggests how individual leaders can develop new skills and new tools to succeed in today's new, speeded-up economy. Indeed, it provides a wealth of advice and approaches you can use, not just to build a strong leadership community within your walls but also to increase your organization's speed, agility, profitability, and productivity.

We're living in exciting times. Not only are we witnessing an explosion of new knowledge and new technology, but we're also seeing those forces drive the fundamental redesign of our organizations and the radical transformation of our markets. The future looks bright for those organizations (and leaders) that can adapt to operate in our new economy. That's the key: creative adaptation to the new and emerging business realities of today.

I'm confident that by reading *Growing Leaders* and applying the tools it contains that your organization can harness its people and resources to compete in this new business environment and achieve world-class excellence as a result. This book will help you and your organization develop the confident, self-aware leaders that will be key to your organization's future success and profitability. What's more, it will provide you the tools to ensure continuous organizational growth and renewal as well.

Audrey Weil
Senior Vice President of America Online
General Manager, CompuServe

Introduction: Leadership Is No Longer a Solo Act

If in the 1950s you asked a corporate CEO for a definition of leadership, you might have heard a middle-aged, white, Anglo-Saxon Protestant male say, "It's about building commitment to business objectives, having personal convictions and self-confidence as a leader, communicating your goals and expectations to employees, controlling the bottom-line expenses of the company, and dealing mortal body blows to your competition in the marketplace."

In the 1980s (the decade of downsizing and the end of the "implied employment contract"), if you put the same question to another CEO, you might have heard him (or her) use different words: "Leadership is about encouraging collaboration in the workplace (that is, building teams), creating new workplace contracts with employees, undertaking corporate reengineering or restructuring efforts, and reducing cycle times."

Today, of course, you hear business leaders describe leadership in still other terms: "Leadership is about managing a company through marketplace chaos and industry convergence," says the 26-year-old CEO of a new dot.com with a price-to-earnings ratio of 150 to one. According to the 34-year-old female director of the international division of a *Fortune* 100 company, "Leadership is about growing your organizational competencies in new areas, rising to the challenges of globalization, and making the transition to the e-business model." Leadership, for an African American CEO preparing to take his start-up, high-technology company public, means "balancing the need to be both a 'click-and-mortar' company and positioning ourselves for an initial public offering six months down the line." Different decades have led to different ideas about corporate leadership. In our view, however, the focus of modern leadership cannot be limited to any of the scenarios just described. Stated otherwise, it is not enough to focus simply on solving today's business problems. Instead, it must focus on the future and on developing the capacity to deal with a growing array of new business challenges. For these reasons, senior leaders today (be they in the private, public, or nonprofit sector) must increasingly concern themselves with nurturing a strong *community* of leaders at all levels in their organizations—not simply in the executive suite.

Creating such leadership communities is not easy, but it has never been more critical to business success. The following are some reasons why:

- ✿ Today's business leaders must deal daily with challenges such as globalization, turbulence in emerging markets, and overcapacity in mature markets, and all this under the watchful eye of the business press and Wall Street community.

- ✿ They must contend with the disruptive influence of new technologies (the Internet, for example) that is rapidly changing the nature and pace of business transactions and radically reconfiguring how people work, think, learn, create, and solve problems.

- ✿ They must lead increasingly diverse, often far-flung workforces and manage new growth all the while championing greater ethnic, racial, and sexual inclusiveness, and showing greater sensitivity to wage and working conditions in foreign countries and to the environment.

- ✿ They must grapple with the reality that "authority"—in its most traditional, top-down workplace sense—no longer exists as it once

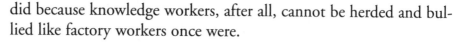

did because knowledge workers, after all, cannot be herded and bullied like factory workers once were.

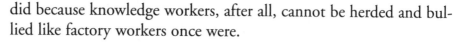 Today's business leaders and their organizations must increasingly struggle with how best to develop and grow their "intellectual capital" because in a knowledge economy, knowledge workers are both expensive to hire and tough to retain.

These business issues are simultaneously global and local, tactical and strategic, technical and high-touch, chronic and quick-changing. No individual working alone can possibly address all of them. Corporate leadership is no longer a solo act. Today, leaders must "act through other people," says James O'Toole, author of *Leadership from A–Z* (1999). And, as author Peter Senge (1990) has suggested, it is time that we give up the notion of "hero" CEOs. Senge notes that the notion of the "hero CEO" is limited in its organizational usefulness particularly today. "Especially in the West, leaders are *heroes*—great men (and occasionally women) who rise to the fore in times of crisis. So long as such [hero-leader] myths prevail, they reinforce a focus on short-term events and charismatic heroes rather than on systemic forces and collective learning."

We agree. Today's business issues are highly complex. Dealing with them requires a team leadership approach. Over the decades, the idea of organizational leadership—truly effective, compelling leadership—has evolved to encompass a concept that is both basic and sublime. Leadership today is about cultivating and nurturing a strong *community of leaders* within the organization's concrete (and virtual) walls—a community that can serve as both the engine and brain trust to drive, guide, and shape an organization's fortunes. Creating such a leadership community is not easy, but it has never been more critical to a company's success because today's top business leaders are under greater pressure than ever to perform, all the while dealing with unprecedented change.

Given these facts, we argue that the first priority of today's leaders is to *develop other leaders at all levels* in their organizations. That is where you come in. We wrote this book to assist OD consultants, HRD professionals, executive coaches, and trainers who increasingly are being called upon to help develop leadership communities within their organizations. *Growing Leaders* provides tools and methodologies that you can use not only to assist your organization with leadership development and coaching efforts but also to accelerate and enhance that process.

Our experience as consultants has taught us that today's most successful companies are those that make a strong commitment to leadership development *at all levels,* not just in the executive suite. Such "leader-builder" organizations:

- ✿ display a strong commitment to leadership development training and development

- ✿ have a strong leadership development "architecture" in place to ensure the consistency of their efforts

- ✿ focus consistently on grooming established leaders and on recruiting and growing new leaders

- ✿ possess deep talent pools and robust talent pipelines that help ensure continued organizational vitality and marketplace competitiveness

- ✿ are deeply committed, on philosophical and practical levels, to enhancing existing organizational capabilities and developing new competencies when necessary

- ✿ exhibit organizational nimbleness and the ability to manage continuous organizational renewal.

The result is that leader-builder organizations (many of which you will meet in this book) are typically showplaces of profitability, organizational vitality, strong internal alignment, and world-class business performance. Characterized by high levels of productivity, collaboration, creativity, top team unity, and innovation, they are also natural magnets attracting new management and leadership talent.

Unfortunately, many otherwise profitable and productive companies today face leadership dilemmas: Because of rapid change, many suffer from one or more organizational problems, any one of which can sap it of productivity or limit profitability. We have identified seven such leadership "challenges" in *Growing Leaders.* These challenges are

- ✿ poor organizational vision

- ✿ inconsistent leadership behaviors

- ✿ lack of a sufficient talent pool and pipeline

❁ insufficient (or obsolete) leadership competencies

❁ bad internal alignment

❁ lack of top team unity

❁ inability to manage effective change.

Dealing with these leadership challenges is critical if organizations are to realize their fullest potential. *Growing Leaders* offers seven ways that you and your organization can effectively address these challenges through the leadership training and development programs you are tasked to build. You and your organization's leaders will be able to assess your organization's leadership challenges, come up with strategies to address them, and build a strong, vibrant leadership community to solve them.

The leadership development and coaching approaches and methodologies outlined in this book are based upon the extensive client experiences of PricewaterhouseCoopers consultants working in the United States and the United Kingdom. They exemplify some of the most innovative and progressive approaches to leadership development being used in companies today; the approaches used are both time-tested and "client-proven." Think of this book as a handbook you can use to "grow and groom" your own population of leaders and build vital core competencies in your organization.

To make *Growing Leaders* a user-friendly reference, it offers a wealth of assessment exercises, sidebars that delve into selected areas in greater depth, case studies, and recommendations based upon our consulting experience. You can use these "tools" to transfer this book's concepts and ideas to your own leadership development programs. You and your organization's leaders will be able to assemble a factual (rather than anecdotal) base of organizational knowledge about your organization's leadership capabilities and the challenges you face. Use them to help guide critical, data-driven decisions about leadership development needs both now and in the future.

Finally, we have provided tips and suggestions about what you, as an OD consultant, HRD professional, or trainer, can do to continuously hone your own professional skills as a leadership development coach. The roles of OD and HRD professionals are evolving so rapidly today that you, as an individual, must continuously reexamine your own professional perspectives and aggressively develop new skills to remain effective to the clients you serve.

You, as an OD or HRD professional, have a critical role to play in framing the debate about leadership issues within your organization and helping your company come up with appropriate solutions. Indeed, it may well fall to you to raise the consciousness of senior leaders in your organization about the leadership challenges your company faces. On the other hand, your company's leaders may already recognize the leadership challenges and are simply looking for tools to help them act on them.

Either way, *Growing Leaders* can serve as a ready reference and road map to help you and your firm's top leaders tackle the specific leadership challenges facing your organization at this point in its history.

So, go for it!

Part One

The Challenges of
Modern Corporate
Leadership

— 1 —

Is Your Company Suffering From a Leadership Crisis?

Most executives remain astonishingly provincial and insular in their outlook, training and experience. This is particularly true for North American CEOs, even in such ostensible hotbeds of business innovation and creativity as Silicon Valley. I am constantly amazed by the number of otherwise brilliant Silicon Valley executives whose world view barely reaches to the other end of the San Andreas fault line. (On a really good day, it might extend as far east as the Hudson River.)

— Michael Kiernan, *The Eleven Commandments of 21st Century Management* (1996).

As every businessperson knows, the leadership demands on today's executives and managers are growing more numerous and complex every day. Globalization, the sustained management of corporate growth, the need to deal with disruptive new technologies, and the need to leverage the benefits of e-business are all requiring a robust new repertoire of leadership skills in today's leaders—at virtually *all* levels in organizations.

This challenge is leaving many companies gasping, not just for executive-level leaders who can chart new business strategies, woo investors, and court closer favor with Wall Street, but also for midlevel managers who possess high-demand skills in Internet commerce, cross-cultural communications, capital markets, and corporate transformation.

The November 8, 1999, cover story in *Fortune*, for example, describes the problems facing old-line companies like Sears, Whirlpool, and Procter & Gamble as they try to grasp the essentials of e-business. The cover shows Arthur Martinez, the Sears CEO, cheek to jowl with the youthful, creative chief of Sears.com Michael Vaughan. The "marriage" of the two was precipitated by the late entry of Sears into Web commerce, the article notes. That fact is forcing many companies, Sears among them, to align traditional leadership approaches with the work styles (and lifestyles) of technology-fluent Generation Xers, who are conversant in online buying habits and Internet-only branding issues.

Meanwhile, far from the *Fortune* 500 (at the other end of the corporate food chain, in fact), many dot.coms are facing leadership challenges of their own today, specifically when it comes to attracting star senior executives to engineer big-time Internet launches and strategic alliances with other firms. The October 26, 1999, edition of *The Wall Street Journal* reported that anywhere from 400 to 1,500 CEO vacancies exist at Internet start-ups today. This gap exacerbates the challenges faced by more and more of these Web companies as they move toward initial public offerings (IPOs) and struggle to compete in the still-virgin marketing frontier of online commerce.

As if these stories were not evidence enough of a burgeoning leadership problem in business today, what should we make of all the CEO "failures" of the 1990s: Eckhard Pfeiffer at Compaq, Bob Stempel at General Motors, and Bob Allen at AT&T, to name three? Consultants Ram Charan and Geoffrey Colvin (1999) concluded recently that these and many other former high-flying CEOs failed because they could not execute strategy, did not put the right people in the right jobs, or, in other cases, did not understand the changing nature of their markets.

Are We Facing a Leadership Crisis?

Clearly there *is* a leadership problem (perhaps a crisis) in the corporate world today for all companies whether they are old-line or online, old guard or upstart. This problem is not likely to disappear anytime soon. For while the pace at which business is conducted today is accelerating, and the amount of "knowledge capital" required to bring new products to the market keeps growing, the competitive interval considered "reasonable" to launch new products, implement new strategies, even complete mergers/acquisitions (M/A) is shrinking. Five years ago, a typical M/A in the high-technology industry took six to nine months to complete. Today that same deal is sealed in days or even hours (McLean, 1999). As for the shortening product development cycle, "Today, the only reliable way to make the proverbial better mousetrap is to embed more knowledge-value in it than your competitor does, and to be prepared to come out with a new, improved and even more knowledge-rich version before the competition has figured out your last one" (Kiernan, 1996).

The Challenge for Training and Development Professionals

In your role in HRD, OD, training and development (T&D), or as an executive coach, you may already have been touched by the leadership crunch your company is facing as it struggles to move faster to market or as it deals with shrinking profit margins or a rapidly shifting business climate. Perhaps you have been asked to introduce a new generation of leadership development programs in your company or to help it get a handle on growing skill gaps in its management ranks. Maybe you have found yourself having to coach your organization's top leaders as they tried to reframe the company's strategy, get a handle on Web commerce, come up with better ways to motivate people, or embark upon a long-range, comprehensive culture change effort. Did you have the tools you needed or even the perspective with which to undertake such efforts?

The specific leadership challenges companies face today typically fall into seven key areas. Take a look at these seven challenges and think about how your own T&D programs for leaders prepare them to meet the challenges described. Do your programs provide leaders with ways to develop a clear vision of the future? Do your leadership development programs deal with the devastating effects caused by leaders who are inconsistent in how they present their vision?

Leadership Challenge 1: Lack of Clear Vision or Future Direction

Many companies today lack a clear vision and sense of their future direction. The reasons are numerous. Change is taking place on a tectonic level and scale in business today, making it hard for any company to develop strong business insight about the future: where its customers, markets, competitors, and suppliers are going to be five months much less five years from now. Moreover, much of the change that is taking place today is of a *discontinuous* nature. Companies are scrambling to find the competitive high ground in today's "new economy." Technical breakthroughs, scientific discoveries, rapid emergence of new competitors, and a host of other factors (economic volatility and industry convergence) can reconfigure marketplace dynamics overnight. The competitive milieu changes monumentally with each announcement of yet another strategic alliance between former competitors or another big industry merger (for example, AOL and Time Warner).

No wonder organizations lose their way or fail to see new market opportunities in front of them. Because this is happening more today, however, it is essential that companies develop the ability to do strategic visioning and re-visioning on a regular basis if they hope to survive through this first decade of the 21st century. The outcome of that visioning must be the development of organizational foresight that a company can then use to stay ahead of its competitors. Any senior leadership team "that [does not make] a substantial investment in creating industry foresight will find itself at the mercy of more farsighted competitors" (Hamel & Prahalad, 1994). That foresight needs to be based on "deep insights into the trends in technology, demographics, regulation, and lifestyles that can be harnessed to rewrite industry rules and create new competitive space" (Hamel & Prahalad, 1994).

For that reason, chapter 3 provides powerful process tools that can help you and your company undertake the "visioning process" to create a new organizational vision and strategy, or to better align people and processes behind *existing* business goals or corporate priorities.

Leadership Challenge 2: Conflicting Behaviors

Another leadership challenge that paralyzes organizations today is the problem of conflicting behaviors which, when magnified across the full spectrum of an organization, can form the basis for a dysfunctional or grossly under-performing corporate culture. Conflicting (or inconsistent) behaviors are a common problem inside companies today. Often, for example, CEOs will call in consultants to help them orchestrate large-gauge organizational change or merger integration efforts. The consultants may find that members of the company's top management team do not agree about how best to proceed with change plans. In other cases, top executives are displaying inconsistent behaviors about the company's priorities, the result being that change messages do not cascade down the organization very well or that employees receive mixed messages about where the company is going. In other cases, the consultants may find members of senior management teams actively resisting the need for change or even sabotaging the company's change efforts before they get off the ground.

Conflicting behaviors can be difficult for a company to root out. Although *active* resistance to change can be addressed forthrightly, it is harder to deal with individuals or groups who *passively* resist change, who mouth agreement with new business goals and directions, but who actually do little to commit themselves to new ways of working. The problem of conflicting behaviors in organizations is further compounded by the fact that in many cases such behavior has been enabled for long periods. A company's top leader may not have known how to deal with it or may have been unwilling to deal with it forthrightly. Doing so takes courage. It also takes tremendous tenacity, more than many top leaders have the stomach for.

An organization suffering from the problem of inconsistent behaviors must use such tools as team-building programs, multirater evaluation instruments, and 360-degree feedback to assess whether leaders at different levels are working synchronously with one another or sending mixed messages to employees, thereby stifling productivity, diminishing morale, and keeping the company from embracing new business goals or strategies. Consequently, chapter 4 discusses these transformation tools in depth and outlines how you can use them to align the behavior of your organization's leaders to support new or emerging business goals and strategies.

Leadership Challenge 3: An Inadequate Talent Pool and Pipeline for Future Leaders

Yet another challenge faced by many organizations today is an inadequate leadership pool and talent "pipeline" from which to draw future generations of leaders or even replacements for people who retire or go to work for competitors. This lack of strategic leadership depth is a problem for several reasons:

❁ Even the most admired companies (for example, Microsoft and Dell Computer) have trouble retaining top-flight executive talent today in the extremely tight job market. An article in *BusinessWeek* by Michael Moeller with Victoria Murphy (1999) pointed to the "brain drain" that has occurred at Microsoft as recruiters have pillaged the company in search of CEO prospects to head up Web upstarts.

❁ Many managers promoted through management ranks today continue to be promoted for technical competence rather than for their "soft" (leadership/people) skills even though these "soft" skills (the essence of emotional intelligence) are increasingly viewed as essential in building new companies and leading diverse work teams.

❁ Many companies have become overly reliant on headhunters and have grown complacent about growing in-house leadership talent.

❁ The downsizing legacy of the 1980s, which derailed traditional career tracks inside many corporations, has, in many cases, never been replaced in these companies with new, more functional approaches to growing and grooming new leadership talent even though companies may have long since recognized the need for it.

New leadership development (LD) initiatives, especially aggressive recruitment, retention, and succession plans, are typically called for in companies that lack strong leadership depth. Such plans can ensure continuity when key executives or product champions leave. They can also be important when it comes to attracting new capital investment and wooing the goodwill of analysts on Wall Street.

Many firms don't make leadership development a priority until dramatic drops in productivity or profitability register on the radar screens of the company's board of directors or until the firm loses what has been a long-held position of marketplace prominence.

To help you and your organization lay the foundation for strong succession planning and leadership development programs, chapter 5 focuses on how to develop a framework for reinvigorating existing LD programs and/or establishing new programs (and succession plans) when necessary.

Leadership Challenge 4: Insufficient or Obsolete Leadership Competencies

In many organizations today, little effort has been made to systematically grow *new* organizational competencies that can serve as the foundation for the firm's future competitiveness. The loss of cutting-edge core competencies can occur in companies for the following reasons:

- gradual loss of funding for LD programs over a period of years

- organizational restructuring that fragments the development or deployment of leadership training

- loss or absence of a strong LD champion inside the organization

- hyper-rapid industry change that alters the nature of a whole industry in a short period of time.

Given these realities, it is increasingly important that companies both protect and enhance their core competencies to remain competitive. One way to do this is by establishing a core competency "agenda" and making it the cornerstone for new LD initiatives and training programs. Another thing organizations must do is use a variety of training approaches and modalities—everything from Web-based training to action learning to one-on-one coaching and mentoring—to effectively tailor LD programs to the diverse needs of individual leaders and, in some cases, entire leadership populations within organizations today.

If you believe your organization has work to do when it comes to developing new in-house leadership competencies, you must first help it:

- define what its emerging leadership competency requirements are

- identify skill gaps that are hindering the company's ability to compete in the marketplace

- identify specific LD approaches and modalities that are most likely to help the organization rapidly develop new leadership capabilities

- determine how to achieve these outcomes as rapidly as possible.

Leadership assessment initiatives and competency assessment instruments are extremely valuable tools that you and your organization can use for these purposes. Also critical to success is the degree to which your company:

- ✿ makes continuous learning for everyone a core organizational value

- ✿ systematically translates new knowledge and know-how into new practices and processes

- ✿ holds all leaders of the organization responsible for the continual recruitment, grooming, and coaching of new populations of leaders.

How to address the problem of inadequate or obsolete leadership competencies is a topic covered in chapter 6.

Leadership Challenge 5: Lack of Organizational Alignment

Still another leadership challenge facing many companies today occurs when different business units or divisions are not properly aligned with one another to support overarching business goals. In other cases, an organization's lack of alignment can reveal itself in management practices that are at odds with new leadership approaches, in performance appraisal systems that fail to evaluate employees based on new work requirements, or in workplace technology that keeps people from working in more efficient ways.

Poor organizational alignment, often the result of downsizing, the sale (or acquisition) of individual businesses, or poor merger integration that leaves an organization in disarray, can negatively affect a company in many ways. Consider what former AlliedSignal CEO Larry Bossidy discovered when he took over the helm as CEO of that company back in 1991. At the time, AlliedSignal was losing money and far from living up to its potential. The company comprised three separate divisions, each of which was an amalgam of previously acquired or merged companies. Bossidy diagnosed the problem as a lack of alignment. In an interview, he said that the company:

> . . . had a curious internal focus. So many things had happened in terms of putting these businesses together that it got a big kick out of analyzing itself, and I thought it had taken its eye off the external environment

which was moving at a rapid pace. It was [also] steeped in technology, yet the time it took to get products to market was way beyond the competitive need. It took pride in being separate companies as opposed to being joined. And its financials [were not] what the public expected; specifically [there was] poor margin performance across all three businesses, hemorrhaging [of] cash as opposed to [the] generating [of] it, and more debt than it should have had, in terms of the size of the company and its ability to realize on [its] potential options. (Tichy & Cohen, 1997)

Solving the problem of poor organizational alignment requires that an organization consciously articulate a new framework of operating principles so that various organizational components—from management practices and workplace technology to organizational structure and mission and strategy—can be harmonized to work synchronously. That was the strategy put into place by Bossidy at AlliedSignal in the early 1990s.

Leadership development efforts become a critical component in helping to achieve this harmonization of organizational parts, which typically takes time and the resolve of top-level leadership to accomplish and sustain. In cases where an organization lacks good alignment, LD efforts typically focus on building leadership competencies in the areas of project management, quality assurance/metrics, conflict resolution, and policy/program deployment. Companies also must emphasize clear, consistent, and frequent executive communication with employees and use of appropriate, effective methods (quality programs and Six Sigma, for example) to drive tight alignment of people's behaviors with business goals. Chapter 7 focuses on how you can create stronger organizational alignment within your company and how LD efforts and approaches are pivotal to achieving this.

Leadership Challenge 6: Lack of Senior Leadership Team Unity

Lack of senior leadership team unity within an organization can have devastating effects on employee morale and organizational productivity and profitability. Often precipitated by the departure of certain key leaders (for example, the CEO, chief financial officer, chief information officer, or a strong product champion), it can cause an organization to drift and to lose quickly marketplace position or competitive strength. Lack of team unity often results when organizations have been restructured without any new organizational vision or mission having been articulated to support it. It also occurs when various business units compete with one another; when executives or managers who operate as "Lone Rangers" fail to cooperate across functional lines in a company; or when there is no strong tradition of team leadership, especially at a workplace level in the organization. Under these circumstances, LD programs become critical in helping to solidify and codify management practices, leadership approaches, and a game plan to carry the organization forward and unify all operating units or business divisions.

Specific LD approaches used in such cases often include 360-degree feedback, executive coaching, communications coaching, and other interventions designed to increase the efficiency and productivity of leadership teams. Chapter 8 deals with the topic of senior leadership team unity and how to make it a reality in your organization or company.

Leadership Challenge 7: Inability to Initiate and Sustain Change

Perhaps the most serious leadership challenge facing companies of all kinds today is the inability to initiate and sustain successful change. As noted earlier, today's business climate is extremely turbulent, and a firm's ability to respond even to minor changes in the business climate can have a significant impact on its long-term resilience and organizational viability. Unfortunately, statistics show that up to two-thirds of all change efforts fail or do not meet expectations. This, studies show, is because leaders do not articulate a compelling need for change, fail to allocate sufficient resources to make it succeed, or fail to create the required "climate of organizational alignment" to support and sustain change efforts over time.

Change leadership is rapidly emerging as the single most critical leadership competency for corporate leaders to develop today. It is becoming increasingly essential because companies are under growing pressure to

❁ develop new business models quickly in response to rapidly developing new technologies (the Internet, for example) and shifting customer requirements

❁ acquire or develop new organizational competencies (branding and e-business expertise, rapid alliance development, customer management, and so forth) to support implementation of these new models

❁ restructure large parts of their existing organizations to support new kinds of relationships and transactions with outsourced suppliers and manufacturers

❁ redesign people's jobs (and performance recognition systems) to support new ways of working with customers, suppliers, and one another.

To help companies acquire the change leadership competencies they need in today's harsh business climate, a growing number of change leadership programs today focus on

❁ building strong, top level leadership commitment to change as a core business principle

❁ developing entirely new skill sets in senior leaders (in collaboration, cross-border alliance building, and strategic partnering, for example)

❁ coaching leaders at all levels who, in many cases, are initiating highly unpopular changes in organizational culture and business approaches. (Such programs typically involve a strong contract of commitment between key executives and the executive coaches or counselors on whom they rely for these kinds of training and coaching interventions.)

The Costs of Ineffective Leadership

Do any of the seven leadership challenges describe the state of affairs in your company? Have you already been called on, perhaps, to develop programs or services to address one or more of these leadership challenges in *your* organization?

In today's rapidly changing business environment, the costs associated with poor or weak leadership cannot be underestimated. It affects virtually all organization stakeholders: employees, stockholders, customers, and others. Poor or weak leadership has led to the premature death of more than a few companies over the years.

Because the consequences of ineffective leadership are huge and growing bigger all the time, many companies are moving beyond the notion of traditional leadership "training" to embrace a new concept called leadership coaching and development (LCD). The LCD approach is the best way to position themselves for the future, build leadership capacity, and create the marketplace edge necessary to compete in increasingly crowded and competitive environments.

Essentially LCD is a leader development approach in which an organization commits itself, in a *strategic and systematic way,* not just to training and preparing a small coterie of leaders at the very top of the organization, but to the ongoing development of leaders across all levels and lines of the business.

Focusing LCD at Two Levels

Leadership development and coaching efforts in organizations can be concentrated at what change management consultant and author Warner Burke of Teachers College, Columbia University, describes as both the large-scale "transformational" level, and the so-called "transactional" or workplace level "where an organization's actual, everyday work gets done."

In Burke's view, the goal of providing leadership coaching and development at the transformational level in an organization is "to equip a company's senior leaders with the tools and skills to chart new business directions, develop and adopt new business strategies, or bring about large-gauge changes in organizational culture, using the lever of strong leadership to do so."

On the other hand, the goal of concentrating LCD efforts at the transactional level, that is, at the level of middle managers and process owners, is often "to help restructure operations, accelerate the introduction of new management practices, bolster work unit productivity, facilitate process redesign efforts, or speed introduction of new procedures, systems, or technology."

In many cases, says Burke, an organization will focus LCD efforts at both levels. It all depends "on a company's needs and the environmental challenges (e.g., increased competition, changes in the marketplace balance-of-power among competitors) with which an organization is confronted." (For more details, see also appendix A.)

Whereas traditional leadership development programs focused on equipping CEOs and their senior leadership teams with new skills and tools, LCD efforts represent a more integrated, organization-wide approach to identifying and developing entire "leadership populations" within organizations. The goal of such efforts is to

- improve operating performance

- increase marketplace strength and resilience

- build overall leadership capacity

- help the company fulfill tenets of its core philosophy and business values

- respond to external environmental forces.

Some companies—the leader-builders—do a very good job at LCD. As chapter 2 shows, they systematically link LD efforts with existing or emerging business requirements. They also align organizational resources to ensure the success of such programs. Chapter 2 examines the characteristics of these leader-builder organizations and how their efforts represent specific responses to the seven leadership challenges.

— 2 —

Characteristics of Leader-Builder Organizations

We have to change our fundamental approach...our DNA.
And teaching does that better than any other way I know. With
the teaching programs we've used over the past three years, our
people have delivered $2 billion to our bottom line.

— Jacques Nasser, CEO of Ford Motor Company, in "Driving Change: An
   Interview with Ford Motor Company's Jacques Nasser" (Wetlaufer, 1999).

M any organizations today suffer from leadership deficits because
one or more organizational problems prevent them from developing strong leadership capacity and leveraging strong core competencies. How can a company deal effectively with these problems? How can a company ensure that it puts robust LCD efforts in place to guarantee the continuous development of current leaders and identify, recruit, and groom new ones?

This chapter lists and describes the traits of organizations that consistently do a good job of developing their leadership populations. Concrete illustrations drawn from the business world demonstrate how some companies exemplify these characteristics. A series of assessment exercises is also included that can help you identify and target challenges that your organization faces as it moves along the path to become a leader-builder.

In addition, the chapter provides a list of potential benefits that organizations can realize by conducting leadership assessments. Leadership assessments can play a valuable role in catalyzing discussions about LCD needs within your organization as you develop your own programs. The data you collect by asking these questions can also be used to develop a core competency acquisition plan and to create a sufficiently deep leadership talent pool and pipeline within your company.

Traits of Leader-Builder Organizations

Companies that do the best job of growing and nurturing new generations of leaders today—the leader-builders—are those that keep the themes of change, speed, resilience, and renewal central to their business strategies and their LD philosophies. Typical leader-builders have a number of traits in common (figure 2-1). The following sections enumerate some of these shared characteristics, cite some examples of companies that demonstrate these characteristics, and offer some assessment exercises to gauge where you and your company are on the leader-builder pathway.

Ability to Articulate a Clear Vision of the Future

Leader-builder companies have invested a great deal of time and energy defining what terms such as *vision* and *mission* mean to them and to developing teachable points of view about these concepts to allow them to be cascaded readily throughout all levels of the organization.

Shell South Africa (SSA) is a good example of a company that has spent considerable time and energy in recent years defining what the words *mission* and *vision* mean to SSA employees of all levels. Within SSA today, getting people aligned with new business goals and a new business mission ("Shell will be the Customer's First Choice") are at the core of CEO Errol Marshall's leadership agenda. This is being necessitated by swift changes in the South African economy that are redrawing the consumer demographics "map" of South Africa and motivating the company to get closer to newly

Figure 2-1. The seven traits of leader-builder organizations.

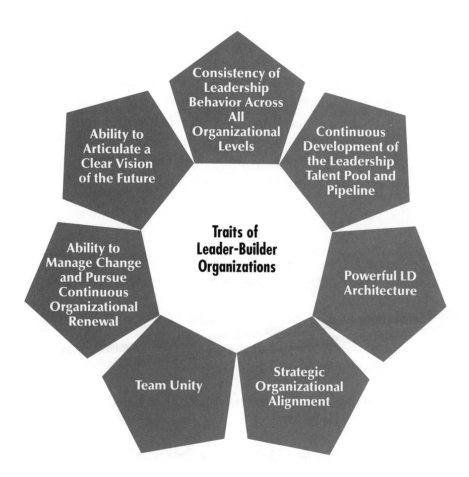

enfranchised black customers who today represent the bulk of the consumer buying power in that country.

To build commitment to change and to align employees behind new business strategies (for example, targeting specific product offerings to specific South African consumer markets), Marshall and his multilevel leadership team spent considerable time in workshops creating what Marshall calls "a common language of change" (Marshall, 1998). This involved fleshing out detailed ideas about how SSA employees could be more responsive in their daily dealings with customers and how the company as a whole could become nimbler in dealing with new market opportunities, as the black consumer market for energy products in South Africa grows more affluent and demanding.

Those ideas are now part of the mindset that all SSA employees apply in doing their daily jobs and fulfilling SSA's new customer mission. "Empowerment of people without alignment breeds chaos," says Marshall. "Our common language of transformation today acts as a framework to keep everyone in the organization moving in the same direction. For example, there are only seven words in our mission statement, but each one of those words has 15 minutes of 'teachable point of view' attached to it" (Marshall, 1998).

You have seen how much time Errol Marshall and employees of Shell South Africa spent on the visioning process. How does your organization compare? Assessment 2-1 can help you gauge how much work needs to be done to build your leadership training programs.

Assessment 2-1. Ability to articulate a clear vision of the future.

Please answer *yes* or *no* to each of the following questions.	YES	NO
1. My organization's leaders do a good job of articulating the organization's vision and strategy for the future.	❑	❑
2. The organization's employees understand the vision for the organization and where it is headed in the future.	❑	❑
3. Employees understand how their daily job roles contribute to the vision of the organization.	❑	❑
4. Employees have concerns about the future direction of this organization.	❑	❑
5. I understand the direction that my organization is taking toward the future.	❑	❑
6. Employees of my organization (at all levels) use common language and terms to describe the organization's future direction and business priorities.	❑	❑

If those whom you queried about the state of leadership in your organization answered "no" to three or more of the above questions about vision, your organization may require assistance with the visioning process. If that is the case, you may want to go directly to chapter 3.

Consistency of Leadership Behavior Across All Organizational Levels

In leader-builder organizations, leaders typically display extremely consistent behavior across all levels of the organization. This helps to drive organizational focus and to create a culture of accountability and commitment.

Executives and managers in leader-builder organizations recognize that displaying consistent leadership habits and behavioral traits fosters trust and telegraphs a powerful message to rank-and-file employees about the degree of leadership consensus that exists around business goals and organizational direction. This makes them credible and effective managers, able to act upon goals and strategies at the "transactional" level in the organization— the level where "actual, everyday work gets done," in the words of change consultant Warner Burke (Burke & Trahant, 2000).

Leader-builder companies send strong signals about the importance of leaders acting in consistent ways regardless of their level. One way they do this is by making frequent use of 360-degree assessments and feedback to build well-rounded leaders and to assess leader behavior on a continuous basis. During an interview with Tichy and Cohen (1997), General Electric CEO Jack Welch asserted his support of 360-degree assessments as a way to drive new behaviors in people. "You ought to see these 360-degree evaluations. They're the roughest evaluations people can get." Thus, "You've got to have self confident people [as leaders] because people hear things about themselves that they've never heard before," according to Welch. That sentiment is echoed by Bill Weiss, former CEO of Ameritech, who says that 360-degree assessments (with peers, subordinates, and superiors evaluating a leader's work performance) are an extremely valuable way to determine if anyone—including the CEO—is a real performer at work or not (Tichy & Cohen, 1997).

How consistent are leaders' behaviors in your organization? Does everybody pull in the same direction? Or, are people at different levels often at odds with each other over business priorities and where the organization is going? Assessment 2-2 offers some questions to help you gauge the consistency of your leaders' behavior.

Continuous Development of the Leadership Talent Pool and Pipeline

In leader-builder companies, there is strong emphasis on the continuous development and replenishment of the leadership talent pool and pipeline.

Assessment 2-2. Consistency of leadership behavior across all organizational levels.

Please answer *yes* or *no* to each of the following questions.	YES	NO
1. All levels of leadership in my organization are in sync with what the organization's top leaders emphasize and do.	❏	❏
2. There is strong leadership consensus within my organization about the organization's priorities, business goals, and strategic direction.	❏	❏
3. Leaders at all levels in my organization are consistent in their management practices, work habits, and workplace attitudes.	❏	❏
4. Leaders at all levels in my organization are held accountable for their behaviors through use of tools such as 360-degree assessments.	❏	❏
5. Leaders within this organization are viewed as credible and honest leaders with integrity.	❏	❏

If you answered "no" to two or more of the above questions about leadership behaviors, your LCD programs may need help with this issue. If that is the case, you may wish to go directly to chapter 4.

The organization publicly demonstrates its strong commitment to developing new generations of leaders with top leaders often modeling the roles of teacher and learner themselves.

Leader-builder companies recognize that in business today learning and leading are closely connected to one another and that both are integral parts of short-term process and profit improvement as well as longer-term organizational renewal and resilience. Thus, in such organizations, one often sees the organization's top leader taking a personal role in the teaching and coaching of others.

In the 1980s, SmithKline Beecham CEO Bob Bauman was very much focused on creating a leader-builder company when he orchestrated the merger between U.S.-based SmithKline Beckman and British-based Beecham to form SmithKline Beecham (SB). To accelerate this transatlantic merger of equals, Bauman put strong emphasis on members of his top management team having intense learning experiences together. One way he did this was to take his entire executive committee to Japan for a two-week field trip, during which time they forged a consensus about future goals and developed hands-on skills in process management and quality assurance that would prove pivotal in speeding SB's merger integration efforts (Bauman, 1998).

Companies such as PepsiCo, General Electric, Honeywell, and Intel are all examples of leader-builder companies that show strong organizational commitment to the ongoing development of new leaders. This commitment is reflected in the fact that their chief executives take regular turns playing the roles of teacher and coach in training classes. It is evidenced too in these companies' constantly-evolving LCD programs, the linkage of the content of such programs with the strategic goals of the company, and the incessantly changing skill requirements of people's jobs.

To what extent does your organization emphasize continuous leadership learning? Use assessment 2-3 to evaluate your organization's efforts to develop new leadership.

Assessment 2-3. Continuous development of the leadership talent pool and pipeline.

Please answer *yes* or *no* to each of the following questions.	YES	NO
1. My organization has made a formal commitment to underscore the importance of leadership development.	❏	❏
2. My organization has systematic LD and succession plans in place to support the continuous growing and grooming of new leaders.	❏	❏
3. Succession plans are linked systematically with recruitment, training, performance evaluation, and promotional procedures in my organization.	❏	❏
4. My organization emphasizes the critical importance of succession plans in helping it to remain competitive in the marketplace.	❏	❏

If you answered "no" to two or more of the above questions about leadership learning, you may wish to go directly to chapters 5 and 10 for guidance on building strong LCD programs in your organization.

Powerful Leadership Development Architecture

Leader-builder companies emphasize the creation of a powerful development architecture to support leadership training and succession planning. They also have a strong, well-developed concept of what effective day-to-day leadership of a company is all about. These beliefs often take the form of leadership operating principles or values that guide the identification, selection, and training of leaders at all levels and provide a philosophical basis for ongoing LD, coaching, and evaluation.

The former AlliedSignal (now part of Honeywell) is an excellent example of a leader-builder company that has developed organizational "intent" about what makes and creates effective leaders. The company uses ongoing development of leaders as an *engine* to drive its research and product development efforts and to achieve aggressive earnings and profitability targets. It has developed a *learning framework* that is the basis for all employee development in the company. Training and development opportunities are all organized under the banner of different "success attributes." Each attribute is viewed as critical to supporting the company's business values. There are 10 attributes. Among them are customer focus; vision and purpose; bias for action, values, and ethics; innovation, and business acumen (Ramelli, 1999).

As part of Honeywell's effort to be a learning leader, everybody from the CEO on down has a development plan in place. A strong organizational learning ethic drives the organization's T&D efforts at all levels. As former president and chief operating officer Fred Poses (1999) puts it, "I've often said that our buildings are no different from our competitors; nor is our machinery fundamentally different. Certainly our dollars are no greener. The thing that has and will continue to differentiate us from our competitors is our people and what they know." Still, Poses is quick to add that that does not mean the company pursues learning for its own sake. "Too many companies check off the boxes and say they've presented training," he says. "Our learning is targeted. I always ask people, 'Are you getting the right learning to do your job?' I'm always seeking feedback on how we can make our learning better" (Poses, 1999).

How much of an emphasis does your organization place on creating a strong LD architecture to support leadership coaching and development and succession planning efforts? The questions posed in assessment 2-4 can help you evaluate the LD architecture in your organization.

Assessment 2-4. Powerful LD architecture.

Please answer *yes* or *no* to each of the following questions.　　**YES**　**NO**

1. A leadership philosophy exists inside my company to help all employees understand what is expected of them as leaders.　❑　❑

2. My organization explicitly stresses key attributes (e.g., customer focus, bias for action, continuous learning, innovation) of effective leadership to which all leaders are expected to subscribe.　❑　❑

3. This organization uses core leadership attributes as the foundation for its training initiatives, LD programs, and coaching/mentoring efforts.　❑　❑

4. Core leadership attributes are used as the basis for performance appraisal, feedback, and reward and recognition systems inside the organization.　❑　❑

5. My organization is committed to the continuous identification and development of new core competencies necessary to support the company's changing mission and strategy.　❑　❑

If you answered "no" to three or more of the above questions, you may wish to go directly to chapter 6 for help with creating a strong development architecture in your organization.

Strategic Organizational Alignment

Inside today's leader-builder companies, strong organizational alignment prevails. Leader-builder companies are committed to the value of developing a broad leadership community and to working from an explicit leadership agenda or plan as part of exercising day-to-day and long-term organizational leadership. At the same time, the organization's various organizational components—its mission and strategy, people, processes and technology—are all tightly aligned to support achievement of business goals or organizational aims.

BAE Systems (formerly British Aerospace) is an excellent example of a company that today puts consistent leadership focus on creating a strong climate of organizational alignment to supports its corporate goals. For the past five years, chairman Sir Richard Evans has been working hard to break down a culture of "separate fiefdoms" within BAE Systems, a vestige from the time when diverse competitive companies first came together to form the aerospace giant. To do that, he has driven top-down culture change in the organization and worked to align leaders at all levels within BAE Systems around five core business values:

- ✿ *People* are our greatest strength.

- ✿ *Customers* are our highest priority.

- ✿ *Partnerships* are our future.

- ✿ *Innovation* and *technology* are our competitive edge.

- ✿ *Performance* is the key to winning (Burke & Trahant, 2000).

This new organizational focus is helping BAE compete in a shrinking marketplace for defense and aerospace products as it goes up against much bigger defense players such as Lockheed Martin and Boeing.

How well aligned is your organization to support its current or emerging business goals, vision, and strategy? Use assessment 2-5 to evaluate your organization in terms of strategic alignment.

Team Unity

Underscoring any organization's ability to attain its vision through strategic alignment is the ability for members of its top leadership team to work together synergistically and to put egos and personal agendas aside for the sake of the organization's overarching goals and needs. Top-team unity goes beyond mere teamwork principles; members of the leadership team must consistently speak with one voice and always achieve more than the sum of their parts.

One prominent business leader who exemplifies strong top-team unity in an organization is Lee Griffin, former CEO of Bank One of Louisiana. In the early 1990s, Griffin spearheaded the restructuring and economic recovery of Premier Bank of Louisiana (today Bank One of Louisiana). Though at the time it was a hugely profitable bank, Griffin realized that his institution was not competitive with other financial institutions in its marketplace.

Assessment 2-5. Strategic organizational alignment.

Please answer *yes* or *no* to each of the following questions.	YES	NO
1. My organization's mission and strategy are aligned to support the business priorities articulated by top leadership.	❏	❏
2. Current management practices mirror new or emerging work expectations of employees.	❏	❏
3. In my organization, technology supports current or emerging work expectations.	❏	❏
4. Policies and procedures support new work expectations.	❏	❏
5. All parts of the organization work toward common goals.	❏	❏
6. Employees generally understand how their jobs support business goals.	❏	❏

If you answered "no" to three or more of the above questions, you may wish to go directly to chapter 7 to learn about ways to improve strategic alignment within your organization.

To keep pace with changing demographics and consumer banking habits, Griffin had to oversee the bank's transition from a branch-based banking institution to one that relied far more on technology to deliver an increasing menu of bank services. That meant redesigning many of the bank's core processes (consumer and commercial lending, new accounts, bank office operations, and so forth).

Mindful of the short-lived success of many corporate change efforts, however, Griffin realized he could not simply mandate such changes. He had to get his senior leadership team on board with his ideas. So, he forged a senior team consensus about the new directions that the bank needed to take after holding a series of strategic, executive-level workshops. Griffin and his team engaged in heated discussions about the bank's future, but eventually they thrashed through their differences to establish a new mission, vision, and set of values for Premier. They also agreed to aggressive, measurable new objectives for reengineering the institution. "We needed to get agreement at the top of our organization about the changes we were going to make," says Griffin in retrospect (1998). He says that team commitment proved vital to the eventual success of Premier's reengineering initiative.

To what extent does team unity exist in your organization? Assessment 2-6 can help you answer this question.

Ability to Manage Change and Pursue Continuous Organizational Renewal

Leader-builder companies display a strong commitment to continuous organizational renewal. One way they do this is by developing change leadership skills in leaders at *every* level. In today's business world, where the nature of change itself is continuously changing, the companies most successful at developing new leaders put a premium not only on constant transformation but also on developing new populations of leaders to drive this.

Consider the example of Royal Dutch Shell (the umbrella organization of all Shell operating companies worldwide). A few years ago, after an internal review of Shell's Service Companies showed that company executives were remote from everyday workers, that the company's culture was insular, and that Shell's attitude toward customers was aloof if not arrogant, the

---

Assessment 2-6. Team unity.

Please answer *yes* or *no* to each of the following questions.

	YES	NO
1. Members of this organization's top leadership team are perceived as putting the organization's business agenda ahead of their own egos.	❏	❏
2. Leaders at all levels in the organization work together.	❏	❏
3. Leaders in my organization rise above turf wars and political infighting because of the detrimental effect on team unity.	❏	❏
4. Leaders in the organization understand their roles.	❏	❏
5. My organization's top team works closely together both to brainstorm future business directions and to act on current business issues.	❏	❏

If you answered "no" to three or more of the above questions about top-team unity, you may wish to go directly to chapter 8 for help with this issue.

company embarked on a massive LD effort across all its lines of business. The goal of this effort was to transform the company's culture and make it customer-friendlier while infusing managers with new skills in team-building, communications, speed to market, and performance management and measurement. "The review showed that we lacked a strong commercial capability," says Mac McDonald, former head of Shell's Leadership and Performance (LEAP) operations. "In our products business, we were a retail organization that didn't have much expertise in dealing with customers. In fact, we acted more like a wholesaler than a retailer"(McDonald, 1998).

Today, Shell's Leaders-Developing-Leaders program is based on three main concepts:

- ✿ adhering to the principle of leaders driving transformation efforts by developing *other* leaders

- ✿ delivering hard business results while simultaneously changing individual and team behaviors to assure the sustainability of those results

- ✿ achieving scale and speed—transforming how the company operates on a process level by touching a critical mass of people in a short period of time, thus overcoming the natural resistance to change that exists in any organization.

How committed is your organization to continuous renewal? Moreover, to what extent is there a strong organizational commitment to developing change leadership skills in leaders at every level? Gauge your organization's readiness for change using assessment 2-7.

The Makings of a Leadership Development Road Map

If you use the foregoing seven traits of leader-builder organizations as an LD road map or template, you will be able to get a handle on the specific issues and questions that must be raised by your organization if it is to address effectively its own leadership challenges and become a leader-builder in the 21st century. Use the foregoing discussion and assessment tools as a platform to develop leadership assessment tools to keep your organization's LCD programs on the cutting edge of industry.

Assessment 2-7. Ability to manage change and pursue continuous organizational renewal.

Please answer *yes* or *no* to each of the following questions.	YES	NO
1. Historically, my organization has been good at reinventing itself by staying ahead of the competition.	❏	❏
2. The leaders ensure that my organization responds rapidly and effectively to changes in business conditions, marketplace demands, and customer requirements.	❏	❏
3. My organization is effective at incorporating new knowledge and information into core processes and business practices.	❏	❏
4. The ability to lead others through change is treated as a learnable, critical key management competency by my organization.	❏	❏
5. The actions of the change leaders in my organization demonstrate a high degree of skill.	❏	❏
6. Change management terms and concepts are understood and are freely used in conversations within my organization.	❏	❏

If you answered "no" to three or more of the above questions about organizational renewal and change leadership, you may wish to go directly to chapter 9 for help with these issues.

Applying Leadership Assessment Tools

Each trait discussed in the foregoing sections represents a critical success factor to a company becoming a leader-builder organization and developing and sustaining strong LD initiatives and programs within its walls. By answering these questions, you and your organization's top leaders can determine the scope and severity of the leadership challenges your organization faces and establish where you rank on the corporate leader-builder scale. You can also determine whether there is strong consensus inside your organization about the leadership challenges the company faces, or if people at different leadership levels have different perceptions about what problems exist.

Use the assessments in this chapter as "scratch pad" exercises to initiate the LCD planning process with your organization's senior leadership team and as a way to bring awareness of specific leadership challenges to others within your organization. In constructing questions for your leadership assessment, try to mix questions that involve responses using a graduated (Likert-type) evaluation scale with those that allow you to capture qualitative and anecdotal information as well. Gathering answers to both types of questions will be critical to successful implementation of new leadership initiatives. From the findings you gather, you can establish priorities and target areas of your organization that need special attention if you are planning to introduce new leadership programs or to revitalize existing program offerings.

Benefits You Derive by Conducting a Leadership Development Assessment

Conducting a leadership assessment serves several important purposes:

✿ *It enables an organization's leaders to identify and prioritize specific leadership challenges that must be addressed if the organization is to build stronger populations of leaders at all levels.* By prioritizing areas of concern, the organization will be in a position to roll out plans over a multiyear period, for example, if financial and organizational resources are limited or if other issues show that a phased implementation of leadership programs is indicated for other reasons.

✿ *It enables you to gather and analyze data that can be used to build a compelling business case for why LD initiatives are important to the organization's future.* Too many organizations never develop strategic intent or organizational resolve around the importance of LD because so many other things vie for attention: internal political pressures, competing business agendas, and near-term concerns about business competition. The data you collect from a leadership assessment may show starkly that all these other issues will be moot unless the company develops new leadership skills to steer it into the future.

✿ *It is an excellent way to help you build a stronger working relationship with your company's top management team and with other managers and process owners elsewhere in the organization.* The format and content of questions can be customized and wording altered, depending on the specific audience and level of individuals with whom you are working. This can be important as a way to build trust in the assessment process and build early support for recommendations that may flow from it.

✿ *It sends a strong signal to employees at every level that the organization is serious about LD initiatives.* Moreover, it conveys the importance of employees at all levels taking a leadership approach and attitude in doing their daily jobs. Part of the reason that assessments are a valuable LD tool is that they serve as an "engagement device." Not only do they engage people with the promise that the input they provide will be used to change how things operate, but they can build employee enthusiasm for such an endeavor at the same time.

✿ *Leadership assessments generate a valuable set of data points, both quantitative and qualitative, that can be used in the actual design and implementation of LD initiatives at the programmatic level.* The qualitative and quantitative data gathered from a properly structured leadership assessment can help you identify specific weaknesses (for example, a lack of one-on-one coaching of leaders or the dearth of follow-up appraisal and feedback) in your company's current LD programs. Review of the data will indicate possible remedies and paths for eliminating these problems and give you a strong organizational grasp of what must be done to enhance your organization's ability to develop leaders on a going-forward basis.

Looking Deeper

This chapter has outlined the attributes of leader-builder organizations. It has also detailed a road map (an assessment process) that you and your organization can use to analyze your organization's current leadership capacity and the degree to which the organization possesses the core competencies it needs to remain competitive in the years ahead. More than anything else, however, this chapter provided you with the tools to begin an organizational dialogue within your company about LCD concerns and the questions your company must ask itself as part of building stronger leadership capabilities.

Chapter 3 explores in greater depth the problem of lack of vision that plagues many organizations today and what they can do to address it.

Part Two

The Solutions

The pentagon diagram shows "Traits of Leader-Builder Organizations" at the center, surrounded by:
- Consistency of Leadership Behavior Across All Organizational Levels
- Continuous Development of the Leadership Talent Pool and Pipeline
- Powerful LD Architecture
- Strategic Organizational Alignment
- Team Unity
- Ability to Manage Change and Pursue Continuous Organizational Renewal
- Ability to Articulate a Clear Vision of the Future

— 3 —

What to Do When Your Company Suffers From Poor Vision

The core values embodied in our credo might be a competitive advantage, but that is not why we have them. We have them because they define for us what we stand for, and we would hold them even if they became a competitive disadvantage in certain situations.

— Ralph S. Larsen, CEO of Johnson & Johnson, in "Building Your Company's Vision" (Collins & Porras, 1996).

What do you think it is that makes a company truly successful? Is it leaders, technology, products, or, perhaps, strategy? Because this is a book about leadership development, you might reasonably conclude that, in fact, leadership is the single most important success trait. You would be right with one important qualifier: It is *visionary* leadership that is the key to a company's success.

Contrasting Vision and Mission

What is the difference between vision and mission? In many ways, the differences are subjective and situational, and many people use the words interchangeably. Here, the word *vision* describes where an organization is going and what it is trying to achieve.

In particular, an organization's success depends on its ability to retain an intense focus on customers, competitors, products, and markets. As a training and development professional, you are uniquely positioned to help your organization develop its future leaders, and to help them find the focus they need to succeed. Consequently, this chapter emphasizes the important role that the visioning process plays in any company's success and on how you can help your organization's leaders acquire the visioning skills they need to succeed in the marketplace over the long term.

The following examples of successful companies and their visions will help you guide your organization through the process of developing a vision. Consider the companies that made *Fortune* magazine's 1999 list of America's most admired companies, for example. Number one for the second year in a row, General Electric, won accolades for its continued value as a long-term investment and, of course, for the leadership prowess of CEO Jack Welch who has focused tirelessly on new markets and on process improvement programs like Six Sigma and e-business. Coca-Cola (number two on the list) and Microsoft (number three) received praise for their consistency of financial performance and for their ability to hire and keep top people. Dell Computer (number five on the list) won kudos for its strong focus on selling PCs directly to customers and for providing high levels of customer service, both of which have created legions of loyal customers. Wal-Mart (number nine) garnered enthusiastic reviews for its blockbuster growth (it posted 1999 revenues of $137 billion) and its commitment to measuring how quickly it gets products into its 3,000 stores, not in days or hours but in minutes (Brown, 1999)!

A Passion for What They Do

What do these companies have in common? In a word, each is *unwavering* and *unrelenting* in its focus on business goals. These companies never pass up an opportunity to emphasize their goals. At Dell Computer, for example, the emphasis on "the direct model" of selling and serving customers has become the company's "only religion," according to vice chairman Kevin Rollins. That business focus has enabled founder Michael Dell in just 15 short years to build his company from a fledgling startup (which he began in his college dormitory room) into an $18-billion-a-year business that sells more computers to medium and large companies than companies like IBM, Hewlett-Packard, or Compaq do. The company's focus on "direct, direct, direct" means it can stay in continuous contact with customers, respond quickly to problems, and gather precious customer data and market intelligence used as the basis for everything from work process redesign efforts to development of new products (Brown, 1999).

Meanwhile, at Wal-Mart a similar, relentless focus on customers means the company goes out of its way to keep inventories low, to streamline supply and distribution processes, and to pass on the savings from those efforts to customers. Despite a low-tech image, Wal-Mart has become a master at using technology to manage its distribution processes, track product sales and consumer trends, and supply inventory on a just-in-time basis to some 3,000 stores. The company briefly lost its focus after Wal-Mart founder Sam Walton died in 1993 but has since come roaring back, posting the biggest-ever revenues in its history in 1999 (Brown, 1999).

Just how do companies like Dell Computer and Wal-Mart (or Nordstrom, Nike, Disney, Southwest Airlines, and 3M for that matter—other companies known for their strong visionary focus) develop such clear ideas of what their business is about? It is one thing to describe best-in-class companies that have "the vision thing" down and do it well in their particular market or industry. It is quite another for a company (maybe yours) that is suffering from poor organizational vision or that is struggling to reinvent itself in a changing marketplace to develop a clear vision of where it goes next. Then, that vision must be translated into a set of values, business best practices, and work processes to support achievement of that goal. This chapter can guide you as you help your company develop a stronger organizational focus and vision of its future, if that vision has not always been clear or if your

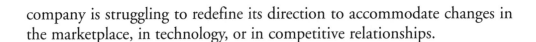

company is struggling to redefine its direction to accommodate changes in the marketplace, in technology, or in competitive relationships.

10 Reasons for a Company to "Re-vision" Regularly (two- to three-year cycles)

1. Changing business climate (globalization, emerging, maturing markets)
2. Failed or floundering business strategy
3. Lack of new business growth
4. Appearance of new competitors
5. Change in the marketplace balance of power among existing competitors
6. Pressure to adopt a new business model (for example, e-business)
7. Emergence of disruptive new technologies (biotechnology, cloning, nanotechnology, and so forth) that alter a company's competitive advantage or marketplace leverage
8. Shareholder dissatisfaction with profit growth
9. Loss of important organizational competencies
10. Lack of internal organizational alignment.

Failure to Vision: Some Cautionary Tales

Given the unprecedented changes taking place in business today—shifts in the business environment precipitated by new technologies, emerging and maturing markets, and other factors that can rapidly alter a firm's competitive position—it is not surprising that a company might lose its way or miscalculate the next big business trend or market development. Many companies do lose their way. For example

✿ Sears misjudged the retail store business back in the 1960s. At the time it was America's preeminent retailer, known for hearty product lines like its Kenmore appliances and Craftsman tools. But, it soon fell victim to boutiques and a growing number of chain stores that offered women consumers (in particular) a wider variety of products, just as women began entering the workforce in droves, buying clothing not just for their families but also for themselves. Only in the last few years have ad campaigns for the retail giant emphasized "the softer side of Sears" and made other attempts to lure women shoppers back to Sears.

❁ IBM is another company that at one point lost its way. Back in the 1980s, it failed to see the market moving toward PCs and away from mainframe computers. Only with the arrival of Lou Gerstner as CEO did IBM begin to get its business house back in order again.

❁ General Motors, too, has faltered in its vision. Back in the early 1980s GM appointed Roger Smith as CEO and was praised widely for doing so. Smith was called a bold and visionary leader. But years later, after GM had fallen behind Ford in earnings for the first time in 60 years, *Business Week* ran a cover story entitled "General Motors: What Went Wrong? Eight Years and Billions of Dollars Haven't Made Its Strategy Succeed" (Bolman & Deal, 1991).

The Characteristics of Truly Visionary Companies

What sets truly visionary companies apart? How do they keep their focus even through times of transition and marketplace turbulence? Visionary companies have a number of things in common, note James Collins and Jerry Porras, authors of the best-selling book, *Built to Last: Successful Habits of Visionary Companies* (1997). First, visionary companies possess a bedrock belief in their business and an uncommon passion about it. These traits are embedded deep in their corporate DNA. Mary Kay Cosmetics, for example, wants "To give unlimited opportunity to women." The Walt Disney Company wants "To make people happy." Wal-Mart seeks "To give ordinary folk the chance to buy the same things as rich people," note Collins and Porras (1996). (To learn more about other visionary companies, see appendix B, which contains some real-world examples of goals and vision/mission statements.)

Second, visionary companies navigate today's treacherous and turbulent business world with uncommon deftness, adapting their strategies, operating goals, and culture as necessary while remaining true to an enduring set of values. Perhaps other things will change for these companies (their leaders, products, management practices, even their culture) but not their fundamental focus. That focus is their ultimate reason for being in business in the first place.

Third, visionary companies possess a core ideology (from which their values spring), which is unchanging and which transcends immediate customer demands or market conditions. Remember the words of Johnson & Johnson CEO Ralph Larsen at the beginning of this chapter? The "unifying" ideology of visionary companies guides and inspires people, according to Collins and Porras (1997), more than it differentiates a company from its competition or gives it leverage in the marketplace. Coupled with an intense, "cult-like" organizational culture, it also creates enormous solidarity and esprit de corps.

Finally, visionary companies subscribe to what Collins and Porras (1997) describe as "big, hairy, audacious goals" (BHAGs) that galvanize people to come together, to team, to create, and to stretch themselves and their companies to achieve greatness over the long haul. Visionary companies commit themselves to stretch goals that may take 10 to 30 years to accomplish (as when the National Aeronautics and Space Administration decided in the early 1960s to put a man on the moon before 1970). "BHAGs grab people," notes Audrey Weil, senior vice president of AOL. "They act as catalysts for team spirit and individual motivation" and often help people move "to the next level of productivity" in their organization (Weil, 2000).

Aligning the Organization to Support the Vision

Once there is clarity and agreement among your organization's leaders about where they want to take the organization, the challenge is to enlist the help of employees to get there. There is in fact an "infrastructure" that leaders must put in place to ensure successful implementation of a new vision, and you must help them do it. The following are some of the infrastructure's component parts:

✿ *Create a feeling of urgency around the visioning process.* Leaders must create "positive tension" by contrasting where the organization is today with where the organization needs to be in the future. When metrics can be used to make this tension obvious to employees, use them.

✿ *Help your organization's leaders harness the power of ideas, symbols, and stories to articulate the new corporate vision.* Look at today's most effective leaders and you will see people who are good at manipulating and using symbols to get their points across. Ronald Reagan's evocation of the "shining city on the hill" is an example of an effective word picture to describe where he wanted to go. John F. Kennedy Jr. evoked the same passion and energy in people when he talked about America going to the moon. Martin Luther King was a master at galvanizing the energy and support of others in pushing for civil rights for African Americans. In helping your organization's leaders articulate a new vision for your organization, help them to use ideas and words effectively to convey where they want to take the organization.

✿ *Involve those who will be most affected by changes in the change process.* You and your company's leaders must design organizational structures and change initiatives so that they provide those who will be most affected by change with the opportunity to influence change plans and action steps. Everybody in the organization should have the opportunity to have his or her voice heard, to offer feedback and input, and to voice concerns or comments as part of the visioning process.

✿ *Know when to move fast and when to go slow.* New leaders are often under tremendous pressure to make changes quickly, and there are times when it's best to act fast (to make personnel changes or terminate programs, for example). At other times, however, leaders must move more slowly to build trust with employees or to get large groups of people to work differently. Help your organization's leaders know the organizational climate and make recommendations about when it is best to vision or re-vision.

Using Strategic Visioning and Process Tools to Discover Your Company's Core Ideology

If, in fact, a company does not *create* its core ideology, but arrives at it through an organic process of self reflection and action planning, it is critical that that company use powerful strategic visioning and process tools to help it periodically re-vision. As part of this iterative process, a company's leaders and its employees must ask themselves why they are in business, what the core philosophy is, and what forms the basis of their company's organizational ideology. That ideology, in turn, affects the company's goals and objectives; how people relate to customers and co-workers; what directions, markets, and products the organization embraces; and how the company wishes to be seen by those outside its walls.

In the past perhaps you were charged—in your role as an OD consultant, T&D professional, or executive coach—to help your organization develop a new vision or mission statement, but the process for some reason did not work. It may have been that there was not enough time allowed for people to contribute both ideas and feelings to the process, so they did not "own" the words of the vision or mission statement. It is possible that people did not feel free to participate fully in the exercise and to offer their own ideas and thoughts. Maybe people thought the whole exercise was simply window-dressing for corporate goals that others had already established.

Cascading the Vision Down Through the Organization

If your organization is to embark on a corporate visioning process in a way that taps people's energy and yields breakthrough commitment to new goals, it must be done the right way. Allow sufficient time for the exercise and make sure people at all levels have a chance to participate in the visioning process. Although visioning workshops typically involve the top echelons of an organization at the very beginning, you must make an effort to involve employees at all levels in some aspect of the visioning process if you expect to gain their trust, involvement, and commitment. Therefore, it is standard operating procedure in most cases, to "cascade" visioning workshops down several levels in an organization, so that you can lay the groundwork for a new set of business goals and objectives based on a broad base of input for such efforts.

This is very hard work. Indeed, it is even harder than it first appears. You cannot, for example, conduct the same kind of visioning work at all levels of the organization, or take the opportunity to reformulate corporate strategy every time you convene a meeting. Instead, as you move down through successively lower levels in the organization, you move from articulating what the vision is to developing plans and taking steps to ensure that the vision is realized (figure 3-1).

At the highest levels of an organization, for example, your work as a facilitator must focus on helping your company's CEO and senior leadership

Figure 3-1. The visioning pyramid.

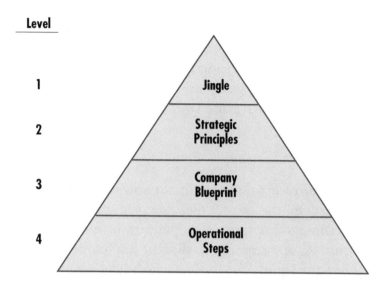

Level

1 — Jingle

2 — Strategic Principles

3 — Company Blueprint

4 — Operational Steps

develop language to describe the new vision (level 1) and articulate the principles upon which pursuit of the new vision is based (level 2). Sometimes level 1 is referred to as "writing the jingle" or describing the company's strategic intent.

As you move further down in the organization, however, and work with middle level managers or process owners, visioning work takes on a different focus. As you engage with project teams, for example, who may be responsible for developing plans to implement the vision (level 3), you must help team members develop detailed implementation "blueprints." At level 4, you will work with implementation managers and teams charged with putting the organizational machinery in place (practices, processes, technology, and so forth) to ensure that the new vision is put into action.

Emphasize the Value of Vision

Stress to workshop participants that the visioning process is not an academic exercise. Rather, it is critical to pointing an organization in new directions and affirming core values that unite people and create organizational resolve. If the goal of the visioning process is for an organization's employees to discover their values, you, as a facilitator, must play an active leadership role in making that happen. Begin the process by challenging your organization to ask (and answer) some challenging questions. For example: "Why are we in business?" "What are the values that really matter to us?" "In what ways do we want these values to drive our daily actions and behaviors with customers?" "What are the overwhelming priorities we face at this point in the life of our company?" The Business Climate Modeling process described later in this chapter (and the question sets associated with it) can help you and your organization drill down and have substantive discussions about the priorities now facing your organization and the drivers of change in the business environment requiring that your company revisit its existing vision and strategy.

Build Consensus

Recognize that in your role as facilitator you must guide discussions so they stay on target. At the same time, however, expect to see conflicting views and ideas come to the fore, as people within your organization storm toward consensus. As any seasoned facilitator knows, helping people reach consensus (about any significant business goal or objective) requires that a group first go through a "storming-and-forming" process before they come to consensus about anything ("norming") and create a set of expectations around which they will then agree (perform). Try to short-circuit this process and you will not build the group cohesion and commitment you need to ensure that a new vision statement for your organization succeeds.

Create a Living Document

Recognize that any vision statement the organization develops must be *relevant* to the needs of the business, *authentic* in what it holds as an ideal, and *clear* in its call to action. If a vision statement has these three attributes, it will become a *living* document that people are willing to talk about after they leave the workshop. It will help to sculpt people's subsequent behavior and influence the development of a new culture inside the organization.

Attributes of Effective Vision Statements

1. Does it motivate and excite people?
2. Does it frame the organization's future and define where the organization is going?
3. Does it embody a "big, hairy, audacious goal"?

4. Is it original?

5. Is it something people can wrap their arms around?

6. Does it elicit a strong word picture (the idea of a "shining city on a hill" for example)?

Become a Lightning Rod for Discussion

Facilitating discussions around vision and values is not easy. As a moderator of discussions about your company's vision and mission, you will need to spur debate among people at times, and, at other times, you will have to move people to come to closure and consensus about what they have been discussing. You may become a lightening rod, from time to time, as the process proceeds. (So, it is important to develop a thick skin!) At the same time, though, you will become a catalyst for change.

Getting Started on the Vision Path

Being an effective facilitator requires that you be viewed as a credible and effective T&D professional inside your organization. In a sense, you will be on stage as the emcee of events, but the real indicators of your success as a facilitator will be the degree to which you:

- engage others in the discussion process

- get people to freely exchange their views with others

- mediate conflicts as they arise

- reframe issues for discussion when necessary

- help the group(s) come to consensus or closure about how to enact the vision or mission upon which they have agreed.

That, in brief, represents the things you must keep in mind as you begin the visioning process in your organization. They hold true, *regardless of the leadership level at which you are working in your organization.* But, to be successful in helping your organization with the visioning process, you also need tools to help you facilitate visioning workshops.

Process tools, such as group facilitation and polling techniques, are an essential component in helping you and your organization implement new strategies and move in new directions. (See appendix C for a description of several powerful tools—polling techniques, electronic meeting technology, and so forth—that you may want to use with various groups in your organization.) Even more important today, however, is applying effective strategic visioning tools that can help you and your organization engage in breakthrough thinking, scenario planning, product "imagineering," and leadership competency building. Using such tools has become essential in today's business world because globalization, rapid growth, and the disruptive influence of new technologies (the Internet, for example) are continuously affecting everything from organization design to the specific leadership competencies a company needs to stay competitive.

An Introduction to the Business Climate Modeling[1] Process

One of the most innovative and useful new tools for strategic visioning is the Business Climate Modeling (BCM) process, a visioning methodology developed by Bill Trahant, a partner with PricewaterhouseCoopers, and W. Warner Burke, of Teachers College, Columbia University, and described in their book, *Business Climate Shifts: Profiles of Change Makers* (2000). Developed in response to the increasing number of "phase shifts" (rapid, discontinuous changes) taking place in today's business environment, the BCM process can be used by companies to discern trends in the external business environment with potentially significant and long-lasting implications for business longevity. Using a technique called "multivector, multivariable" assessment, it analyzes the business environment from the perspective of four key vectors:

- ✿ a technology vector

- ✿ an economic vector

- ✿ a political vector

- ✿ a demographic (consumer/customer/culture) vector (Burke & Trahant, 2000).

---

[1] Business Climate Modeling is a proprietary term of PricewaterhouseCoopers.

Each of the four vectors comprises different variables (drivers) that influence how that vector affects a given industry, company, or the economy as a whole. The aggregate of these individual variables is what creates the overall impact of that vector on a company or industry at any given point in time. The four vectors can be viewed as being positioned on a matrix and as being related both directly and indirectly with each other. An analysis of the four vectors for emerging trends can help an organization answer any of numerous strategic visioning questions with which it may be grappling. Perhaps your company is

- ✿ concerned about how overseas political instability could potentially affect its profitability in emerging markets

- ✿ concerned that a competitor's new technology could eventually leapfrog its own and, thus, fundamentally change the balance of power among business competitors

- ✿ concerned about developing the long-term leadership bench strength it will need to compete in the rapidly emerging world of e-business.

By developing and answering question sets directed along the four vectors, the BCM process can help your company's top leadership team develop an informed and shared point of view about these and other consequential business issues.

The BCM process begins with a company's top leadership team asking itself key questions in each of the vectors and ultimately linking the questions together to create appropriate cross-references to understand the interrelationships of these factors—how disruptive new technologies and economic volatility in emerging markets can affect a company's profit picture, for example, or how political instability in developing nations or new consumer trends in a developed economy does so. These factors have enormous implications for a company's profitability, sustainable growth, market share, and organizational vitality. Leaders need to become aware of the deeply subtle interplay among these vectors in today's global business environment, because emerging trends and long-term currents can be hard to discern, in many cases, or even discontinuous in nature.

Table 3-1 lists some questions directed along the four vectors of the BCM process. These questions might be asked of an organization's leaders as they go about the visioning process. Real question sets (including vector cross-connects) are developed only after intense discussion with a client and determination of specific needs.

Table 3-1. Sample question set built upon the four vectors of the BCM process.

Understanding the *technology* vector's *effect* on a given industry or company requires that leaders ask questions such as:

1. How are technological advances (e.g., e-business) in the economy as a whole (and in our company's industry specifically) putting pressure on the company's business performance?

2. Which specific technologies (individually and in combination) are driving the redesign of business processes and customer relationships for our company today?

3. Historically, how quickly has our industry/company integrated new technologies into its work processes or organizational design? (Is it an early adopter or late adopter of new technologies?)

4. In what ways are customers putting pressure on the company to adapt technologically?

5. What core technologies are driving change and transformation in our industry and to what extent is our company staying abreast of these advances?

6. In what areas is technology particularly critical to our company's bottom-line business performance (e.g., research and development, distribution, sales, marketing)?

7. Are there technological breakthroughs on the horizon that are likely to radically transform our industry when the technology is applied to business operations and work processes?

Understanding the influence of the *economic* vector on a given industry or company requires that leaders ask questions such as:

1. What macrotrends in the economic environment (economy-wide) are putting specific pressures on our company's business performance at this time?

2. What microtrends (i.e., industry-specific) are putting pressures on our company's business performance at this time?

3. To what extent is our company a global company?

4. In what ways is our company vulnerable to fluctuations in exchange rates, capital flow changes, and other factors that affect capital availability and cost of capital?

5. To what extent is our company financially leveraged in emerging markets? Where is it leveraged? (See also the political vector.) To what extent is there financial volatility in those countries or economies where it is leveraged?

6. How good is the infrastructure in the emerging markets where our company does business?

Understanding the *political* vector's influence on a given industry or company requires that leaders ask questions such as:

1. What political developments (global/local) are of most concern to our firm at this time?

2. How might these events potentially affect the climate for doing business in those countries or areas where our company operates?

3. In what "problem" countries does the company current operate? Specify.

4. To what extent is there political instability in these countries? Specify.

5. What is the climate of relations between the United States and the various foreign "host" countries in which the company operates? Specify.

6. Are there latent political forces at work in the countries where the company operates that could potentially cause business interruptions, a breakdown of laws, seizure of company assets, or other conditions that could discourage investment? Specify.

Understanding the influence of the *demographic* (consumer/customer/culture) vector on a given industry or company requires that leaders ask questions such as:

1. Describe the nature of the company's customer base in country _____.

2. To what extent is the company's bottom-line business performance in country _____ _____ being driving by changing demographics, changing consumer habits, or increased/decreased consumer/customer affluence?

3. What is the current proportion of business-to-business and business-to-consumer commerce that the company engages in country _____?

4. What is the likely proportion of business-to-business and business-to-consumer commerce in country _____ in 2 years? 5 years? 10 years?

5. To what extent is rapid wealth redistribution taking place in country _____? Specify.

6. Is the company struggling to adapt to changing customer/consumer demands in country _____?

7. To what extent are changes in the country's culture (e.g., laws, customs, public policies, political leadership) affecting consumer buying behaviors and preferences?

Summary of the BCM Process

The BCM process can take the form either of a macroeconomic scan (the entire business climate) or can be tailored to forecast developments in a specific industry or vector. In any case, companies are forced with increasing frequency to reassess their marketplace position, their competitive strategy, their technological strength, and whether they have the leadership skills necessary to compete in an increasingly turbulent marketplace. The role of the OD consultant or T&D professional will undoubtedly be that of helping to facilitate the visioning and re-visioning process. The BCM process and other visioning tools can go a long way toward helping you and your organization clarify goals, identify challenges and opportunities, and ultimately articulate a new and compelling organizational vision and direction.

Think Big

This chapter explored the characteristics of companies that enthusiastically embrace their vision and mission. Such companies share several important characteristics: strong values, a core ideology, and an ability to think big about their future goals and business direction. To help your organization follow in the footsteps of these proven successes, use the visioning pyramid and robust visioning tools to undertake the visioning process and brainstorm your organization's future.

There is no one best way to translate a new vision into a set of action plans, of course, but doing the things suggested in this chapter will help enormously. Strategic visioning and process tools will help focus the attention and energies of your organization's senior leadership team as it tackles visioning activities and will help improve your effectiveness as a group facilitator and leadership coach in that process.

Although many companies today struggle with articulating their vision and identifying the steps needed to realize it, these are not the only leadership challenges facing modern organizations. Far from it! Indeed, to actually implement a vision, an organization needs first to understand and articulate a set of values and then align people's behaviors at all levels with those values on a consistent basis. Chapter 4 will discuss the importance of using 360-degree assessments to help align people's behaviors behind the vision and values that an organization articulates for itself.

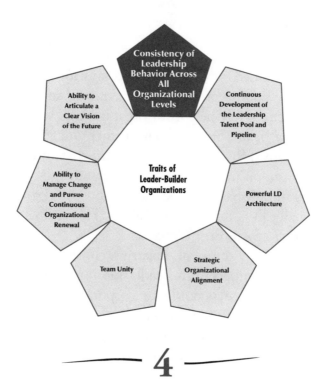

Consistency of Leadership Behavior Across All Organizational Levels

Ability to Articulate a Clear Vision of the Future

Continuous Development of the Leadership Talent Pool and Pipeline

Ability to Manage Change and Pursue Continuous Organizational Renewal

Traits of Leader-Builder Organizations

Powerful LD Architecture

Team Unity

Strategic Organizational Alignment

— 4 —

How to Create Positive, Consistent Leadership Behaviors in Your Organization

Starting with the board of management, we have each taken complete psychological assessments so that we all understand our own work behaviors better. At first, there was an awful lot of fear associated with this, until we began to realize how valuable a tool it [360-degree assessment] was for understanding human motivations and actions in the organization. Now these activities are normal process.

— Sir Richard Evans, Chairman of BAE Systems, in *Business Climate Shifts: Profiles of Change Makers* (Burke & Trahant, 2000).

Chapter 3 explained why it is so important for your organization to pursue the visioning process, and it outlined some of the tools you can use to effectively help your organization's senior leaders to not only articulate a new vision, but also to implement it at the workplace level. One question remains: How do you actually do that in the programs you create? First, it is important to realize that any effective vision is underpinned by an organization's espoused values and the degree to which the organization actually lives up to those values. This leads to the matter of *behaviors,* the primary focus of this chapter.

In today's business environment, ensuring consistent leadership behaviors among all of the members of the leadership team can speed innovation, enhance market responsiveness, and ease corporate transformation efforts. They are critical if your organization wants to send unambiguous messages to employees about your company's operating goals and business priorities. And, they are vital to ensuring efficient knowledge management and effective vision setting.

Knowledge, power, and influence have become diffused throughout organizations as never before—the result of enabling technologies and the demise of traditional hierarchies. How do you go about creating training programs for a large population of leaders within the organization so that they march in the same direction, say, for example, to follow a new CEO, or to support an important new business strategy, or to change how they interact with their subordinates, customers, and organizational peers?

More companies are turning to 360-degree assessments as a tool to transform leadership behaviors within organizations and to align entire leadership populations behind new business goals and operating priorities. Many business leaders today, from GE's Jack Welch to former Ameritech CEO Bill Weiss, are strong proponents of 360-degree assessments, especially when a company's very survival is at stake. BAE Systems (formerly British Aerospace) chairman Dick Evans is another business leader who has become a vigorous evangelist about the importance of 360-degree assessments in transforming how a company operates. In the last few years, Evans has used 360-degree (and peer) assessments to help drive culture change at BAE and fundamentally redesign how everyone within that company works with everybody else.

Introducing Your Organization to the 360-Degree Assessment Process

What is the best way to introduce use of 360-degree assessments to the organization? How do you use them to transform or align leadership behaviors across all organizational levels? To answer these questions, first consider the contemporary nature of corporate leadership and "followership" in organizations and why the changing nature of each is requiring use of tools like 360-degree assessments to create leadership cohesion and team discipline.

Although notions of leadership vary greatly, most people agree that modern leadership requires more than just sound management (Zalesnik, 1977). Effective leaders influence others in different ways than do managers and supervisors. Think about how your own experience validates this. A manager's function and power derive primarily from the formal authority and control conferred by his or her position, but a leader is usually thought of as someone who works and influences people through other means: the force of his or her personality, persuasive powers, charisma, energy, and "likeability."

The Difference Between Leadership and Management

Social psychologist Herbert C. Kelman (1974) describes three mechanisms by which people are influenced to do things: compliance, identification, and internalization. In Kelman's view, compliance is attained through authority and "means-control." In other words, people agree to do things because they perceive the order-giver to have legitimate authority or because it is in their best interest to do so. In the case of identification, however, people agree to do things when the act itself is presented in an appealing way or because the presenter is someone whom the individual likes or wishes to emulate. When people come to endorse a behavior or goal on their own, they have *internalized* it; they "own" it.

Kelman's modes of influence can help us distinguish between management and leadership; think of compliance-based influence as management, and consider commitment-based influence (identification and internalization) as leadership. This idea is not new. About 1,500 years ago, the Chinese philosopher Lao Tzu (Mitchel, 1988) wrote:

> A leader is best
> When people barely know that he exists
> Not so good when people obey and acclaim him
> Worst when they despise him
> "Fail to honor people,
> They fail to honor you;"
> But of a good leader, who talks little,
> When his work is done, his aim fulfilled,
> They will all say, "We did this ourselves."

The Downside of Using Compliance-Based Leadership Tactics

Compliance-based tactics (the basis of traditional-style, top-down management) are typically the easiest and fastest ways to achieve short-term changes in behavior in organizations, but there are costs associated with them. Compliance-based influence tactics do worse than just fail to gain true commitment, they create resentment and, over time, will lead to active resistance. Research has shown that when people attribute their own behavior to compliance with authority or with a desire for rewards, they are less likely to engage in or endorse such behaviors when they are no longer being directly monitored and rewarded (Deci & Ryan, 1985).

What does all this have to do with modern notions of leadership based on organizational values? Contemporary concepts of leadership—values-based leadership, servant leadership, principle-centered leadership, and so forth—emphasize the importance of *involvement* and *commitment,* rather than acquiescence or compliance. The emphasis is on helping subordinates by coaching and empowering them rather than controlling them by coercing or cajoling.

The idea of "manager as leader" creates an environment in which committed, capable followers can flourish. By setting a good example, acting with integrity and courage, garnering the respect and admiration of others, establishing trust and openness, and helping others to do well, the best leaders today are driving forces for personal and organizational excellence.

Today, too many LD programs still train people to *manage,* not *lead.* Yesterday's managers relied on hierarchical authority, rules, incentives, and the threat of punishment to influence subordinates. This worked relatively well through the 1950s and into the 1960s, when work was relatively straightforward, output was tangible, and the business environment was stable. Today, relying too much on traditional management approaches is a surefire way to go out of business. Managing for compliance ignores the realities of today's uncertain business environment; it undermines some of the most important aspects of knowledge work and hinders an organization's ability to adapt to new market forces.

Employee Commitment: The Leadership Imperative in the New World of Work

Perhaps the most compelling reason for companies to do away with compliance-based management and adopt commitment-based leadership approaches today is the new world of work in which we now live. Now that the information age is upon us, it is clearer than ever that knowledge workers must be led, not just supervised.

Listed below are six important reasons why knowledge workers must be managed through leadership and not traditional supervision. This is important information to keep in mind as you develop leadership programs for your organization.

1. *It is difficult to measure the value that a knowledge worker adds to an organization.* The value of today's professionals lies in their ability to create meaningful information out of idle data; the benefits of such contributions tend to be equivocal in the short run if not entirely worthless. Traditional yardsticks used to measure the output of manual laborers (productivity, conformance to standards, and so forth) do not apply to knowledge work. Therefore, setting precise and easily measurable performance expectations, and then rewarding or punishing accordingly, is not realistic for knowledge work.

2. *Knowledge workers often know more about their area of expertise than their supervisors do.* Under conditions where a manager is less capable and less knowledgeable than a subordinate, the "do as I say" approach is hardly feasible.

3. *Knowledge workers must be innovative to be effective.* Given that work is more and more in the mind of the worker, rules would be difficult to enforce even if it were advisable to do so; strict adherence to rules is probably not a good idea in the first place. Blind obedience to existing rules is a sure way *not* to invent the next best thing. The best

employees of the 21st century will question rules and obey only those that make sense. Employees and companies on the cutting edge will discard these irrational rules and invent their own.

4. *Managers may not have direct control over the workers upon whom they depend the most.* As the complexity of organizational structures evolves, mirroring the increasing complexity of the business environment, learning to influence colleagues who are not direct reports (that is, those who are "sideways" or "diagonal" on an organizational chart or even in different organizations altogether) is fast becoming a necessity for managerial effectiveness. Even for direct reports, bosses should use caution when employing compliance-oriented influence tactics. Tight labor markets leave skilled knowledge workers in a strong negotiating position when it comes to the rewards and perquisites of their job, rendering traditional carrot-and-stick methods of managing others weak at best. If rewards are withheld, these workers can simply move on to another employer.

5. *The power bases that managers have traditionally used to control their subordinates are not effective in managing knowledge workers.* Because the effectiveness of knowledge workers cannot be judged by mere observation and because subordinates often know their work better than anyone else does, it is nearly impossible for bosses to sustain performance by barking out commands and doling out rewards and punishments. To do so would be so time consuming as to be impractical. Without spending inordinate time in oversight and performance assessment, knowledge workers could seek and achieve desired rewards by misleading, distorting information, and managing expectations and impressions rather than actually producing results. When managers achieve compliance in the short run, they sow discontent, passive resistance, and deception in the long run. Ultimately, knowledge workers excel not because they are coerced, but because they are inspired, internally motivated, highly committed, and highly involved in their work.

6. *Tomorrow's knowledge workers will themselves be leaders.* The winning companies of tomorrow will go a step further than effective top-down leadership; their knowledge workers will not only be committed and involved, but, within their own spheres of influence, they will be leaders in their own right. In the 21st century, the best managers will need

to be more than just leaders of workers, they will have to be leaders of leaders. A leader of leaders nurtures and develops the leadership skills of others, even those in the lowest ranks of the organization, coaching and teaching them to set their own direction and helping them react to an ever changing market place.

Passion, values, integrity, decisiveness, respect, courage, trust, vision, empathy, loyalty, humility, service—these are the "soft stuff" upon which the commitment of followers is built. These are also some of the most difficult things to do. In their landmark book, *In Search of Excellence,* Tom Peters and Bob Waterman (1982) argue that deep-rooted values and a distinct culture, shaped by transformational leadership, are perhaps the most important factors differentiating America's best-run companies from the also-rans. Only through "clarity on values" and "the right sorts of values" is it possible for a company to achieve excellence.

Transformational leaders play a central role in actively shaping the values and cultures of organizations, but they can only do so by exercising personal and interpersonal competence. So, what skills must today's leaders possess to shape values and lead change? How can these skills be acquired? What values must a leader have to lead successful transformation? It is these questions that will be answered in the remainder of this chapter.

Skills for Shaping Values and Leading Change

Over the years, business writers and consultants have suggested many different traits, skills, and abilities as being important factors for leading leaders, leading change, transformational leadership, principled leadership, and values-based leadership. Peters and Waterman (1982) suggest that the two most critical characteristics for transformational leadership are believability and excitement. In his book *Leading Change,* leadership guru James O'Toole (1995) offers a different set of characteristics: integrity, trust, listening, and respect for followers. Others offer even longer, more robust lists of characteristics and abilities; adding these to the growing list yields a seemingly bewildering number of candidate characteristics that are "essential" for fostering follower commitment.

A synthesis of the characteristics (table 4-1), however, suggests a basic underlying pattern of six basic skill sets:

- ❖ self-awareness

- ❖ self-regulation

- ❖ positive energy

- ❖ integrity and commitment

- ❖ social awareness

- ❖ interpersonal skills.

Of these, self-awareness and self-regulation are perhaps the most important skill sets, as they provide the foundations for developing the others. Self-awareness refers to one's ability to be aware of and know oneself. Without self-awareness, one cannot accurately judge the gap between where one is (one's current level of ability or achievement) and where one wants to be (one's desired level of ability or achievement). Self-regulation is the ability to control and change one's behaviors, including self-control, willpower, adaptability, and learning. Through self-regulation, one is able to learn and change in order to close the gap between current self and desired self.

Positive energy refers to one's optimistic outlook, which is critical to motivating and creating excitement in others. Individuals with positive energy tend to be described as energetic and decisive, which Bray and Howard (1983) have linked to leadership effectiveness at AT&T. Hogan, Curphy, and Hogan (1994) list "surgency" among their "big five" personality traits. They define surgency as assertiveness, energy, activity level, and sociability.

Leaders with integrity garner respect from others and are better able to build commitment to a cause. These individuals tend to be described as responsible and hard working, which Bentz (1990) linked to leader effectiveness at Sears. The integrity skill set is similar to the "big five" personality trait conscientiousness, defined as responsibility, achievement, initiative, personal integrity, and ethical conduct by Hogan, Curphy, and Hogan (1994).

Thus far, the skill sets discussed have been primarily *personal* in nature. Although energy and integrity tend to be effective only to the extent they are demonstrated with others and perceived as such by others, both can be practiced in the absence of other people. The remaining two skill sets are fundamentally *interpersonal;* that is, they can only be practiced with other people. Social awareness refers to one's empathy and sensitivity to others, one's ability to listen, and a service orientation. Interpersonal skills refer to the ability to cooperate, resolve conflict, and influence others.

Table 4-1. Leadership characteristics proposed by different experts.

		Emotional intelligence (Goleman, 1998)	Values-based leadership (Kuczmarski & Kuczmarski, 1995)	Principle-centered leadership (Covey, 1990)	Executive EQ (Cooper & Ayman, 1997)
Personal skill sets	**Self-awareness**	Self-awareness	Recognizes self-doubts and vulnerabilities	Self-awareness and self-knowledge	Emotional feedback
	Self-regulation	Self-control Adaptability Innovation		Volition and willpower Continual learning	Resilience and renewal
	Positive energy	Optimism Initiative	Energy level is high Attitudes are positive and optimistic	Positive energy	Emotional energy
	Integrity and commitment	Trustworthy Conscientious Committed	Delivers on promises and commitments	Service-oriented	Integrity Trust Honesty Commitment
Interpersonal skill sets	**Social awareness**	Empathy Communication Service orientation	Empathetic Sensitive to others' needs, values, and potential Listens actively	Listens with empathy Service oriented	Intuition
	Interpersonal skills	Influence Conflict management Collaboration and teamwork Building bonds Inspiring and motivating		Synergistic Believes in others	Influence without authority

As managers climb the corporate ladder, those unable to develop these skill sets often fail. Based on a review of 10 years of accumulated research, Hogan, Curphy, and Hogan (1994) concluded that leaders who are otherwise capable derail because they are perceived as abrasive, aloof, arrogant, compulsive, emotional, insensitive, overly controlling, or untrustworthy.

Regardless of the specific character flaw, promising fast-track leaders who derailed all have one thing in common: Because of deficiencies in personal or interpersonal skill sets, they alienated subordinates in ways that kept them from building an effective team.

Top Eight Things That Keep Competent Managers From Becoming Great Leaders

8. *They lack the vision and energy to lead.* People want to know where they are going before they will follow.

7. *They fail to empower subordinates.*

6. *They do not interact with their team as a team.* Leaders need to get to know people as people, not just as subordinates. They need to get to know their team as an interdependent group, not just as a set of individuals.

5. *They are not very socially astute.* Therefore, their effectiveness within the organization is severely limited.

4. *They lack the integrity and character required to lead.* People want to follow someone they look up to and respect.

3. *They mismanage people and cannot create and sustain an effective team.*

2. *They are "control freaks" who try to control everyone's thinking, ideas, and behavior.*

Finally, the number-one reason that competent managers fail to become great leaders is

1. They fail to apply consistently and effectively the people skills they *already possess.*

Developing Leadership Skills Using 360-Degree Feedback

Are leaders born or are they made? The premise of this chapter is that, although certain inherent traits may be prerequisites (intelligence, for example), people *learn* to be excellent leaders. They develop and hone their skills over time by setting ambitious goals, stretching themselves, and, most important, by learning from their successes and mistakes.

Experience means nothing without feedback that is specific and action-oriented. Feedback helps learners make the association between specific behaviors and their effects. That way, learners can train themselves to perform better and better over time and with less effort. This concept holds true whether the learner is developing basketball skills (Was the shot too high, too far to the right? How was the player's stance?) or mastering a new language (Do others understand what I'm saying? Do I know how to use idiomatic expressions correctly?). As is true in these examples or for anything else a person can learn, feedback is a critical process in developing leadership skills. The fact is, without developmental feedback along the way to target specific behaviors, it is very difficult for anybody to improve his or her performance in any area of endeavor!

In organizations today, people get feedback in various ways. Rarely, however, do they get the kind of feedback that is most useful: clear, specific, actionable feedback on their skills as leaders and managers. Managers who are interested in this type of feedback (how well they set performance expectations, how well they delegate work to their subordinates, how they are viewed by their peers, or whether they inspire and motivate others) will find traditional feedback mechanisms, such as the annual performance review written by their boss, lacking.

Meanwhile, informal feedback methods present their own problems. Many people find it hard to talk freely and honestly to other people about their weaknesses and are reluctant to give feedback openly. At the same time, recipients of feedback may react defensively when confronted with negative feedback. Subordinates offering comments about a boss, fearing retaliation or the souring of an important relationship, may tend to sugarcoat their feedback to superiors. Still others are too busy to spend the time and energy necessary to give good feedback to others, or they may lack the requisite skills to give feedback in a useful way. If they give feedback at all, they:

- ❀ provide too much, too few, or the wrong details

- ❀ misapply examples or use none at all

- ❀ emphasize immutable personality traits rather than changeable behaviors

- ✿ offer the recipient what first comes to mind rather than what is first in importance

- ✿ deliver feedback either too passively or too aggressively.

As an OD consultant, executive coach, or trainer, you are ideally positioned to introduce or perhaps expand use of 360-degree assessments within your company as it pursues a new mission, embarks on new business directions, or tries to respond effectively to a changing business environment. Therefore, it is essential that you become familiar with how best to use them for LD and coaching.

The 360-Degree Assessment: A Multidimensional Snapshot of Leader Behavior

The results of a 360-degree assessment (also known as multirater or multi-source feedback) offer a useful alternative to the hits and misses of other feedback methods. The process is quite simple. A behavioral survey is prepared and completed for a target individual by superiors, peers, subordinates, and the "ratee." Sources of feedback typically end here, but other people (clients, customers, suppliers, or others with whom the target individual works) can also provide input. Raters typically complete the survey anonymously and then send it to a third party who processes the data. Scores from each rater are averaged with others in the same "constituency" group (peers, subordinates, teammates, or clients) and summarized in a feedback report. This report, which highlights the strengths, weaknesses, and major discrepancies between self-perceptions and the perceptions of others, is then shared with the target individual perhaps by a consultant, a supervisor (or other superior), an HR specialist, or an executive coach. This person typically discusses the report with the target individual, identifies improvement objectives, and helps develop an action plan for achieving them.

Usually 360-degree feedback is used for developmental purposes only and is not used as an appraisal tool linked to pay, promotions, or other incentives. This distinction encourages honest feedback and discourages people from trying to handpick or influence their raters.

Raters should be advised to provide feedback that is

❀ behavioral—comments should focus on behaviors, not issues related to personal style or personality traits

❀ work related—comments should describe behaviors that are directly related to work effectiveness and team performance

❀ performance oriented— behaviors should be explicitly tied to their impact on performance

❀ specific—comments should be as specific and descriptive as possible, including examples, if applicable

❀ actionable—feedback should emphasize things that others will be able to change

❀ constructive—feedback should be phrased constructively.

Anatomy of the 360-Degree Assessment Process

Putting together 360-degree assessments can take time and organizational resources. Still, the wealth of descriptive and quantifiable data generated by the process will be of great assistance in driving tighter alignment of leadership behaviors within your organization, identifying key leadership competencies, and determining leadership skill gaps or deficits. In general, use of 360-degree assessments consists of 10 key steps, which are discussed in the following sections.

Step 1: Develop Meaningful Behavioral Rating Scales

❀ The target individuals, as well as those at least one level up and one level down, should be involved in creating and selecting questions used in the 360-degree survey instrument.

❀ Questionnaire items should include top-down input, reflecting what senior managers would like to see in the target individual's behavior. For example, is the target individual's behavior aligned with the organization's vision, mission, strategy, and so forth?

✿ Questionnaire items should also include bottom-up input, reflecting important and meaningful behaviors to the manager's direct reports.

✿ Questionnaire items should include "sideways" input, reflecting important and meaningful behaviors that peers and teammates would like to see.

Step 2: Decide Which Questions Are Intended to Address Weaknesses and Which Are Intended to Build Strengths

✿ Is the item intended to represent a basic minimum competency? Is it reasonable to expect *everyone* to consistently exhibit this behavior? If so, use competency modeling to identify key minimal competencies for relevant groups of managers and professionals.

✿ Does the behavior represent the difference between an adequate performer and a star performer? If so, prior identification of high, medium, and low performers followed by critical incident interviews and content analysis can help determine which behaviors separate the adequate from the outstanding. These behaviors can turn solid managers into stars!

Step 3: Decide Whether to Use One or Several Versions of the 360-Degree Rating Instrument

✿ Tailor the surveys to different types of target managers. Thus, a technical supervisor might be rated by self and others on different behaviors than would an HR professional.

✿ Surveys can be tailored to different constituency groups of the target manager/professional. It may make sense to have subordinates or direct reports rate the target manager on some behaviors that are not relevant for peers or supervisors (and vice versa).

✿ If you use different versions of a survey instrument, it is usually a good idea to have a few core items that remain constant on all versions. This facilitates normative comparisons across groups.

Step 4: Group Items Into General Categories

✿ Combine items on the survey instrument into appropriate categories, such as communication or leadership. This can help managers overcome the information overload that can result from feedback on too many survey questions.

🌸 Groupings can be developed ahead of time based on logical categories.

🌸 Alternatively, a statistical procedure known as factor analysis can be used to identify basic themes underlying the data. These themes or factors can then be used to create categories that are statistically reliable.

Step 5: Create the Survey Instrument

🌸 Consider whether to rate behaviors on the basis of frequency or on the basis of effectiveness. For basic competencies, build minimal effectiveness into the behavioral description itself and use a Likert-type, six-point scale to measure frequency. For behaviors that go beyond minimal competency, it may make sense to use effectiveness ratings.

🌸 For ratings by others, consider whether the importance, or significance, of the behavior should be rated. If so, is it important that the target individuals do it at all, important that they do it well, or is it important that they do it often?

🌸 For ratings by self, it is sometimes useful to include not only "what I think" but also "what I think others will say about me." Managers are inclined to look at areas where there are discrepancies. Where such discrepancies exist, managers may say, "I knew they would say that about me, but that's because they just don't know. . . ." (In fact, this is often a defense to being surprised that others do not see the manager favorably and having to address it.) If a manager rates him- or herself highly both on "what I think" and "what I think others will say about me" and then finds a discrepancy, it is harder to use the defense, "Well, of course they would say that."

🌸 Individuals can also complete various individual difference assessments, such as the Myers-Briggs Type Indicator assessment, which are not directly related to observable behaviors that others evaluate. These assessments can enhance self-insight around more basic personality constructs. This kind of self-assessment often enhances the "total package" of a 360-degree feedback process.

✿ Solicit open-ended responses and anecdotal comments. Such responses can better describe the nature of problems, why especially high or low scores were given, and specifically how the manager could improve his or her performance in the future.

✿ Consider using a start-stop-continue format. Which behaviors should the individual start to do or do more? Which behaviors should the individual stop doing or do less? Which effective behaviors should the individual continue to demonstrate?

Step 6: Pilot Test the Instrument

✿ Pilot testing is critical to developing a successful assessment instrument. Choose several cooperative individuals to go through the process ahead of the full rollout.

✿ Collect comments on paper right after the surveys are completed.

✿ Hold debriefing sessions, either individually or in a group setting, to stimulate discussion about how the process can be improved.

Step 7: Collect the Data (Survey Administration)

✿ Be sure your organization's top leaders articulate the importance of 360-degree assessments to the organization's future.

✿ Notify the target individual and raters about the 360-degree assessment well in advance.

✿ Take all steps necessary to ensure confidentiality and anonymity.

✿ Distribute the survey instruments.

✿ Establish and staff a "hot line" to answer questions, address problems, issue reminders, and so forth.

Step 8: Analyze the Data and Generate Reports

✿ Conduct an item analysis, generating one report per target individual. Each item lists five means (averages): self-effectiveness rating, top-down rating of effectiveness, top-down rating of importance, bottom-up rating of effectiveness, and bottom-up rating of importance.

✿ Summarize the items by category to yield a broader picture of the target individual.

❂ Analyze the different versions of the assessment completed by different constituency groups.

❂ Carry out a statistical evaluation to assess variance: the extent to which subordinates agreed with one another in their ratings of the target individual.

❂ Undertake more complex analyses of how various factors interact with one another, such as effectiveness ratings at the dyad level versus group level, differences within and between constituency groups, interactions between importance and effectiveness, correlations of ratings and other performance measures, and so forth.

❂ Create ways to present findings in graphical format, but do so judiciously. Although clients usually prefer graphic representation, it comes at a considerably higher cost when the graphics are complicated or highly tailored to client preferences.

❂ Present qualitative data. Comments and open-ended responses can be categorized in a number of ways. One method is to simply present a list of verbatim responses (in random order to protect anonymity). Another approach is to have a consultant or analyst summarize the feedback presented by others. This approach has the benefit of sanitizing and synthesizing feedback and avoids potentially caustic responses. However, the authenticity of the data may be questioned; people may wonder if the feedback has been altered or distorted. Data can also be presented according to themes. Either the summaries or the verbatim responses can be listed under the general categories or themes that have emerged from the total set of responses. Organizing comments by major themes can help managers more quickly assimilate feedback.

Step 9: Distribute Reports

❂ Disseminate reports in ways that protect the anonymity of raters and the target individuals alike. Follow-up should occur simultaneously or very shortly after dissemination of reports.

❂ Remember that feedback can be very difficult to receive. Depending on the sensitivity of the survey items, clinical professionals may need to be available for personal counseling, if necessary.

Step 10: Conduct Appropriate Follow-Up Activities

✿ Dialogue with the target individuals. Also useful may be discussions between the target individuals and the raters. Such discussions must be facilitated by a professional with group process skills.

✿ Stimulate dialogue among target individuals. Managers can share tips and tactics on how they have improved or maintained performance in particular areas, and managers can support each other as they come to terms with organizational difficulties and potentially harsh feedback.

✿ Institute developmental action planning. This can be a useful way to channel post-feedback energy for constructive development. It relies on training and on building accountability into development plans.

✿ One-on-one management coaching sessions, either by an internal mentor or from an external consultant, can be an extremely helpful post-feedback approach to facilitate development.

✿ Identify training and development opportunities. There may be areas that need development across the board. Here, managers and professionals may be offered training targeted to specific areas identified by the 360-degree assessment. Note that it is not a good idea to differentiate high versus low performers and require only the low performers to attend the training. Attendance should be either voluntary or mandatory for everyone.

✿ Use results to make an organization-wide impact. The organization may deem that deficiencies or issues identified by the survey require some broader organizational intervention that goes beyond training, such as restructuring, clarifying roles and responsibilities, and so forth.

Building Values Into the 360-Degree Feedback Process

Three-hundred-sixty-degree feedback is useful as a leadership development tool for many reasons, but it is especially valuable when organizations are trying to inculcate new business values or work habits into new generations of leaders. Ultimately, the "bottom line" for values is not what is dreamed up as part of a company's official values statement. Rather, it is whether people live and breathe certain values inside the organization as they go about their jobs, work with others, and pursue the organization's goals. As Chris Argyris (1962) pointed out years ago, the values that really matter are not espoused values or what is said, but rather *enacted* values. It comes down to walking the talk, and the only way to measure this is to ask the people who work with the target individual each day.

For this reason, individuals evaluated in 360-degree assessments should be "tested" for two types of values. First, they should be evaluated in terms of values that relate directly to leadership skill sets (integrity, self-awareness, and so forth). Second, they should be evaluated relative to specific values deemed critical to the organization's future operating effectiveness or business goals (customer focus, innovation, risk-taking, entrepreneurship). It is not hard to list values that everyone agrees are "good things." Rather, the difficulty lies in stating how values are expressed and demonstrated behaviorally, then determining which values are most important, and focusing on these to the exclusion of others.

The way to do this (and to lay the groundwork for developing a customized 360-degree survey instrument) is through the process of values clarification. Simply put, this is a process whereby an organization articulates, clarifies, and measures the values of an individual or a group. For a full description of how you and your organization can go about the values clarification process, please refer to appendix C.

Once the values clarification process is complete, it is important to prioritize values and translate them into observable behaviors. Being too vague or too inclusive leads to a list of platitudes and usually amounts to a generic call to all employees to be nice, be effective, be efficient, be profitable, help people, and do good. Instead, a values statement should help people decide how to set priorities, allocate time and resources, and make choices. Therefore, it is crucial to select the handful of values that best reflect those current and desired aspects of the culture that will enable the company to achieve its mission.

Perhaps you are wondering how 360-degree feedback can actually be used as a transformational change vehicle inside an organization. Consider the following case study.

Case Study: Using 360-Degree Feedback as a Change Lever

The most often-cited reason for why mergers and acquisitions fail is that enigmatic foe known as "culture clash." Although this is sometimes used as an excuse to disguise what were really strategic or financial blunders, culture and related "soft" issues—values and leadership, for example—are the main reasons why strategically sound mergers unexpectedly fall apart. Values clarification and 360-degree feedback can be used to address these problems.

In the mid-1990s, two financial services companies merged. At the outset, the combined leadership team laid out a new direction for the company. Following a reorganization and the rollout of a new mission statement, the company commissioned an organizational assessment to track the progress of its strategic initiatives and to assess other aspects of the organization and its members.

The assessment was conducted using surveys, interviews, and focus groups. Results highlighted general support for the merger and the direction set by top leadership, a strategic fit between the two legacy firms, and a well-articulated mission and strategy that were supported and understood by employees. The assessment, however, also pointed to several shortcomings including culture, values, leadership, and management. Inconsistent cultures, a lack of strong values, and inadequate leadership to support the new strategy were jeopardizing the success of the merger.

Values-based 360-degree feedback to improve leader and manager effectiveness was one of the key initiatives the company undertook to address these issues. Senior leaders began by defining and communicating a set of values and corollary behaviors intended to support the mission. A group of senior managers, including the CEO, initially created a list of five values representing core elements of a culture that would enhance and support the new mission. The draft was then shared with others in the organization who made several modifications, including the addition of a sixth value. The final set of values included the following:

- ✿ performance
- ✿ customer focus
- ✿ shareholder value
- ✿ diversity

Table 4-2. Values and related behaviors used by a financial services firm.

Value	Representative managerial behaviors
Performance	Inspires others to perform at the highest level Provides clear direction regarding performance goals
Customer focus	Demonstrates that being the best in the eyes of the customer is our most important job Solicits and responds regularly to customer feedback regarding the quality of our products and services
Shareholder value	Creates clear strategies that enhance the long-term franchise value
Diversity	Maintains a productive environment that values and appreciates differences among people Strives for synergy in teamwork by encouraging the exchange of different perspectives and points of view
Positive and challenging work environment	Maintains a challenging, motivating, and rewarding environment to attract and retain a superior workforce
Growth and innovation	Monitors on a regular basis the external marketplace for new business opportunities

✿ a positive and challenging work environment

✿ growth and innovation (table 4-2).

These values were also tied to specific outcomes, such as recognition, participation and empowerment, and intended business results. Each core value was translated into six specific leader behaviors and incorporated into the 360-degree feedback instrument. The first round of the leadership development program targeted the top 125 executives and involved leadership training, a personality assessment, a leadership style assessment, and management coaching in addition to 360-degree feedback.

After collecting and processing the survey data, feedback reports were prepared and used as part of a two-day leadership development program. Customized feedback reports for each leader included an average of the ratings from themselves, their bosses, their peers, and their subordinates on each of the 36 items. Leaders compared how they viewed themselves with the perceptions of others on each of the six values. These feedback results helped leaders understand gaps between their values and intended behaviors on one hand and their actual behaviors on the other. Related initiatives helped managers learn how to improve these and other behaviors essential to realizing necessary improvements.

Other Ways to Ensure Consistent Leadership Behavior in Your Organization

- Codify a set of prescribed behaviors based on vision, values, and competencies.
- Measure leaders and provide feedback (based on 360-degree assessments), then roll up the scores into an organization-wide balanced business scorecard.
- Incorporate desired behaviors into such HR processes as recruitment, placement, promotion, and appraisal.
- Reward leaders in monetary and nonmonetary ways (including "punishment" for nonperformance).
- Reinforce desired behaviors through an action-based culture change program.

The efficacy of this program was clear: The company successfully navigated its merger in terms of people, organizational culture, and assets. The leadership development program was eventually expanded to include managers at lower levels in the organization with a similar set of manager behaviors (in addition to the leader behaviors) developed and set around the same six values. When a second organizational assessment was conducted two years after the first to track progress, improvements were noted on each key indicator and on all but two of more than 100 survey items.

Several factors were essential to the success of this effort:

✿ *There was support from the top.* The CEO was committed to the effort, led it, drove changes in core processes, communicated desired outcomes, and modeled desired behaviors.

✿ *Change efforts were data-driven.* Although led from the top, changes were always planned based on input from the entire organization. Data was carefully and systematically collected by external consultants using surveys, interviews, and focus groups.

✿ *There was management alignment.* At the top, executives supported and actively participated in the program. Executives who were either unwilling or unable to support change were replaced.

✿ *Feedback was one element within a larger program.* The effectiveness of 360-degree feedback suffers when not integrated with other leadership development initiatives such as training, goal setting, and coaching. Values-based 360-degree feedback facilitates change best when it is used as one leverage point within a larger change program.

✿ *Expertise was provided by external consultants.* Consultants who were uniquely qualified to provide an integrated set of services including strategic change, leadership development, organization assessment, values clarification, and 360-degree feedback, offered advice and provided key services over a two-year period following the merger.

Emerging Trends in 360-Degree Feedback

More and more companies are using and experimenting with 360-degree feedback, so much so that emerging trends are too numerous to count. Among these emerging trends are the use of electronic surveys, multisource feedback, and the application of 360-feedback to development and assessment purposes.

Use of Electronic Surveys

Technological advances are making 360-degree feedback easier and cheaper than ever. By administering surveys electronically, via an intranet or the World Wide Web, data can be gathered, entered, stored, and analyzed automatically. Although the up-front costs to set up such a system are greater, the variable costs associated with including additional managers, longer surveys, or additional administrations of the survey over time are substantially lower. The major result is that programs formerly limited to the higher echelons of management due to cost considerations can now be expanded or repeated at a reasonable cost.

There are some potential drawbacks to electronic surveys. For one, people may be somewhat fearful of using electronic assessment methods. If employees fear that their responses can be traced to them, it will be difficult to get honest input, especially if there is already a lack of trust. It may help to allow people to provide feedback over a secure Web site that is run by an external firm so that the data can go directly from any computer with Internet access, even a home computer, to an external consultant who guarantees anonymity.

From 360-Degree Feedback to Multisource Feedback

Another emerging trend in 360-degree feedback is the use of more and different types of feedback sources. Originally, performance appraisals tended to be done by one's immediate supervisor. Following the advent of bottom-up appraisal (whereby subordinates began to evaluate their bosses), peer and self-assessments were added to the mix, generating feedback from all sides, hence, the term 360-degree feedback. Recently, additional raters have been added and new terms have been coined. Multirater feedback conveys the idea of multiple raters but does not specify how many. Raters can include one's immediate supervisor, other superiors, subordinates, peers, critical internal or external customers, suppliers or other business partners, and team members from different functions or business units.

Feedback that integrates subjective assessments with other performance information is called multisource feedback, reflecting the many data sources that are incorporated into the feedback. In a kind of balanced scorecard for managers, multirater feedback can be combined with such performance measures as customer satisfaction, product innovation metrics, employee turnover, profitability, market share growth, or cycle time. Such broad-based feedback approaches have many advantages. For the same reasons that balanced scorecards are so useful to keep an organization's performance on track with its mission and strategy, so too can multisource feedback be used to keep the behavior and performance of leaders and managers strategically focused.

The primary disadvantage of feedback that emanates from many sources and involves types of information is the risk of information overload. Beyond a critical threshold, increasing the complexity or the volume of feedback information may paralyze a manager's ability to assimilate the feedback and make changes. With so much feedback to examine, an overloaded manager may do nothing at all or may choose to selectively address only particular aspects of the feedback.

Combining the Development and Appraisal Purposes of Feedback

Multirater feedback has traditionally taken one of two forms. In one form, feedback has been used as a shot in the arm to improve management and leadership. This form typically has focused exclusively on leadership development, has been done once or twice only, and the results have been confidential; that is, they have not generally been available and have not been a factor in performance assessments, pay raises, or promotions. The other form has been appraisal-oriented and used on an ongoing basis as a significant element in annual performance assessments. Here, a formula has been used to combine various ratings into an overall performance index that is used to decide promotions, pay raises, and bonuses. Although ostensibly for purposes of both appraisal and development, appraisal usually turns out to be the more important dimension. When development is the goal, people are just as interested in honest feedback as they are in positive feedback; but if promotions and pay are on the line, people tend to forget about honest feedback—they just want high ratings. For this reason, feedback has usually focused on either development or appraisal, but not both.

Consider how one company used a complex hybrid feedback model to meet its dual goals of development and appraisal. The research division of a large pharmaceutical company used multirater feedback for developmental purposes. However, managers were also required to generate a set of performance goals based on their feedback and to share these goals with their research teams. Then each manager discussed the feedback results and their goals with their respective supervisors. Supervisors were then responsible for following up by periodically discussing progress with the managers, their peers, and their subordinates. The conventional performance appraisal system was used at the end of the year with one change: In making their assessments, senior managers were asked to consider the progress their direct reports had made toward the goals they had set based on the multirater feedback. (As of this writing, follow-up surveys indicate that people's behaviors within the division continue to improve, becoming better aligned with organizational values, and that interpersonal effectiveness improves as well.)

Linking 360-Degree Assessments to Other Behavioral Tools

No doubt 360-degree feedback is a powerful tool in helping to fashion a consistent set of behaviors within an organization. Reinforcing it with other

HR practices can make it doubly effective. The approaches we recommend to our clients include the following:

1. Incorporate desired behaviors into your firm's appraisal system to ensure that people are evaluated not just in terms of what they achieve but how they get the job done. Getting a job done at the expense of working relationships is a surefire recipe for short-term success but long-term failure.

2. Incorporate desired behaviors into salary calculations, as well as internal promotion and succession systems. People take their cues from high flyers, and organizational stars are rewarded for specific leadership traits and work behaviors.

3. Incorporate desired behaviors into the recruitment process. This enables an organization to identify people who will be good role models from day one. As the old adage goes, "If you can't change the people, change the people!"

4. Ultimately, if coaching and counseling fail to help individuals change their ways at work, it is often better that such people seek employment elsewhere. Arguably, the most powerful message about being "consistent in one's behavior" gets sent to others when someone who is otherwise a top performer is asked to leave because their behaviors simply are not aligned with the organization's vision, values, and goals.

Putting 360-Degree Assessments to Work at Your Organization

In this chapter, we have showcased the benefits you can derive by using 360-degree assessments to assess leadership competencies, help individuals grow personally as leaders and motivators of other people, and to align leadership behaviors behind new or emerging business goals and priorities. We have discussed how use of 360-degree feedback can benefit an organization as it becomes more intentional about leadership development and works to build leadership competencies that are aligned with the organization's goals or emerging business priorities.

Perhaps the single most important benefit that can be derived from using 360-degree assessments (and similar tools) is that they can be used to develop not just more effective but also more *reflective* leaders—individuals who possess the competence, confidence, and emotional awareness to be all that a leader must be today. Leadership is more than the sum of a set of skills. Effective leadership is an amalgam of intuition and intelligence, judgment and maturity, talents and temperament. The cultivation of these things in human beings is no simple task, yet doing it has never been more critical to the success and vitality of organizations than it is today.

Chapter 5 points out another big challenge facing organizations today: the problem of how to construct effective leadership development and succession planning programs.

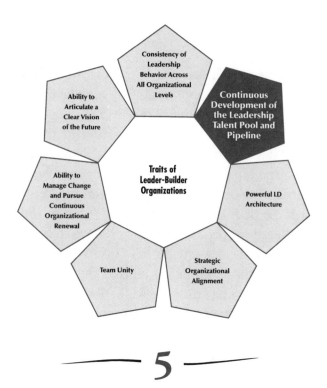

Traits of Leader-Builder Organizations

- Consistency of Leadership Behavior Across All Organizational Levels
- Continuous Development of the Leadership Talent Pool and Pipeline
- Ability to Articulate a Clear Vision of the Future
- Powerful LD Architecture
- Ability to Manage Change and Pursue Continuous Organizational Renewal
- Strategic Organizational Alignment
- Team Unity

— 5 —

How to Develop Your Company's Talent Pool and Pipeline

Without robust leadership development and succession plans in place, a company overlooks two of the potentially most powerful tools at its disposal, not just to grow and groom new generations of leaders, but to motivate high-quality individuals with key competencies to stay with the firm for the long term. In today's business world, the value of providing such inducements to key personnel is not to be underestimated.

— INSIDEDGE, Conference Board of Canada (June 1999).

I f your CEO suffered a heart attack tomorrow, would your company have leaders in reserve to potentially fill his place? If your company's chief information officer suddenly received an attractive job offer from a competitor, would you have somebody waiting in the wings that could step into her shoes? If a headhunting firm suddenly scooped up one of your firm's bright young stars in Internet commerce or snatched away somebody with critical expertise in global branding or capital markets, would you have replacements for these people who could readily step to the plate?

"As the next millennium begins, leaders will have to be made because not enough have been born." So wrote Robert Grossman in a February 1999 article in *HR Magazine* in which he noted that three quarters of the corporate officers polled as part of a study by McKinsey and Company said their firms lacked sufficient reserves of management talent or suffered from a chronic lack of leadership bench strength across the board.

The evidence of this leadership deficit is clearly visible from even a cursory examination of today's business landscape. As companies grapple with a variety of new business challenges—globalization, growth, e-business, global branding, and other issues—it is clear that many lack the in-house talent they need to deal with today's brave new business world. Many companies are not doing the kind of core competency development or succession planning necessary to compete in an increasingly complex business environment. As noted earlier in this book, companies such as Sears and Procter & Gamble have their hands full today in ramping up to the challenges of e-business. Meanwhile, in a poll of 500 HR executives, half the respondents indicated that their companies were not doing a good job of succession planning and were unprepared to replace key executives if and when it became necessary (Grossman, 1999).

The initial part of this chapter discusses the current state of succession planning to give you some context and marketplace signposts to use as you develop your leadership and succession plans. Later in the chapter, we provide a list of important marketplace trends that will serve as important background for developing cutting-edge LD programs. This chapter also uses the example of General Electric to demonstrate its intentional approach to developing leaders with global perspectives and skills. Finally, this chapter offers 10 ways to demonstrate your own leadership to management by articulating how to build consensus for building a pipeline of qualified leaders.

When Tragedy Strikes

Sometimes a company's lack of leadership depth becomes painfully (and publicly) evident. When U.S. Commerce Secretary Ron Brown died in a plane crash in Croatia in 1996, for example, 16 corporate executives were among those on board who died with him. Most of the organizations they led suffered from a cavernous leadership gap immediately after the crash and for a considerable time thereafter. Meanwhile, in the United States, companies such as AT&T and Apple have had a tough time managing successful CEO successions in recent years. Overseas a similar problem has plagued the likes of Barclays and EMI. Even in firms where no succession crisis looms, a latent leadership dilemma exists according to Grossman (1999), who cites findings reported by *Business Week* that of the 500 companies in the Standard and Poor's Index, 17 percent have CEOs aged 63 and older.

Nevertheless, the leadership problem facing companies today is by no means limited to the executive suite. In an age of marketplace chaos and industry convergence, when knowledge workers and information-driven business strategies have become key to sustained market dominance, more and more firms are grappling with how to recruit, retain, train, and groom future populations of leaders at all levels. Two main reasons explain why U.S. and European firms have, in many cases, failed to develop the infrastructure to ensure either the development of new populations of leaders or the creation of succession plans to ease transitions when key executives depart or retire.

First, years of downsizing in the 1980s depleted many companies of their best and brightest middle management talent and virtually destroyed traditional career paths in many organizations. This occurred when companies shed staff to ratchet up profits and at a time when people believed it good for virtually all companies to become leaner and meaner in how they operated. The problem is that no one recognized that in gutting themselves of their middle management ranks, these companies were, in many cases, removing both the people and expertise that would later be needed to occupy more senior level positions. "A lot of companies are recognizing that middle management was more important than we thought it was," notes Tammie Snow, manager of training for UNUM Corporation, a Maine-based insurance company (Grossman, 1999).

Second, many companies today have become heavily reliant on head-hunting firms to supply them with leadership talent from the outside. In the continuing age of lean and mean outsourcing, the recruitment function is viewed by many of these companies as a cost-effective way to conserve corporate resources for other priorities. Using outside recruiters seemingly ensures that an objective perspective is brought into the executive recruitment process, one that is ostensibly untainted by the firm's own organizational politics, the competing agendas of board members, and other factors.

Yet, if outsourcing the recruitment function seems sensible for these reasons, there are other reasons why it is unlikely to benefit an organization in the long run if it serves as the sole channel for filling top leadership jobs. Not only does it keep a company from developing inherent leadership capacity at the top of the organization (thus making it a ripe takeover target in many cases), it can also keep a firm from establishing the embedded organizational competencies that it needs at a *process* level to pursue sustained business growth and organizational renewal. In today's business environment, where knowledge "edge" is a key marketplace wedge, "A company must be viewed not only as a portfolio of products or services, but [as] a portfolio of competencies as well" note Gary Hamel and C.K. Prahalad in their book, *Competing for the Future: Breakthrough Strategies for Seizing Control of Your Industry and Creating The Markets of Tomorrow* (1994).

Firms that fail to practice the principles of sound LD and succession planning often reveal themselves in the insular corporate cultures they retain or in old-style management approaches that over time yield diminishing returns. Consider the uphill struggle of British retailer Marks & Spencer as it tries to compete in today's increasingly crowded and Internet-driven world of retailing. "Dragging Marks & Spencer into the 21st century is a task that would tax even a retailing genius," notes a recent article in the November 3, 1999, issue of *The Economist*. Hinting at the lack of leadership depth inside the firm today, the article continues, "But the British clothes and food chain has only Peter Salsbury as chief executive, an M & S lifer, desperately learning at top speed what it might take to correct some elementary mistakes." Certainly there are high hopes that the external appointment of chairman Luc Vandeveld, together with a large management restructuring and an ambitious change program, will help turn around the fortunes of this mighty high street retailer.

By contrast, in that same issue of *The Economist*, there is an article outlining the steps that two other supposedly "old-line" companies (Ford and General Motors) are taking to step up to the challenges of the Internet age.

The article details the plans that Ford and GM announced on November 2, 1999, to put their purchasing operations on the Web, "connecting suppliers, business partners and customers from all over the world."

As the foregoing discussion suggests, there is a growing need for companies of all sizes and in all industries today to undertake systematic LD and succession planning efforts. Moreover, it is essential to do this before key executives leave or before a firm becomes so overwhelmed by riptides of change in its industry that it is unable to retain competitive strength because of a lack of important organizational competencies.

Your Role in the LD and Succession Planning Process

As an HRD or T&D professional, you will likely have a role in framing the debate about the importance of LD and succession planning in your organization. It is possible that you will be called on

- ✿ to undertake an environmental scan to see how changes in the external business environment are affecting the leadership competencies your leaders must possess today

- ✿ to identify specific critical competencies that leaders at all levels in your organization must possess if they are to do their jobs effectively

- ✿ to develop profiles of the types of individuals your company must either acquire or groom from within to replace the current generation of leaders

- ✿ to put together a leader development curriculum and succession plan that envisions leadership needs over two-, three-, five-, and 10-year timeframes.

How can these things best be accomplished? Numerous developments in today's business environment are driving companies to look at leadership issues in a new light. Among the most important are these trends, which are addressed in detail in the sections that follow:

- ✿ Trend #1: Globalization is driving market growth and emergent business opportunities in virtually all industries today.

✿ Trend #2: Within today's increasingly global business environment, industry convergence is becoming a predominant trend, necessitating a different set of skills in business leaders.

✿ Trend #3: E-business is driving fundamental redesign of all kinds of business transactions today.

✿ Trend #4: In today's "new" economy, knowledge is the ultimate product, and leveraging it effectively to create new products and services is the only thing that will give a company a competitive edge.

✿ Trend #5: There will be intense competition for highly qualified knowledge workers. For this reason, leaders will need to create organizational environments that are both challenging and highly "developmental" in the sequence of work assignments they offer to people.

Trend #1: Globalization

"Today's global economy is in a constant state of growth and expansion characterized by both incremental change and longer-term systemic transformation" (Burke & Trahant, 2000). In this environment, business leaders must often handle numerous new leadership tasks at once. As they grow and lead increasingly global companies, for example, they must often grapple with the complexities of international economics, cross-cultural communications, fluidity in financial markets, and diverse workforces—often without having had formal training in any of these areas. At the same time, they may have to deal with volatility in emerging markets, overcapacity in mature markets, and an increasingly savvy business press which, driven by 24-hour news cycles, covers companies and industrial issues with far more vigor and sophistication than in years past.

Dealing with myriad leadership tasks in a climate of nonstop change can be tricky for even the most seasoned and sophisticated of business leaders. It requires that leaders "look beyond the chaos of the moment to the opportunities being opened by instability" (Rhinesmith, 1996). Translation: Leaders must turn market turbulence into marketplace opportunity. They must know how to leverage knowledge of customers and their needs to create new products and services, and must exercise extraordinary visioning skills and risk-taking abilities in the process.

Trend #2: Industry Convergence

Convergence is dissolving the boundaries that once kept many businesses (banks, financial services, telecommunications firms, and entertainment companies, for example) from doing business with each other, and is redefining many industries and markets. The merger of America Online and Time Warner is a perfect example of this trend toward convergence. In this business climate, traditional competition is giving way to strategic partnerships and marketplace alliances—arrangements that may be foreign territory to traditionally trained leaders and that require new skill sets (and mindsets) in leaders if they are to succeed. Today's leaders, therefore, often need experience in more than a single industry. They need to

- possess cross-market business perspectives

- know how to work collaboratively with strategic partners

- be skillful in leveraging their companies' core competencies as part of doing new business deals and finding new opportunity arenas.

Trend #3: e-Business

Disruptive technologies like the Internet are remaking the business world today by redefining virtually all business processes and functions, and changing conventional concepts and rules about strategic alliances, outsourcing, competition, customer relationships. In this environment, according to Burke and Trahant (2000), companies must increasingly deal with what they call "phase shifts"—critical discontinuities that occur in the life of a company or business as the result of advancing technologies or the rapid emergence of new competitors. Phase shifts can quickly cause a company to be unseated from a position of long-held market dominance if, for example, it is shown to have made long-term investments in the wrong kind of technology or suddenly finds itself losing marketshare to a company that is more "Internet enabled."

In the contemporary world of e-business, therefore, business leaders need to be skilled in Web commerce, rapid product development, brand and customer management, and continuous best practices improvement if they hope to keep up with increasingly complex customer demands driven by the Internet's speed, functionality, and ease of use. They also need to effectively foresee the long-term implications of e-commerce (looking beyond the media buzz and popular thinking of the moment) to determine how it will affect their existing business models as well as their strategic marketing mix.

Trend #4: The Knowledge Advantage

In today's "new" economy, knowledge is the ultimate product, and leveraging it effectively to create new products and services is the only thing that will give a company a competitive edge. As today's world economy shifts away from traditional assets (bricks and mortar) and toward intellectual assets, companies will increasingly be judged (and valued) based on their knowledge capital and their use of these assets to create value. Given these circumstances, leaders will face daunting decisions about how to leverage industry knowledge to enhance market value and increase human and organizational performance.

Leaders will have to determine, for example, how new discoveries and technologies can best be exploited to yield new generations of products and services. They will have to rapidly and frequently reinvent their organizations from the perspectives of research and development and the supply chain to keep their business practices on a par with their competitors'. Most important, they will have to become more intentional about creating organizational environments that encourage innovation, information sharing, and collaborative work approaches. This will be essential to optimizing the use of people, and creating strong employee commitment to business goals and long-term business directions in the process.

Trend #5: Competition for Knowledge Workers

There will be intense competition for highly qualified knowledge workers. For this reason, leaders will need to create organizational environments that are both challenging and highly developmental in the sequence of work assignments they offer to people. Those in the HR field have known for some time now of the new attitudes in the workforce relating to workers' desire for a healthier balance between work and life.

Given this reality, leaders will need to fashion new style employment "contracts" with employees that encourage continuous development, career resilience, and at least short-term corporate commitment. Company leaders must avoid the old psychological contract (pre-1980s), which promised job security but did not emphasize peak performance in people. They will also need to think far more about attracting, developing, and retaining women and minorities than they ever did in the past.

Unfortunately, even in many companies known for their robust approaches to LD and succession planning, there are often few corporate initiatives or programs targeted specifically at advancing the careers of women and minority employees. Yet, such initiatives and programs are becoming critical in developing broad-based leadership populations within organizations today.

Firms that do a good job of LD and succession planning (GE and the former Honeywell, for example) pursue a long-term, comprehensive approach to growing and grooming their leadership talent (figures 5-1 and 5-2.) Figure 5-1 depicts an integrated approach to LD and succession planning. Individuals who are assessed as being of high potential early in their careers are carefully tracked and monitored over time and, if job performance merits, are then put into a high-performance pool from which the company's most senior leaders can eventually be selected. Figure 5-2 offers a more detailed examination of the institutional approaches practiced by high-performing companies. As this illustration shows, many high-performing organizations are extremely intentional about assessing the skill sets and job performance of key individuals. They identify skill gaps using competency profile instruments and develop individual development plans (IDPs) to help high potential individuals address gaps in their skill sets or experience. In many fast growth, rapid changing industries, this disciplined approach to LD ensures that leaders' skill sets stay in step with emerging business requirements.

How Companies Are Developing Women and Minority Leaders

A growing list of companies now identifies and mentors high-potential women and minority leaders. Charles Schwab & Co. and IBM, for example, both have specific LD initiatives in place to target and promote women and minority managers and executives for advancement. Each was recently recognized for its efforts in this area (along with other firms) by Catalyst, a nonprofit research and advisory group that studies women in business.

Charles Schwab & Company's program "Building a Culture: No Ceilings, No Barriers, No Limits" has been a core component in the company's operating philosophy since its founding 25 years ago. The program is built on the premise of creating a truly equitable

workplace. Hiring, retention, turnover, time in grade, and participation rates in training are all tracked by race and gender, to
ensure that women and minorities have equal promotional/
development opportunities with those of men. As a consequence,
36 percent of corporate officers at Schwab today are women, as
are two of the company's five vice chairs (Catalyst, 2000).

At IBM, "Big Blue," the company's "Global Women Leaders
Task Force: Creating the Climate to Win" program specifically targets women and minorities for LD nationally and globally. Begun
in 1995, this initiative, which includes special mentoring and
development opportunities for minorities, as well as a global
women's leadership conference, has received strong top-down
leadership support from CEO Lou Gerstner. IBM managers are
required to attend diversity training courses and are also held
accountable in performance reviews for meeting diversity goals.
As a consequence, women's representation at executive levels in
IBM has increased from 1 to 8 percent in the company's Asia
Pacific region, from 0 to 5 percent in Latin America, and from 2 to
8 percent in Europe, the Middle East, and Africa. In North
America, women's representation has grown from 14 to 20 percent (Catalyst, 2000).

Still other organizations, ranging from Apple, EDS, and Time
Warner to AT&T, Ben & Jerry's, and Eddie Bauer are reaching out
to support career planning, mentoring, and coaching for
Hispanics, Latinos, Asians, gays, and lesbians. At EDS, for example, numerous employee networking groups have been formed
in recent years including the Hispanic Employee Resource
Organization (HERO) and Gay and Lesbian Employees at EDS
(GLEE). (Diversity/Careers in Engineering & Information Technology, 2000a). The company has also offered domestic partner
benefits for several years now. Meanwhile, firms like Eddie Bauer
are aggressively hiring handicapped individuals, and others, such
as Hoffman La Roche, are coming to see the integration of
recruitment, diversity, development, and retention policies as key
to their long-term business success. "The attraction and retention
of talented people are strategic issues for us," says Steve
Grossman, vice president of human resources. "We want talented people from diverse backgrounds, whether that's gender, sexual orientation, race, age, national origin or geography. This commitment to diversity makes our company stronger and better able
to compete in today's marketplace" (Diversity/Careers in
Engineering & Information Technology, 2000b).

Figure 5-1. An integrated approach to LD and succession planning: spotting the winners in a big company.

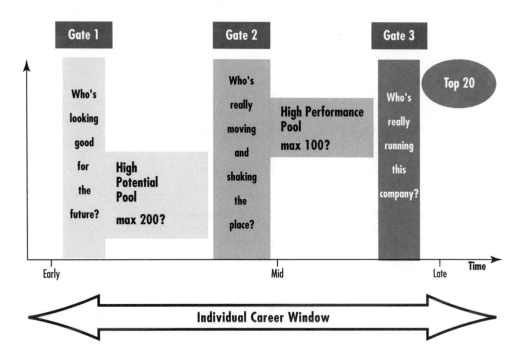

Nobody Does It Better: The Example of General Electric

Today, few companies are as intentional about integrating LD and succession planning activities as is GE. Under the guidance and watchful eye of GE CEO Jack Welch, the company has long had a reputation for focusing time, energy, and organizational resources on developing new generations of leaders.

Welch takes a tremendous personal interest in coaching and developing other leaders; he spends some 30 percent of his time teaching and developing other GE executives at locations all over the world, much of it at GE's world-renowned Crotonville management development center in New York state, where he interacts not only with senior-level executives but frequently with new hires and first-time managers, too. Welch has long stressed that for companies like GE to survive and thrive in the 21st century, there must be a strong organizational commitment to the idea of leaders developing other

Figure 5-2. An integrated approach to LD and succession planning: filling the development gap.

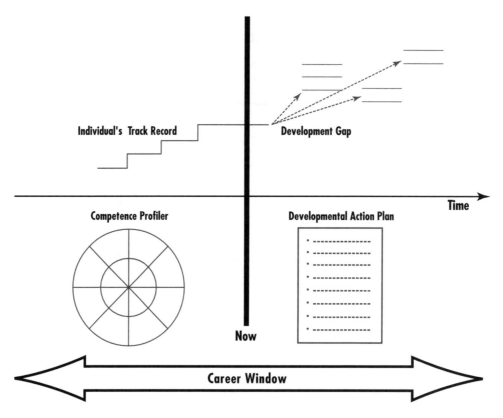

leaders at all levels in an organization. To that end, he has been intensely involved in moving Crotonville away from being just another corporate training facility that packages course materials and teaches technical skills into a state-of-the-art teaching organization that puts a premium on feedback, testing, coaching, and developing leaders.

Welch's goal in doing all this is to develop and nurture a strong talent pool and pipeline to meet not only GE's current business needs but also its future leadership requirements especially in the areas of growth, globalization, and e-business. Since becoming CEO of GE 19 years ago, Welch has built an LD program at GE that consists of the following core elements:

❁ *Detailed career maps to monitor and drive leader development are used.* All managerial-level GE employees have career maps that indicate where they are in their careers and what positions they might potentially hold in the future. These maps, which are used for career planning and tracking, include detailed assessments of people's current skills, as well as future skills that they will need to move into more responsible positions. The maps are an important element in the employee coaching and mentoring process. One of their key functions is to help GE know what skills its leaders currently possess and what future skills will need to be developed or acquired for the company to remain competitive.

✿ *Leadership coaching and development are emphasized.* General Electric puts a strong emphasis on developing leaders at all levels; the top 500 managers in the company are singled out for special treatment. Welch insists, for example, that the skills of his top 500 managers be refreshed constantly. Whenever top job openings occur, Welch typically solicits numerous job candidates (some of them from the outside) to compare GE's resident talent pool with that available "on the street." Senior executives who are identified as having high leadership potential are put through a series of executive development courses at Crotonville to gain the necessary leadership skills to run the global and competitive sides of the organization. Courses in this curriculum emphasize development of skills in change management, team leadership, and increasing customer satisfaction.

✿ *Regular—and ruthlessly honest—performance feedback is given.* Welch is a big believer in giving top-level managers and executives feedback on their job performance. He is known for his legendary handwritten notes to certain subordinates, for example, detailing both their accomplishments and shortcomings during a given job year. Such handwritten notes are accompanied with face-to-face meetings during which people are expected to demonstrate the ways in which they live out GE's business values ("customer focus," "passion for excellence," "empowerment of others," and so forth).

✿ *The organizational structure encourages enterprisewide LD.* In line with the priority of making GE a truly global company, Welch has long stressed the need for people to adopt "boundaryless" behavior and to work across corporate levels, divisions, and functions to meet customers' needs and solve business problems. To that extent, he has done away with GE's hierarchy and replaced it with the corporate executive council (CEC), made up of the top 25 executives in the company. The council meets to share ideas and best practices and to facilitate information exchange and learning among its members. This same CEC operating structure has been inaugurated in many parts of GE, creating an informal and fluid way for managers and executives to meet, learn, share ideas, and solve problems together regularly. At meetings of these groups, senior managers normally coach, mentor, and interact with more junior-level leaders, helping to create tight workplace and collegial bonds.

✾ *Processes, policies, and procedures of HR all support the GE LD process.* As you might expect, GE's HR systems and procedures are all geared toward identifying, training, and developing leaders. Promotional opportunities within the company are pegged to the early display of leadership ability, including the ability to form teams, manage and motivate people under changing business conditions, and coach and mentor individuals. Moreover, yearly performance appraisals and salary considerations are all pegged to the ability to motivate, mentor, and lead others (Cohen & Tichy, 1998).

Building Consensus About the Importance of Leader Development Planning

It can take years for a company to grow new core competencies in-house. That is why taking a strategic approach to core competency identification and development is key to the long-term welfare of firms today. With your CEO or some other high-level leader in your organization acting as a champion, you will need to spearhead the development of a strong, internal consensus about the core competencies your organization needs in the future. This consensus will then become the foundation for developing LD programs and succession plans that are in lockstep with both current business priorities and with longer-term strategic business needs.

We recommend a series of steps to make this consensus building process easier and more effective within your organization. Use these guidelines (in tandem with the visioning approaches outlined in chapter 3) to engage your company's senior leaders in a useful dialogue about LD and succession planning issues:

1. *Be ready to make the business case for why LD programs and succession plans are critical to your company's future commercial viability.* In today's rapidly changing business environment, implementation of

LD programs and succession plans provides a safety net and insurance policy that ensures business stability and continuity, should a senior executive die or retire or if other significant leaders in the organization (subject matter experts, product champions, and so forth) depart for new professional opportunities. At the same time, promises of fast-track career opportunities and special "developmental" experiences can serve as incentives for high-quality individuals with key competencies to stay with your firm for the long term. This is important. Executives often jump from one company to another in relatively short timeframes. Indeed, this is a problem even in some of the world's most prestigious companies. Yet, the future of many businesses today depends on their ability to attract and retain core expertise that often resides in a relatively small pool of committed individuals. "Growth in [today's] knowledge-intensive economy will come less from technology than from employee commitment and ingenuity" (Benimadhu, 1999).

2. *Emphasize why your company must develop a core-competence perspective when it comes to LD and succession planning.* Ironically, in this age of the knowledge economy, many companies today still lack this perspective when it comes to business competition. "The core competence perspective is not a natural one in most companies. . . . The most basic sense of corporate identity is built around market-focused entities" (strategic business units) or around end products rather than around core competencies (Hamel & Prahalad, 1994). Yet many dangers await the organization that fails to take a competency-focused approach to leader development. For example, a company may not be able to act on new business opportunities when they arise if its leaders lack core competencies or experience in emerging opportunity arenas. As companies fragment into smaller and smaller business units (a popular trend in business today), it may also weaken or stretch thin certain critical competencies essential to the success of all business units within a firm (Hamel & Prahalad, 1994).

3. *Focus on developing "strategic leadership depth and diversity" within your organization.* Leadership development and succession planning require that your organization allocate both resources and intent to developing leadership strength and diversity at all levels where the company's ability to compete effectively in the marketplace is potentially at risk. "The success of a company should never revolve around

the abilities, supposed or real, of one person" (Heller, 1999). Unfortunately, this scenario is too often the case, even in many large organizations with ostensibly robust reservoirs of intellectual talent within their walls.

4. *Use appropriate tools to build consensus for the specific leadership competencies your company needs in the future.* Your toolkit can include a leadership assessment (outlined in chapter 2), a competency assessment instrument (Barborek & Brown, 1999), or a competency-product matrix (Hamel & Prahalad, 1994) to determine the competency profiles that today's and tomorrow's leaders must possess. Competency assessments have long been used in industry for workforce planning, employee recruitment, T&D, and compensation planning. Increasingly, they are being used for a variety of larger-gauge strategic reasons including market repositioning, organizational restructuring, job redesign, and long-term LD. They provide a means to profile and inventory existing skills and identify potential skill gaps, thus helping organizations identify both their competitive strengths and the new skills they must either recruit or develop. Such tools provide a means for focusing your organization's attention on identifying the core competencies essential to the organization's future commercial viability. The findings from such efforts then become a blueprint for the design of LD programs and for constructing succession plans. Provide a thorough overview to your organization's leaders of how such matrices can be used to help define core competency requirements and existing or emerging skills gaps.

5. *Make sure that the leadership assessment/competency assessment process is a companywide exercise.* It does you little good to implement a leadership assessment or competency assessment unless it is an enterprise-wide exercise. The downside of such an undertaking is that it can take time to identify strong existing leadership competencies as well as skills and knowledge gaps. You will probably have to mediate conflicts among different corporate divisions or groups and deal with dueling political agendas around what are considered essential leadership skills for the future. Still, the engagement of a wide variety of individuals in this process can lay the groundwork for strong employee commitment and belief in such efforts, once they reach the implementation stage.

6. *Establish leadership development and succession planning efforts within a larger context of ensuring that effective recruitment, development, training, and retention processes are in place across all levels of your organization.* The most successful companies today integrate LD and succession planning into other HR processes such as employee recruitment, training, and performance evaluation. Big global companies (Honeywell and General Electric, for example) pursue a strong matrix approach to training design and LD. This involves linking the developmental experiences of executives, managers, and employees with the constantly changing needs of the business, customer requirements, technological advances, and other factors that affect the competency requirements of leaders. Honeywell's emphasis on its learning framework (chapter 2) provides a wonderful model of the kind of organizational template that can help align any company's succession planning, recruitment, training, appraisal, and retention policies. At Honeywell, all employees from the CEO on down have individual development plans in place that focus on helping individuals continuously enhance their skills and tailor their learning to meet the changing requirements of their work and the customers. This approach has helped Honeywell to dramatically improve its leadership capacity. Current employees now fill 65 percent of all job vacancies that come up internally, compared to just 30 percent that were filled in-house back in 1991 (Burke & Trahant, 2000).

7. *Identify explicit "champions" in your organization to help you push planning and implementation of LD and succession planning efforts forward.* You will need the help of your CEO or another powerful senior leader in the organization who can help cascade responsibility and accountability for LD and succession planning efforts as far down in the organization as appropriate.

8. *Benchmark your existing and envisioned LD and succession planning efforts against what your competitors are doing.* Good firms to study as part of these activities include companies such as Motorola, PepsiCo, and GE, each of which links LD efforts to process improvement projects, customer relationship programs, or quality initiatives such as Six Sigma. This tight linkage of LD with process improvement and quality initiatives ensures that LD initiatives in these companies (and others like them) are robust in content, results-driven, and

effectively aligned to support the strategic needs and goals of the business, creating strong populations of leaders in the process.

9. *As you proceed with LD and succession planning efforts, evaluate your progress regularly.* This way you can stay focused, ensure momentum, and guarantee that agreed-upon timeframes are not jeopardized or derailed.

10. *Finally, be sure there is strong team unity at the top of your organization about the importance of inaugurating LD efforts and succession planning if they do not exist.* Strong team unity at the top of your organization is essential, not just for guaranteeing that LD programs and succession planning get priority but to ensure that resources are dedicated to these efforts and that efforts are leveraged across all business divisions or operating units of your company.

The Next Step Beyond Leadership Development: Succession Planning

The preceding steps are essential to undertake, especially when it comes to developing and inaugurating LD programs in your company. Good succession plans need to evolve from and be a logical extension of these planning efforts. As a consequence, they will require things that go beyond the purview of most training or HR departments. For example

- ✿ When it comes to executive development and succession planning at the highest levels, your company's board of directors must be involved in identifying key skill sets and experiences that are essential for both the CEO and his or her senior management team to possess. The board's members should be tapped as critical resources that can help identify external candidates for critical jobs and offer advice and counsel about the leadership qualities most needed by the organization at its highest levels.

- ✿ Your company's board and its senior leaders need to agree on executive "profiles" that can serve as templates in selecting the company's most senior level leadership team. These can then be subjected to further scrutiny and critical fleshing out at lower levels in the organization as competency assessment or leadership assessment efforts proceed and verify new or emerging leadership requirements. Ideally, there will emerge a common "leadership profile" that can be used (in various iterations) as the basis for filling leadership roles at virtually all levels in the organization.

❖ Training and succession plans for key executives must involve placement of candidates in critical developmental assignments where they can enhance their skills in areas that leadership assessment efforts identify as critical to the firm's future. Ideally, developmental job opportunities can be combined with other kinds of learning opportunities: action learning; executive retreats; one-on-one coaching and mentoring; university-based programs; and collegial, Web-based interaction among people of similar leadership levels. You may find it critical to use some kind of software package (either customized or off the shelf) to effectively plan and track the development of executives and managers and to integrate succession planning activities with recruitment and performance appraisal activities.

❖ It is critical that all senior leaders in your organization understand that the development of *other* leaders is a core responsibility of their jobs. Too many LD and succession planning programs fail because the organization puts no emphasis on the importance of leaders developing other leaders in the organization. This process must be woven tightly into the fabric of your organization's culture, not just as an important programmatic initiative but as a core work value (and performance requirement) of senior leaders.

As you initiate discussions in your organization about LD issues and succession plans, you need to pose certain questions to attract people's attention and to focus leadership energies on these topics. Table 5-1 consists of question sets you can use for that purpose.

Galvanizing Commitment to LD and Succession Planning at Your Company

This chapter has explored why adopting a "core-competency" perspective to business competition is critical to a company's ability to survive and excel in

Table 5-1. Question sets to bring LD issues and succession plans to the fore.

Corporate Learning Requirements

1. Do we have a succession planning strategy and process in place that is driven by our company's business goals, strategies, opportunities, and threats?

2. Are people in this organization effectively grouped into different talent pools?

3. Is there a learning strategy in place that focuses on who needs to learn what and by when?

4. Do we have the right technology and systems in place to turn data about people's leadership profiles, training histories, and individual competencies into accessible information that can be used for succession planning?

5. How (and how well) do we measure the effectiveness of our training programs and the learning capabilities of our leaders?

6. When it comes to succession planning, how well are we doing at stimulating internal dialogue about the organization's core competencies and the relationship of these competencies to the company's goals and strategies?

Recruitment, Selection, and Assessment

1. In what ways do we embed our competency frameworks in our recruitment, selection, and assessment processes?

2. How do we create and implement the performance indicators or metrics that are used in our selection and assessment processes?

3. What kinds of benchmarking do we do to compare our succession planning/LD efforts against those of our competitors?

4. How do we use the results of our benchmarking studies to continually (and at times radically) improve our recruitment process?

5. Are we making appropriate efforts to attract and develop women and minorities as prospective leaders?

Talent Development

1. To what extent do our LD programs and processes supply all business units within the company with the talent they need?

2. What kinds of metrics are used to assess the effectiveness of our LD programs and processes? How do we manage the continuous improvement of these programs and processes?

3. Do we have talent pool development processes in place serving all critical capability needs of the company?

Core Competency Development

1. How do we ensure that knowledge and skills gaps (identified through the leadership assessment process or competency assessments) become the focus for major T&D interventions?

2. What processes do we have in place to ensure that our training interventions are state of the art in content and processes used?

3. Are our training interventions richly varied, the best fit for purpose, or restricted in their variety? Are they specifically tailored to meet the needs of leaders and of the jobs they're performing now (or will perform in the future)?

4. What steps do we take to ensure that our talent pool development efforts are responsive to and focused around business, marketplace, and customer needs?

5. Do we measure the return-on-investment in training? What is our training return-on-investment?

6. What steps do we take to ensure that training offerings are based squarely on the goals and strategies of the business? Are our training interventions based on clear ideas of the capabilities the company needs to support its business strategy?

7. How could creation of a corporate university improve our company's business performance?

today's turbulent business environment. Included was a list of the steps you can take to introduce strong LD and succession planning efforts into your organization and reasons why it is critical that LD and succession planning efforts be integrated with your company's recruitment, staff training, job performance evaluation, and retention policies.

Today, the importance of developing greater leadership capacity and of aligning employees' skills (regardless of level) to serve the long-term needs of a business cannot be overemphasized. In light of increasing global competition, and in many cases skyrocketing costs for recruitment, training, turnover, retraining, and poor job fit, companies are looking more closely than ever at the critical links between an individual's job performance on the one hand and overall corporate performance and profitability on the other. When it comes to identifying, developing, and evaluating leaders, the stakes in this process rise dramatically and have huge implications for a firm's sustained competitive strength and marketplace success.

Chapter 6 covers the specifics of LD programs and suggests ways that you can create powerful development architecture to grow and groom future generations of leaders in your organization.

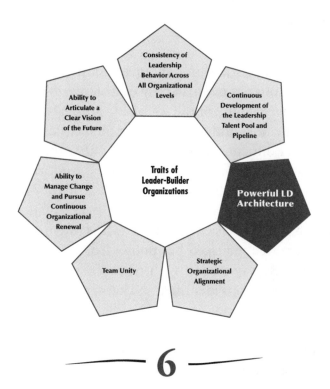

Consistency of Leadership Behavior Across All Organizational Levels

Ability to Articulate a Clear Vision of the Future

Continuous Development of the Leadership Talent Pool and Pipeline

Ability to Manage Change and Pursue Continuous Organizational Renewal

Traits of Leader-Builder Organizations

Powerful LD Architecture

Team Unity

Strategic Organizational Alignment

— 6 —

How to Create a Powerful Development Architecture

As the rate of change increases, the willingness and ability to keep developing becomes central to career success for individuals and to economic success for organizations.

— John Kotter, *Leading Change* (1996).

In chapter 1 we addressed the issue of whether there was a leadership crisis in the business world today and concluded that there was. We concluded, in fact, that it is a problem that exists at every level in organizations today—not just in the executive suite but at the process and team level and on the factory floor. Later, in chapter 5 we drilled down to understand the underlying reasons for this worsening leadership crisis. It is being driven by a confluence of trends including globalization; business growth; an exploding shortage of knowledge workers; and the emergence of new, disruptive technologies that are rapidly changing the nature of organizations and the relationships they have with customers, competitors, and suppliers.

The effects of poor leadership can manifest themselves in dozens of minuscule ways that often prove massively destructive to a company's strategic goals and objectives. Think of the so-called "ostrich" managers who bury themselves in routine tasks and ignore the big picture or the "buck-passing" executives who defer difficult or awkward calls rather than acting decisively on matters that are rightfully their responsibility. And, then there are the executive "cowardly lions" who never quite made it to Oz: top-managers who are motivated more by fear of punishment than by a desire to succeed. The result in each case is the same, and the fact is oftentimes even successful organizations are well managed but poorly led.

So, what is the best way to deal with these leadership deficits and with the other leadership skill gaps identified in chapter 5? Chapter 5 provided a framework for posing the kinds of questions that one must ask in organizations today, as they grapple with LD and succession planning issues. But as an outcome of that process, it is vital that an organization decide on a training architecture to support its LD and succession planning efforts. In other words,

- ✿ What kinds of leadership training programs should an organization put in place to support leadership training goals?

- ✿ How do you make the best use of modern technologies (Web-based training and distance learning, for example) to support LD goals and objectives?

- ✿ What principles or methodologies should undergird actual development of leadership training programs?

The foregoing chapters have equipped you with essential background information and some useful tools to help you, as a representative of the T&D, OD, or HRD function, play an active part in both developing the right LD programs and leading your company out of the leadership crisis. This chapter goes further and provides you with a step-by-step guide to developing the right leadership competencies within your organization.

The New Definition of Leadership

The definition of *leadership* has changed radically in recent times because of rapid change in the business environment and the flattening of the organizational pyramid. Whereas people once thought leaders were needed only at the top of an organization, the new thinking is that any employee can be asked to assume responsibility, show initiative, take risks, and learn to build consensus and trust among equals and subordinates. John Kotter (1996) of the Harvard Business School describes this as "leadership—not only at the top of the hierarchy with a capital *L* but also in a more modest sense (*l*) throughout the enterprise."

A clear imperative exists for this new kind of leadership. In a brutally competitive age, where speed and responsiveness count more than ever, a company must be responsive, flexible, and "transparent" down to the lowest organizational level. This requires empowered employees who understand that they can influence their work environment. This power motivates them and boosts their commitment to the company.

Eight Steps to Developing Leadership Competencies in Your Organization

So, are great leaders born with their special talents or can they be created? It is an age old debate. Many would argue for the former. They would say the skills of a legendary leader like those of former Chrysler chairman Lee Iacocca could never be taught but are simply a part of what makes him who he is. Others take the opposite stance. The late Vince Lombardi, coach of the Green Bay Packers (and a legendary leader in his own right), used to say that leadership could be developed. "Leaders are made, not born," he would intone in his speeches. "They are made by hard effort, which is the price all of us must pay to achieve any goal that is worthwhile" (Maraniss, 1999).

In all likelihood, the answer lies somewhere in between these two polar opposite schools of thought. Leadership undoubtedly can be taught and learned, but the issue comes down to aptitude. Some people are more naturally inclined to it than others. One of the keys to developing leadership competencies is to identify those with some innate leadership ability and then cultivate it. Even so-called "born" leaders can benefit from recognizing their skills and working to improve upon them. Complacency is never a good state of mind, even for the naturally gifted!

Make no mistake about it, developing leadership capabilities is no easy task. Anyone who has tried it knows that managing human interaction is a lot tougher than crunching numbers on a profit-and-loss statement. There are, however, eight steps that an organization can take to develop leadership competencies. Use these as a template to create LD programs in your organization, and you will ensure program variety and effectiveness, learning richness, tight alignment with business goals, and, ultimately, strong relevance to the needs of your organization.

Step 1: Define What Leadership Means to Your Organization

Before you can identify your organization's potential leaders or devise plans to "grow and groom" them, the goal of leadership training must be clearly identified. Just what does your organization mean by leadership? What are the competencies required for it? How will those competencies be developed in individuals? Which metrics will be used to measure learning effectiveness?

You can probably recognize a leader when you meet one, but how would you describe what makes him or her who they are? In the past, defining leadership was easy: The leader in an organization was the person who had all the answers or at least acted as though he or she did. Now we know better. No one person has all the answers. Instead, a leader is someone who knows how to empower employees and challenge them to do their very best and stretch their limits. A leader is also responsible for providing people with the resources they need and holding them accountable for their actions.

Today, some management experts define leaders based on readily discernible skills. A leader is someone who can resolve conflicts, process information, make unstructured decisions, and influence others. Trendier types often opt to use new-age lingo to describe leaders. For example, leaders are those who know how to "think outside the box." Others are described as possessing abilities such as "musical listening," meaning they are intuitively equipped to divine the emotions behind the words someone is expressing, and brave—or foolish—enough to act upon this same mystical prescience.

Defining a Formula for Leadership

Not surprisingly, companies that are well-known for their leadership capabilities have actually come up with formulas for defining leadership. Hewlett-Packard, for example, developed a checklist of 26 leadership characteristics. This checklist is used to evaluate employees and enables the company to recognize its leaders of tomorrow from within and without the organization.

Even the best screening systems can be imprecise, hit-or-miss undertakings. A company might hire 500 promising applicants and end up with only 100 leaders or possibly fewer. For this reason, organizations that seriously undertake leadership training eventually end up training employees at all levels.

For example, in 1986 General Motors launched a massive leadership training effort with a series of discussions among the company's 50 top-level people, each of whom clearly recognized a need for a cultural makeover. The result was "Leadership Now," a week-long program for top executives designed to develop leaders skilled at communicating vision; promoting empowerment; and engendering trust, personal responsibility, and teamwork throughout the GM organization. The goal was to turn managers into leaders. But, the company did not limit the program to the top echelon of executives. Instead, over time it rolled out programs with similar themes and made them available to middle managers, supervisors, and other salaried employees. Long known for its antediluvian top-down management style, GM also decided to create a people-centered culture. It embedded this new philosophy not just into its leadership training programs, but into other HR systems, such as hiring, employee evaluation and appraisal, and its employee reward system.

Step 2: Decide Which Approaches Are Most Appropriate for Your Company's LD Programs

There is no one best way to approach leadership training. Different approaches have distinct strengths and drawbacks. Conger (1992) divides leadership programs into four distinct categories:

- ❂ the personal growth approach to learning
- ❂ the conceptual approach to learning
- ❂ the feedback approach to learning
- ❂ the skill-building approach to learning.

The "personal growth" approach to leadership development has attracted the greatest interest and notoriety in recent years. Unlike traditional skills training that is lecture-driven or based on conceptual programs, personal growth approaches to LD offer the tantalizing novelty of psychological interventions and exercises. Much of the work done in these programs is on an emotional level.

Personal growth approaches are based on two simple premises. First, many people have lost touch with their innermost values, talents, passions, and sense of power because of societal and work-life expectations. Through personal growth experiences fostered in an LD setting, people can reconnect with those inner qualities and allow them to emerge, so that they can infuse their daily work with newfound energy, passion, and authenticity. A second premise of personal growth programs is that fear of rejection or failure prevents people from using their inner potential—be it at work, at home, or in pursuit of their own continuing growth and development. By addressing these fears in LD programs, people can move beyond them and experiment with fully developing themselves. Conger (1992) believes that personal growth programs make an important contribution to leadership training because they directly challenge people to examine their most entrenched values and deeply felt emotions. And, if leadership is in part the emotional manifestation of one's passionate interests and aspirations, it seems only logical that this training "modality" is one that should be used far more extensively than it is today as the underpinning for LD programs and learning experiences.

A "conceptual" approach to learning Conger (1992) holds that leadership is a complex art, one that sometimes is understood only poorly. Therefore, the best that training can accomplish is to build training participants' awareness about the central ideas that contribute to effective leadership. With that awareness, managers can begin a lifelong process of learning to be leaders. For example, one person might focus on developing his or her visioning skills, and another might focus on the idea of inspiring others. Conger believes that the corporate world has downplayed the importance of ideas and concepts in training in recent years. Nevertheless, he says that ideas are critically important in framing the notion of leadership within organizations today, especially as the world of business experiences increasing amounts of change. This approach is also one that needs to get strong focus, though Conger argues that it should not be the sole philosophical framework for the delivery of LD programs.

It can be argued that a "feedback" approach to learning (Conger, 1992) is an important element in helping managers identify the strong and weak points of their leadership styles. Experience shows that this is not always the case, especially if the feedback to a person is off target, irrelevant to the behaviors one is trying to change or adopt, or lacking in "teachable moments" whereby the person can see himself or herself as others do.

Skilled, disciplined use of feedback, on the other hand, can often heighten an individual's sensitivities in areas where competencies are weak and eventually build confidence through a series of improved performances and positive evaluations. The degree to which feedback is a useful learning vehicle, however, depends largely on a person's individual (often highly personal) motivations to change certain behaviors.

A "skill-building" approach to LD (Conger 1992) emphasizes the basics, transforming leadership into a practical, teachable reality. In other words, it demystifies leadership by breaking leadership abilities down into actual mechanical processes that anyone can perform. There are indeed certain skills of leadership. But, many of the skills currently associated with leadership are quite complex and three- or five-day programs offer little time to truly develop these in lasting ways.

In our view, good leadership training incorporates all four of these approaches in a series of seamless learning experiences that build upon each other. Learning, after all, is a matter of both *task* and *process,* of concrete skill acquisition, and of mental and intellectual conditioning that predisposes the human mind to be open to future learning experiences, be they structured or informal, on-the-job or social. Nurturing such learning fluency in leaders today is at least as important as transmitting specific content in a training course because the pace of change in business is so rapid today that learning and leading must be intertwined.

Step 3: Select Training Programs and Experiences for Your Company's LD Curriculum

Regrettably, one size does not fit all when it comes to LD, and leadership formulas do not translate very well from one organization to another. A company's training has to be built around what leaders do in that particular company; training cannot be generalized any more than personalities can be. In any organization, the idea is to get everyone to work together to "pull the wagon up the hill," with the understanding that no two wagons, or hills, or groups of individuals putting their collective hands and talents to the task are ever going to be the same. The goal of leadership training in a company should be to align people to common goals and empower them to take the actions needed to attain those goals.

Often a multifaceted approach to leadership training works best, as exemplified by a program that Royal Dutch Shell initiated in 1997. The company had long been known for its iron-fisted, autocratic leaders who preferred to dictate rather than seek consensus and agreement. But after Cor Herkströter took over as chairman, he quickly recognized that the organization's mediocre financial performance was directly related to its bureaucratic, inward-looking corporate culture. It was technocentric and wholly bled dry of entrepreneurial spirit and initiative. Nobody made a move without a memo that explicitly authorized each and every required motion.

The company launched what it called a grassroots leadership program. It brought together teams of six to eight people from a half-dozen operating companies worldwide for an intense retailing boot camp. In one of the best examples of the strategy that underlies this approach, one cross-functional group consisting of a service station dealer, a union trucker, and four or five marketing executives was brought in to team up and solve a hypothetical business problem. Their objective was to devise a plan to improve service station revenues along major highways in Malaysia. During a five-day workshop, program facilitators introduced a problem-solving model for doing this, along with the necessary leadership tools that the team needed to enlist co-workers' cooperation in the strategic plan. The workshop prepared participants to apply and adapt their newly acquired skills to exploit emerging business opportunities back in their home markets, for example, to improve performance at filling stations on the major highways in Malaysia or to sell liquefied natural gas elsewhere in Asia. As teams completed their work and returned home, other groups of teams rotated in to take their places. Results from these workshops reached around the world. Countries where losses were mounting and marketshare was eroding saw improvements that were nothing short of dramatic. It all happened because people were introduced to new problem-solving skills and given structured, hypothetical scenarios in which to apply them. The result was the development of new competencies to use back in their real-world working environments.

Royal Dutch Shell had other programs that were unique in their approach, to say nothing of their outcomes. One February day in 1997, teams from Shell's gasoline retailing business in four countries spent six boot-camp-like hours in a lowland country downpour, building rope bridges, dragging one another through rope lattices, and helping one another scale 20-foot walls. Another month, the top 100 Shell executives took a soul-searching personality test to determine how and why they made certain decisions.

As these examples illustrate, good leadership training entails much more than rote memorization or classroom-based lectures. Indeed, those elements are invariably a part of most LD activities, but the most successful approach integrates these elements with other training modalities as part of a well thought-out training design, or "architecture." Ideally, this architecture should encompass action learning and challenging work assignments, in which real-job accountability and performance metrics are involved, one-on-one coaching or mentoring, and a growing variety of technology-driven training and Web-based learning alternatives. All of these elements enhance personal growth and professional effectiveness in the workplace.

Action Learning in Organizations

Action learning has become the training vehicle of choice in many organizations in recent years. In essence, the approach involves organizing learners into groups of five or six people, who are tasked to come up with solutions to real-life business problems. The approach is predicated on the philosophy that at the beginning of the learning experience, people do not know what to do next because the answer to the group's "problem" is not available from current expertise. By working together, learning participants solve problems through a systematic and collaborative process of asking questions, testing hypotheses, taking action, and analyzing results—all of it done in a risk and blame-free environment. According to author and consultant Reginald Revans, who is often credited with conceiving (or at least popularizing) the concept of action learning, it is the most effective way to introduce new learning into an organization today and then translate that new knowledge into improved business processes and organizational best practices (Marquardt & Revans, 1999).

The learning modalities outlined in figure 6-1 were recently used with a professional services firm to inaugurate new training and career development programs for its employees. The following modalities are just some of the different kinds of learning that can be encouraged or provided to employees as part of fostering a continuous learning ethic in an organization:

Figure 6-1. Core elements of professional development programs.

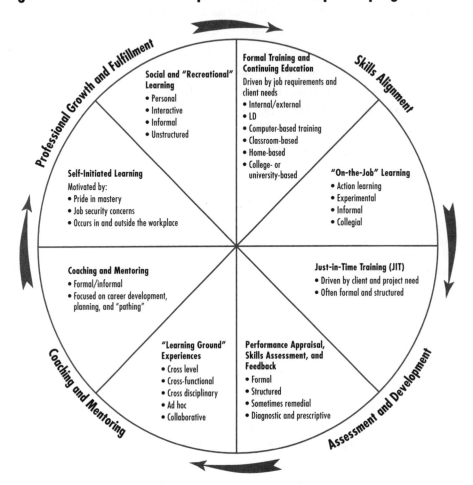

❋ *Formal training and continuing education.* This modality encompasses traditional types of learning and training, both classroom-based and workplace-based. The types of training and learning here include distance-learning, computer- and classroom-based learning, home-based learning, and college and university programs for which tuition reimbursement may be offered.

❋ *On-the-job learning and just-in-time (JIT) training.* On-the-job learning and JIT (Web-based learning, Webcast events, and so forth) refer to more informal and ad-hoc ways of learning that you may want to formalize or otherwise emphasize in your organization as important adjuncts to traditional and structured learning options. These are increasingly being used in many workplaces today, especially as more and more work becomes client-specific and project driven. At Honeywell, for example, combined employee-client teams typically work together on real-life customer process or quality problems, using Six Sigma methods to brainstorm solutions to difficulties (Burke & Trahant, 2000). At PricewaterhouseCoopers, project teams made up of consultants work together online as part of "collaboratories" to enhance group learning, to resolve client issues, and to improve client and intragroup communications.

✿ *Coaching and mentoring.* An organization's performance appraisal, reward and recognition systems, and the ways that managers coach and mentor employees are also important systemic supports for new learning that organizations may wish to emphasize, particularly as they undertake job redesign, competency assessments, or alignment tasks. As part of doing this, organizations may also want to look at ways in which managers and employees can work together to create "learning ground" opportunities—informal opportunities for learning that help employees to broaden or deepen their skill port-folios, particularly at a time when formal career ladders and paths have disappeared from many organizations.

✿ *Self-initiated, social, and "recreational" learning.* This learning modality represents the kinds of informal ways that adults often enjoy learning. These ways of learning are basically experiential and social in nature, and are normally motivated by self-interest (job security, the desire to keep one's skill set current, and so forth). These ways of learning, though seldom emphasized on a formal basis inside organizations, nonetheless represent an important channel through which individuals can continue to grow and develop all of their working lives. Conse-quently, organizations can benefit from stressing these kinds of learning channels to employees, along with more formal, task-oriented and process-specific training programs.

Ideally, with many, if not all, of these training approaches or learning modalities, employees are given responsibility (and a real risk of failure) if they fail to complete programs or projects satisfactorily. The success of such training approaches, however, relies heavily on bosses willing to give subor-dinates a long leash to build new skills or acquire new experiences.

How to Create Winning LD Programs in Your Organization

Wondering how to create effective LD programs in your organization? As a general rule, LD programs fall into one of three categories, according to LD consultant Howard Ross of Cook-Ross, Inc., in Silver Spring, Maryland. The categories are "informational, transformational, or experiential"; using these approaches singly or in combination can provide varied and content-rich programs to participants.

Informational programs, which typically are targeted at first-time managers or supervisors, usually include basic leadership skills training in managing time and tasks, supervising others, managing teams, and communicating effectively. Informational LD approaches also include use of leadership books, tapes, and externally provided classes by groups like the American Management Association to supplement an organization's internally offered courses and programs.

Transformational programs, typically the next step up in complexity, involve helping program participants better understand themselves through analyzing their belief systems and the ways these beliefs drive their leadership behaviors. Normally aimed at mid-level or senior level managers (many times those viewed as rising stars in their organizations), the goal of such approaches is to provide an organization's most promising, up-and-coming leaders with unique learning experiences or opportunities as part of an organization's long-term succession planning efforts. In other cases the goal is to help participants develop enhanced awareness of their leadership styles (strengths and weaknesses) or address leadership blind spots that may be keeping them from performing to full potential.

Experiential programs, sometimes referred to as action learning, involve providing program participants with specific problems to solve or projects to manage. Sometimes these are undertaken as part of course participants doing their everyday jobs, and sometime the assignments take place under hypothetical circumstances that nonetheless stretch course participants developmentally and help them develop skills that the organization sees as critical to its future. Examples of action learning include assigning people to manage high-priority project teams or charging them to develop action plans to cut costs or manage rollouts of new products or services. Normally such assignments are given with strict dead-lines for completion but with significant accountability attached to successful completion of the projects. One-on-one coaching is normally an intense part of action learning experiences. So, too, is feedback that program participants receive from their peers who are taking part in identical or similar training programs.

Step 4: Encourage Leaders to Develop Other Leaders

One of the very best ways to grow new leaders in a company is to encourage the great leaders that a company already has to develop *other* leaders. And though it may sound like "trickle-down" economics, it is a responsibility that needs to start at the top and gravitate throughout an organization. Put another way, good leaders must not only set an example for their subordinates, they must also create an environment wherein others can learn to be good leaders. That means recognizing teaching opportunities whenever they present themselves, and not only passing on knowledge through formal training, but conveying those intangible traits that serve to differentiate great leaders from mediocre ones.

One of the most effective ways leaders can develop other leaders is by making it a personal mission to do so, as Bob Bauman did at SmithKline Beecham in the early 1990s and as Dick Evans, chairman of BAE Systems, has done as well. Leaders who take on this task often discover it brings them big personal benefits. A leader's personal involvement in leadership training often serves as a catalyst for his or her own growth and development. Bauman, for one, believes that personal renewal stimulated by continuous and intense on-the-job learning is the key to sustained leader effectiveness in organizations especially in times of great change.

Companies known for their leadership capabilities usually have top executives who take this responsibility very seriously. We have already discussed the hands-on leadership development approaches of CEOs like GE's Jack Welsh and former Honeywell CEO Larry Bossidy. PepsiCo's renowned CEO Roger Enrico is another leader in this same mold. While Enrico heads a $30 billion corporation with 450,000 employees, he still spends nearly 100 days a year personally conducting workshops for senior executives. He is very serious about the notion that the most important responsibility of a leader is to personally develop *other* leaders.

PepsiCo has also developed a reputation for delegating rather than allocating important business decisions to new managers. This might qualify as baptism by fire, but new hires are entrusted with meaningful managerial responsibilities practically from their first day on the job. Not surprisingly, talent runs deep at PepsiCo thanks to this emphasis on cultivating leaders and on-the-job training that delegates real authority.

Step 5: Promote Mentoring

Mentoring is another step in the development of a good leader. Anyone can be a mentor although quality does vary usually according to motivation. Mentoring involves a combination of instruction and action. A senior person teaches a more junior person how to identify and grab the initiative, practices authority that is appropriate to a given situation, and then encourages him or her to do likewise. It is ideal if a "mentee" can have a variety of mentors so as to be exposed to a wide range of perspectives. This approach helps to create balanced, broad-gauge leaders, who have effectively integrated learning experiences in adult contexts with a number of more senior and seasoned leaders. The learning experiences that the new leader has interacting with various individuals ideally provides a fertile milieu of perspectives and wisdom from which an individual can draw, as necessary, in the course of his or her career, as he or she is confronted with various issues and challenges.

Hewlett-Packard is one company that has taken mentoring to uncharted territory. The company sometimes assigns one executive to shadow another who possesses qualities worthy of emulation. Other firms take a more holistic approach. At the McKinsey consulting firm, consultants work on teams of mixed rank, with more senior executives expected to help the more junior people along. Part of the development process is quite formal; it is customary for inexperienced associates, not partners, to make presentations to clients, and mentoring is an important criterion in partners' appraisals. Long hours and plenty of travel provide opportunities to cement mentoring relationships.

Step 6: Align Leaders with Jobs

Once leaders are developed, the next step is to align individual leaders in your organization with the right jobs. As Edward Gubman (1998) explains in his book, *The Talent Solution,* a person who likes things (a "things" leader) might best be directed toward manufacturing, distribution, finance, and some sales jobs. An "idea" person (an "ideas" leader) might best be directed into research and development, product development, systems development, or some aspects of marketing. Meanwhile, a "people" person (a "people" leader) should be put into HR or some marketing and sales jobs, according to Gubman. The most effective leaders are versatile, even though they have their own strong core orientation. Versatile CEOs can meld people of diverse styles and backgrounds, leading their employees to greater understanding of the marketplace and what it takes to win.

A company needs all three types of people in leadership positions to be successful. General Electric devotes enormous energy to matching managers with jobs in a process called "Session C." Each January, GE employees fill out the front and back of one-page internal résumé forms, describing their skills, career goals, and development needs. Between March and May, senior executives conduct one-day personnel reviews at each of GE's 12 operating units. Meeting mainly with the top leadership, they consider the prospects of about 500 GE senior managers. Pairing people with job assignments is part of the process.

Step 7: Grow Tomorrow's Leaders

Aligning leaders with their key interests (matching job slots to "talents and temperament") is as important as a company sticking with its core competencies. This does not mean, however, that leaders should forgo efforts at personal improvement in areas where they are not quite as accomplished or skillful as they need to be. It is important to "grow people." That means creating and cultivating a climate within organizations where people are actively given the opportunity to test new talents, perhaps fail, and try again.

George B. Weber, secretary general for the International Federation of the Red Cross and Red Crescent Societies, the world's largest humanitarian organization, is an advocate of this approach. In the book, *The Leader of the Future* (The Drucker Foundation, 1996), he says the process can begin on a small scale, by asking promising staff members to serve on task forces and committees for example, where their thinking and judgment can take shape and find expression. Alternatively, they can be given tasks that expose them to the entire organization. They can be asked to share their thoughts and feelings about their work. A belief in diversity of experience means that promising managers can be moved from division to division to develop as diverse and wide-angled a set of leadership experiences as possible. This diversity of experience can come in handy later on when these individuals are candidates for higher-level positions with wide organizational purviews.

Step 8: Establish Guidelines for Evaluating Leadership

As most executives now know, the use of 360-degree assessments has spread well beyond the top executive ranks where they initially took hold. Not only are they a powerful tool for ensuring consistency of leadership behaviors across organizational levels. They are also critical to the development of an organization's leadership training architecture and to the alignment of LD training with current or emerging business priorities.

Conclusions

Some of the various approaches to LD design and implementation that you may want to consider using in your own organization were outlined in this chapter. We have stressed why it is important that a company take time to determine what leadership traits it most wants to stress, why a company's senior leaders must be intimately involved in the LD and leadership evaluation process, and why it is critical that a company develop core values around growing people, matching them to the right jobs, and encouraging the growth of a learning ethic within the organization. To check your company's leadership capability, use assessment 6-1.

The whole point of developing leadership capabilities is, of course, to improve the performance of an organization. Ultimately CEOs and their subordinates will be judged on the financial performance of their organizations, which depends on the individual judgments, attitudes, and competencies exercised by those at multiple levels within the organization, each doing his or her own job. To achieve the level of personal job performance and job ownership necessary to ensure strong financial performance, a company's top leaders must make sure that there are leaders throughout the organization, not just job holders. They must empower those at all levels in the organization to take responsibility for aligning their own performance with the overarching goals (both short-term and long-term) of the organization. And, they must realize that the key to doing this is to nurture a learning and leadership ethic within the organization that ensures consistently high levels of individual, team, and organizational performance.

Assessment 6-1. Does your organization have problems with its leadership capability?

Ask yourself the following questions:

1. How do we define leadership at this company?

2. Do we have employees who demonstrate these leadership qualities at all levels of the organization?

3. What steps are we taking to empower employees and cultivate leadership qualities?

4. Are we encouraging the organization's known leaders to pass on their knowledge, not only through formal training, but by conveying those intangible traits that serve to differentiate great leaders from mediocre ones?

5. Have we considered leadership training that is built around what leaders will actually be doing at our particular company?

6. Do we have a system in place for developing mentoring relationships?

7. Have we developed a strategy for aligning leaders with jobs that will benefit from their particular strengths?

8. Is our organization one in which people are actively given the opportunity to test new talents, perhaps fail, and try again?

9. What tools have we put in place for evaluating our leaders and ensuring that they are contributing to the company's excellent financial performance?

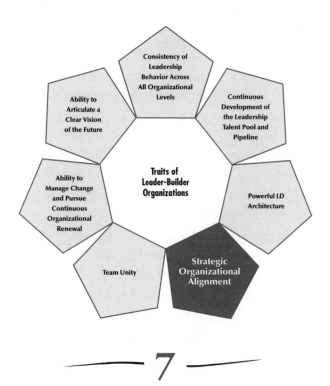

— 7 —

Creating Strong Organizational Alignment in Your Organization

Close your eyes and imagine a company that always produces defect-free products within planned time frames. Or, imagine that an organization's call-center operation never loses a single call, that a firm's sales people turn every quality lead into booked business, that a company's billing department produces error-free invoices every time, or that the baggage handlers at the airport never, ever lose a bag. Do these results sound impressive? These kinds of results are achievable in virtually any area of a business...

> — Jerome A. Blakeslee Jr., "Implementing the Six Sigma Solution" (1999).

P revious chapters have dealt with the importance of vision, strategy, values, behaviors, leadership training, and other organizational components, all working together to create the climate of alignment an organization needs to optimize its performance. But, just how do you go about creating leadership training and development programs that engender and sustain this alignment over time?

This question is not easy to answer, and it poses one of the most subtle (if also fundamental) leadership challenges to organizations today. How do you get a company's leaders, resources, thinking, and behaviors to all move *in the same direction*, not for a split second or even a business quarter but on a sustained basis? This chapter will answer this question and give you help to make it happen in your organization. But before this chapter addresses the question of how to build leaders' organizational alignment skills by familiarizing them with Six Sigma principles and techniques, you should have some background about how companies traditionally have fostered organizational alignment.

The Challenges of Creating Strong Organizational Alignment

1. Your company's leaders may all agree that your organization needs to be aligned, but they may differ on priorities or on the problem areas that are causing the misalignment.

2. Your company's leaders may have all agreed on a strategy to address the problem but never bothered to engage line employees to actually implement it. The result is a lack of ownership for problems below the level of the executive suite.

3. Company leaders may try to "force" quality or process improvement solutions on the organization but without putting the right metrics (or any metrics) in place to evaluate results.

4. Company leaders may be able to argue forcefully that they are in business to serve customers, but they really do not have a substantive understanding of customer requirements or of how they are evolving.

5. Your organization is good at undertaking isolated quality or process improvement projects, but it has never been able to undertake organization or enterprisewide efforts, because of insufficient leadership commitment to such efforts.

Traditional Approaches to Building Organizational Alignment

Traditionally, companies have used a variety of techniques to drive alignment among different corporate divisions or units or to align people's behaviors and attitudes on the job in support of business goals and strategies.

Performance Measurement/Management

Compensation systems can be designed and standard performance management systems implemented to drive shifts in business goals and to encourage changes in everyday employee behaviors on the job to support those goals. "Performance measurement is the bridge between value measurement and strategy on one side, and the operational level on the other," note Bill Dauphinais, Grady Means, and Colin Price in their book, *Wisdom of the CEO* (2000). "A value-based performance management framework provides a company with measures that combine lead (predictive) and lag (result) indicators, and identifies the linkages between the different measures." Because leading-edge companies are normally highly sensitive to customer perceptions and requirements, say Dauphinais, Means, and Price (2000), performance measures traditionally have been translated into "financial targets that are historically focused and reflect current issues to be addressed immediately." To this end, individuals within such companies typically work "in concert to achieve ... specific target[s] in the company's operations, processes, and service capabilities, and [build] their performance management framework to include measures covering all these aspects."

Traditional performance measurement/management systems have helped many organizations manage change, drive alignment of people and processes to support new goals, and transform organizational culture. They have played a notably effective role in transforming many public sector organizations, notes PwC consultant Trish Thomson (1999). "By systematically documenting and reporting performance, many public sector organizations [which are often perceived to be run with little or no accountability] have been able to demonstrate how much they do, how well they do it, and how much progress they have made over time in achieving goals," she says, thus "bridging the credibility gulch," as Morgan Kinghorn, former chief financial officer of the Internal Revenue Service puts it (Thomson, 1999).

Enhancing Internal Communications

Another approach many companies have used to enhance organizational alignment has involved beefing up communications efforts and ensuring that existing communications channels are working effectively.

Become Aware of the Communications Disconnects in Your Organization

Behind most organizational problems—diminished productivity, deteriorating customer service, low morale, or the inability to manage change initiatives effectively—there is usually a communications issue lurking in the woodwork, keeping the organization from operating at full capacity. Some of the more common communication problems are

- The company's leaders do not know how to communicate the imperative of change to rank-and-file employees. So, they do not get employee buy-in for change efforts.
- Middle managers lack the skills to manage and motivate employees effectively in times of downsizing or restructuring. Thus, employee morale sags and the rumor mill runs rampant.
- Training does not prepare people adequately for new and emerging job requirements. In essence, there is no alignment between what the organization needs people to do and the skills they learn in training.

Why do communication problems arise so often in companies? One reason is that CEOs do not always make communication with employees a business priority. For example, studies show that during downsizing, CEOs often focus more on number crunching than on people issues. The unfortunate result is the failure of organizational restructuring efforts. Another reason is that, despite emphasis on teams, people still operate within functional stove-pipes, and too many managers still practice "mushroom management"—controlling employees by keeping them in the dark. Finally, because companies tend to focus on results at the expense of operations, the process by which an organization communicates internally does not get much attention, at least not until the bottom line is adversely affected or customers scurry to competitors (Koonce, 1996).

Other Traditional Approaches to Foster Alignment

Still other traditional approaches companies have used to enhance organizational alignment have included conducting major reviews of current initiatives and removing individuals (blockers), who, in some cases, have resisted change either actively or covertly. Each of these approaches to enhancing organizational alignment has its benefits, and each has its drawbacks. Most notably, none of them provides for the kind of rigorous (and continuous) measurement of organizational performance against the requirements of customers. Nor do any of them contain the necessary infrastructure to ensure that, once achieved, better line-of-sight alignment (of strategy, people, processes, and technology) can be sustained to support marketplace needs or specific customer requirements.

For that, other, still more robust tools for building organizational alignment, are needed, and, in our view, the most powerful and effective of these is Six Sigma.[1]

The Ultimate Key to All Productivity Improvements?

Six Sigma is a high-performance, data-driven approach to analyzing the root causes of business problems and solving them. It ties the outputs of a business directly to marketplace requirements (figure 7-1). At the strategic, or *transformational*, level, the goal of Six Sigma is to align an organization keenly to its marketplace and deliver real improvements (and dollars) to the bottom line. At the operational, or *transactional*, level, Six Sigma's goal is to move business product or service attributes within the zone of customer

---

[1] Six Sigma is a registered trademark of Motorola.

Figure 7-1. Six Sigma business improvement.

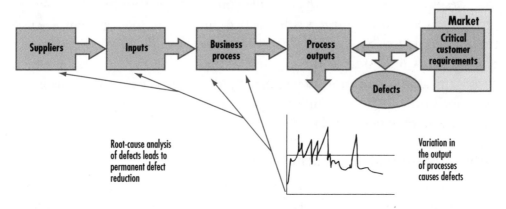

specifications and to dramatically shrink "process variation"—the cause of defects that negatively affects customers (figure 7-2).

Six Sigma appears to hold the key to guaranteeing consistently higher and higher levels of corporate performance (by meeting customer requirements) when it is linked to a company's strategy and when a detailed implementation plan is constructed (with appropriate feedback loops and other mechanisms) to gauge and monitor the company's customer performance over time. First introduced at Motorola, Six Sigma soon spread to other companies. At the former Honeywell (now part of GE), Six Sigma has been responsible for helping that company achieve annual productivity improvements of 6 percent or more. At GE Medical Systems, introduction of Six Sigma approaches recently produced a new generation X-ray tube with 10 times the life expectancy of existing tube technology. And, in GE's Aircraft Engine division, Six Sigma has helped cut paperwork for exports, cutting border delays during shipping by at least 50 percent.

What Is Six Sigma?

- *Definition:* Six Sigma is a vehicle for driving both transformational and transactional change in organizations today.
- *How it works at the transformational level:* Six Sigma provides a framework that potentially can be used to bring about large-scale integration of a company's processes, strategies, culture,

and customers to achieve and sustain breakaway business results.

• *How it works at the transactional level:* Six Sigma provides specific tools and approaches (activity-based accounting, statistical process control, lean processes, variation elimination, and so forth) that can be used to reduce defects and dramatically improve processes to increase customer satisfaction and drive down costs as a result.

Six Sigma requires that companies build their business around an intimate understanding of their customers' requirements, bringing as much discipline and focus to this external activity as they do to internal process-improvement efforts. The payoffs from these activities can be huge, enabling a company to achieve "quantum leaps in quality and competitiveness" (Blakeslee, 1999).

Impressive as these results sound, the challenges to a company in actually implementing Six Sigma practices can be enormous. According to Harry (1988), many companies today operate at about three sigma, which translates into roughly 67,000 defects per million opportunities (products, services, process steps, or transactions). If a company can move from two sigma

Figure 7-2. Six Sigma's objectives.

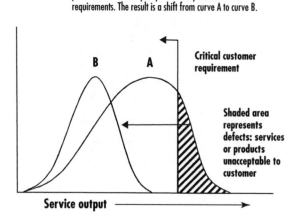

An objective of Six Sigma is to reduce variation and move product or service outputs permanently inside customer requirements. The result is a shift from curve A to curve B.

to Six Sigma it can achieve a reduction in defects from 308,000 defects per million opportunities to a mere 3.4 defects per million opportunities (Hunter & Schmitt, 1999). Manufacturing companies often get to four sigma, and service firms often operate at one or two sigma. Getting to a Six Sigma level of product, process, or service quality requires a rigorous, even "muscular" approach to business improvement. For example, top management must drive the effort, sufficient resources must be allocated for it, the culture must support change, and employees must develop new skills and behaviors to reinforce Six Sigma at the level of individual jobs and work processes (Blakeslee, 1999).

Your role in implementing Six Sigma approaches in your organization may very well involve introducing it to your company's leaders as a powerful and proven way to drive organizational alignment, to boost business performance, reduce cycle times, improve customer satisfaction statistics, or improve product or service quality. So, how do you get started doing that? Implementing Six Sigma successfully in any organization requires scrupulous attention to each of seven steps (figure 7-3), according to Blakeslee (1999).

Figure 7-3. Six Sigma implementation success factors.

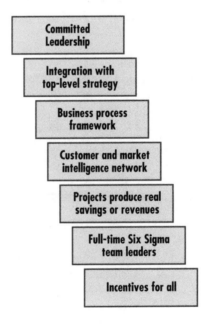

Step 1: Understand That Successful Six Sigma Implementation Is Driven by Committed Leaders

Leaders who possess what leadership consultant Noel Tichy describes as "edge" are the ones who have the tremendous energy that is required to implement Six Sigma approaches in their organizations. Six Sigma requires leaders who can make tough decisions affecting the long-term success of their businesses. Such leaders challenge conventional thinking, often push unpopular ideas, and are willing to push through the reluctance, resistance, and sometimes outright rebellion that can occur as part of championing truly transformational change in an organization. Two leaders whose efforts drove Six Sigma implementation in their organizations are GE CEO Jack Welch and former Honeywell CEO Larry Bossidy. How did these leaders do it?

Each man's commitment to Six Sigma was demonstrated through time, energy, resource allocation, and behavior on the job. Jack Welch makes it clear at GE, for example, that implementing Six Sigma is not optional. Forty percent of executive bonuses, for example, are tied to Six Sigma annual achievements. In GE's 1997 annual report, Welch described "the drive for Six Sigma quality" as the "centerpiece" of GE's "dreams and aspirations" (General Electric, 1997). Before retiring from Honeywell, Larry Bossidy used to tell employees and shareholders that continued emphasis on Six Sigma was central to the company's drive of realizing "6% productivity improvement forever" (AlliedSignal, 1997).

Step 2: Integrate Six Sigma Efforts With Existing Initiatives and Programs

Companies successful with Six Sigma make great efforts to integrate Six Sigma implementation with other corporate quality initiatives, improvement programs, business strategies, and performance metrics. Honeywell extended the use of Six Sigma tools and approaches outside manufacturing to back-office operations. It applied those tools to improving product development processes, for example, to get products to market faster.

Much the same is happening today at GE, where Welch enunciates three top corporate strategies for the foreseeable future: globalization, services, and Six Sigma. Consequently, at GE Capital Services, Six Sigma is being used to drive greater efficiency and productivity in all areas of GE's extensive financial services operation.

Figure 7-4. Integrating Six Sigma with business strategy.

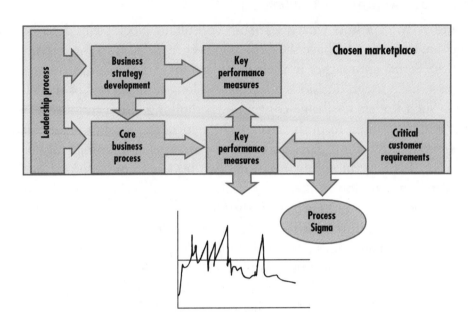

Integrating Six Sigma improvement strategies (at the business unit level) into a company's larger-gauge business goals is key to realizing Six Sigma success (figure 7-4). Like leadership, this alignment process cannot be delegated. Instead, it must be spearheaded by the senior management team to drive home its importance to all employees.

Step 3: Successful Six Sigma Implementation Is Supported Within a Framework of Process Thinking

Because it is such a robust approach to quality improvement, Six Sigma can, as noted, help a company realize quantum leaps in quality and competitiveness. But getting there requires a highly focused approach. For example, because it is based on quantitative analysis of a business and comparing a company's performance to critical customer requirements (CCRs), Six Sigma cannot be implemented effectively in an organization without rigorous mapping of existing business processes. Moreover, there must be agreement as to what those processes are and what kind of output customers expect from them.

It is the intersection of these outputs with CCRs that ultimately defines process sigma as well as long-term business success for any company. Being able to examine and close the gap between what a business produces and what customers demand is the essence of Six Sigma. The width of the gap can be used to set priorities for Six Sigma efforts because the lower the process sigma, the larger the gap. Organizations that identify improvement projects not as isolated endeavors but as part of this hierarchical framework realize a faster improvement rate.

Step 4: Six Sigma Requires Disciplined Customer and Market Intelligence Gathering

To make its Six Sigma efforts work, a firm must have a disciplined process for keeping in touch with existing levels of customer satisfaction and loyalty. It must also have an up-to-the-minute grasp of what the market is doing and where it is going. Anecdotal information about what customers want is not sufficient; CCRs must be known and measured.

How does one determine those requirements? First, the company must have a closed-loop process in place to gather customer and market intelligence data. Then, it must translate the data into hard measurements that can be analyzed regularly and compared to business process outputs (figure 7-5).

Gathering information, analyzing it, and acting on it regularly can ensure that the company's feedback loop remains closed and that the company is consistently measuring against current market requirements. Keep in mind that both current customer data and data gathered from competitors' customers should be used to help analyze what the market is doing.

Step 5: Six Sigma Projects Must Produce Real Savings or Revenues

"This Six Sigma thing has to pay its own way!" This is the cry of most business leaders when they first hear about Six Sigma. The reaction is appropriate. Over the years, improvement initiatives have promised a great deal but often delivered little. For that reason, any Six Sigma project a company implements should be designed to pay its way at least from the second year of implementation onward.

After a small net loss on GE's Six Sigma investment in 1996, the first year it was in place, the company's payoff from Six Sigma had reached more than $750 million by the end of 1998 (General Electric, 1998). Welch believes that savings of $8 billion to $12 billion per year can be realized by eliminating

Figure 7-5. Defining customer and market requirements.

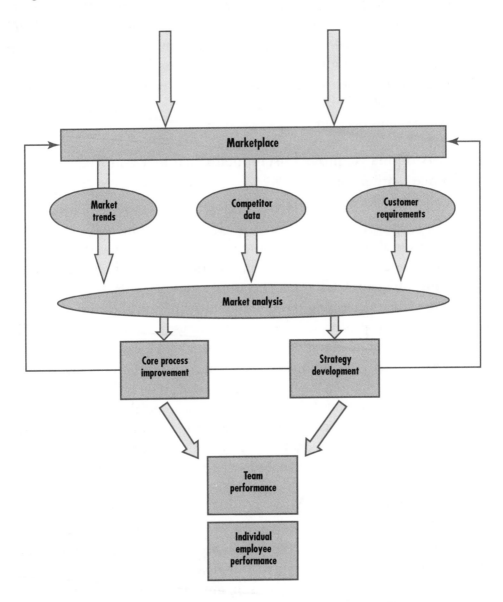

inefficiencies and lost productivity across GE (Byrne, 1998). Likewise, Honeywell has documented $1.5 billion in savings from Six Sigma since 1991 (Anonymous, 1998).

When putting together a portfolio of improvement projects to work on, it is important to design many to have short-term paybacks. This way an organization is forced to put Six Sigma principles to work immediately, thus quickly generating improved levels of service and quality, which, in turn, improves customer satisfaction and generates increased sales in the long term. Short-term payoffs from Six Sigma projects can include anything from improved process efficiency and increased capacity to lower operating costs and reduced costs from rework.

Design other improvement efforts to yield longer-term paybacks. For example, working to improve customer satisfaction over time creates a more robust revenue stream. Developing a more motivated workforce creates a stable foundation for sustaining long-term Six Sigma success.

Step 6: Lead Six Sigma Efforts With a Trained Corps of Team Leaders

Because Six Sigma is such an intense approach to quality improvement, it requires the disciplined training of dedicated practitioners. Known as Black Belts and Master Black Belts at GE and Motorola, the full-time trained professionals who drive Six Sigma improvement projects go by a variety of less exotic names at other companies.[2]

At GE, Black Belts are full-time leaders of teams responsible for measuring, analyzing, improving, and controlling critical processes that influence customer satisfaction or productivity growth. GE's Black Belts, who currently number more than 5,000, receive rigorous training in quality tools, root-cause analysis, and statistical methods. Because they are dedicated Six Sigma experts, Black Belts often manage or take part in numerous projects at once. A typical GE Black Belt, for example, leads three to five improvement teams, and a Master Black Belt will advise 10 to 15 (Blakeslee, 1999).

Master Black Belts are considered the most seasoned and senior of Black Belts. They review and mentor Black Belts. Selection is based on strong quantitative skills and on their teaching and mentoring abilities.

A typical curriculum for improvement team leaders includes four weeks of training, delivered just in time as a team begins its first project. Motorola developed an additional 1,400 Black Belts in 1999 during five weeks of training interspersed with project work as it strengthened its commitment to Six Sigma.

Companies considering Six Sigma should give careful thought to selection and deployment of improvement team members and leaders. The number of teams established should be weighed against the number of improvement

---

[2] Black Belt and Master Black Belt are trademarks and/or service marks of Sigma Consultants, LLC.

projects the company plans to run simultaneously and the amount of change the organization can absorb.

By requiring all its business leaders and aspiring business leaders to complete the equivalent of black-belt training before they are qualified for promotion, GE has produced a cadre of more than 70,000 part-time improvement team leaders. This sends a signal that Six Sigma is tightly aligned with the organization's values, not just for the short term but for the long term.

Step 7: Sustain Six Sigma With Continuous Reinforcement

Reward leaders who support initiatives and the improvement teams that carry them out. Companies get what they measure and reward, and Six Sigma business improvement is no exception. Because Six Sigma is fundamentally different from other quality programs, new incentives must be devised to get organizations moving in the right direction.

As noted, GE's CEO Welch requires any employee who wants to be considered for promotion to be Six Sigma trained—even executives. In addition to giving executive bonuses for achievement of Six Sigma milestones, Welch includes quality professionals at the Master Black Belt level and higher in GE's variable incentive compensation program.

GE's infamous audit staff includes an assessment of Six Sigma implementation in its overall management audit conducted regularly in all business units. Additionally, recipients of GE's Pinnacle Awards for outstanding individual performance include many who have embraced Six Sigma approaches in their business results.

The Implications of Six Sigma for Training and HRD Professionals

Clearly, as we have suggested in this chapter, Six Sigma is a powerful and proven tool for driving tight organizational alignment in any organization today. Indeed, its use has begun to extend well beyond manufacturing and electronic companies (where Six Sigma originated) to other types of businesses, from banks and financial services companies to chemical and pharmaceutical firms, utilities, health care, and even entertainment companies such as NBC.

We have outlined some of the factors that must be in place if you are to implement successful Six Sigma projects in your organization. To incorporate Six Sigma practices into an organization typically consists of four key phases:

1. analyzing your company's current capacity and strengths in meeting customer requirements and its readiness to implement Six Sigma approaches

2. planning how Six Sigma approaches can be integrated into the company to support the existing business strategy

3. focusing on developing Six Sigma skills and moving toward a better understanding of customer requirements

4. building the infrastructure and climate to support and sustain Six Sigma business approaches over time.

Phase 1: The Analysis Phase

In the analysis stage, you and your organization's top leaders need to evaluate the overall readiness of your organization to implement Six Sigma. This will involve profiling the organization's current alignment with its marketplace and identifying crucial gaps that may exist, typically through undertaking a Six Sigma readiness assessment. For example, are process performance targets tied directly to customer requirements as evidenced by error-free invoicing, 100 percent on-time delivery, and zero manufacturing defects in products rolling off the line? In the analysis stage, you must also determine what barriers or supports exist. For example, is there a change vision in place that can help guide the direction of your company's Six Sigma efforts? Are appropriate business structures and systems in place that may facilitate introduction of Six Sigma practices into the organization? Finally, you must determine whether customer requirements and competitive intelligence are gathered systematically and upgraded and analyzed on a continuous basis.

The analysis stage involves benchmarking what other companies have done with Six Sigma and using customer surveys, focus groups, and one-on-one interviews with both customers and internal company "process owners" to determine an organization's specific challenges around Six Sigma implementation.

Phase 2: The Planning Phase

After you and your organization's leadership team have completed the analysis stage, it is time to move to the planning stage. In phase 2, your goal as a training or HRD professional is to help your organization's leaders put together a Six Sigma implementation plan, complete with as many steps as necessary. In this stage, you (and they) must determine how Six Sigma tactics and thinking can best be used to support the company's overall business strategy. For example, "How do we want Six Sigma to help us achieve our business strategy?" and "What processes must we redesign to help us achieve these goals?" You will no doubt have to facilitate conversations (at many leadership levels) to determine performance targets for various core business processes that have been identified for improvement. You will also need to facilitate conversations around the specific roles and responsibilities that leaders and process owners will play in implementing Six Sigma approaches in the organization.

Finally, you will need to focus a great deal of leadership attention and energy on how best to introduce Six Sigma methods and approaches throughout all levels of the organization. Implementing Six Sigma approaches always involves a radical redesign of people's jobs, especially around issues of accountability and performance metrics. It is conceivable that many core work processes will be redesigned to better meet the current and emerging needs of customers. This will necessarily entail new work behaviors, training, and attitudes on the part of front-line workers, process owners, and virtually everyone else in the organization if Six Sigma implementation is to proceed successfully.

Phase 3: The Focusing Phase

In the focusing phase, you and your company's leaders will get into the actual details of Six Sigma implementation. This stage involves providing leaders at different levels with the training they will need to implement Six Sigma approaches. Thus, Six Sigma workshops are commonly a part of this stage. Once training is completed, it becomes important to create project improvement teams and identify potential Black Belts and Master Black Belts. At this stage, hands-on work by Six Sigma teams to develop core process and subprocess maps also takes place, the result of the previous analysis and planning steps. Finally, it is at this stage that you and your organization's leaders will implement approaches to build closer continuous connections with customers for purposes of performance feedback.

Phase 4: The Building Phase

With all the elements for successful Six Sigma implementation now in place, it is in phase 4 that organizations typically launch Six Sigma projects, some with short-term end dates in mind and others that will continue for longer periods of time. At this stage, your organization's leaders and employees, armed with Six Sigma knowledge and techniques, become fully engaged in the daily tasks of process management and improvement, measurement of business performance against customer requirements, and the work of tweaking and redesigning processes and subprocesses in accordance with customer feedback. Experience has shown us that once Six Sigma projects are fully in place and a company's leaders and employees are deployed to manage them, a company can begin to generate results (shortened cycle times, reduced costs, improvements in productivity) within just four to six months. In addition, short-term "quick wins" may result from immediate changes to procedures and work routines. Moreover, our experience suggests that each Black Belt within an organization has the potential to produce up to $1,000,000 in Six Sigma gains annually.

Your Tools for Building Organizational Alignment

No doubt, implementing Six Sigma methods and approaches in an organization is a formidable undertaking, albeit one that can generate enormous benefits once Six Sigma business practices are in place.

Six Sigma is the single most powerful vehicle we have found to drive tight organizational alignment within companies today. Indeed, its use in organizations today is spreading because it is a powerful tool not only for helping to ensure ongoing process and productivity improvement, but also for driving organizational renewal and transformation as well. For these reasons, we recommend that you (and others with whom you work) invest time and resources in becoming qualified in Six Sigma techniques and approaches. Doing so will position you, in powerful ways, to help your organization achieve the climate of internal alignment that will be the key to its business success in the 21st century. And, it will help you address one of the most fundamental of all leadership challenges facing companies today: how to better meet the current and emerging needs of customers in an increasingly competitive business environment.

Nevertheless, more traditional alignment tools—traditional performance measurement/management systems, better communications, project reviews, and removal of those resistant to change initiatives—are also approaches that you and your organization may find useful in driving stronger organizational alignment. By all means, you should consider using these as part of your initial arsenal in achieving greater organizational cohesiveness, short of undertaking the ambitious Six Sigma approach.

Regardless of which tools you choose to drive tighter organizational alignment, it will be necessary to galvanize the energy of people inside your organization to make it happen. Indeed, it will be critical that you *connect* people with one another for this purpose, and that you then *create* and *channel* leaders' energies to achieve this goal. That is the topic addressed in chapter 8.

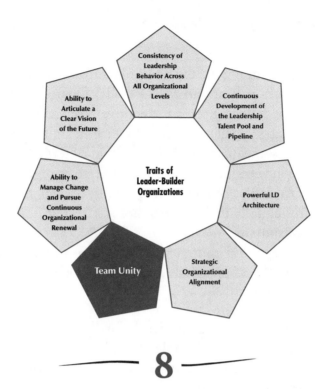

The image shows a flower-like diagram of pentagons arranged in a circle around a center labeled "Traits of Leader-Builder Organizations". The pentagons contain:
- Consistency of Leadership Behavior Across All Organizational Levels
- Ability to Articulate a Clear Vision of the Future
- Continuous Development of the Leadership Talent Pool and Pipeline
- Ability to Manage Change and Pursue Continuous Organizational Renewal
- Powerful LD Architecture
- Team Unity
- Strategic Organizational Alignment

— 8 —

Building Top Leadership Team Unity

The first step in putting together the kind of team that can direct a change effort is to find the right membership. Four key characteristics seem to be essential to effective guiding coalitions. They are:

1. *Position power:* Are enough players on board, especially the main line managers, so that those left out cannot easily block progress?

2. *Expertise:* Are the various points of view—in terms of discipline, work experience, nationality, etc.—relevant to the task at hand adequately represented so that informed, intelligent decisions will be made?

3. *Credibility:* Does the group have enough people with good reputations in the firm so that its pronouncements will be taken seriously by other employees?

4. *Leadership:* Does the group include enough proven leaders to be able to drive the change process?

— John Kotter, Leading Change (1996).

Creating unity among the members of a top executive team is no small feat. Whether you are an HRD or T&D professional, a business executive or manager, or an executive coach, this is probably the most significant change challenge you may face in building your LD programs. Frankly, it is the biggest challenge that external consultants face when they first begin working with a new corporate or organizational client. This reluctance to unify is largely the result of top executives acting autonomously throughout their careers and not seeing it as being in their best interest to collaborate.

The following are typical comments that OD consultants (both internal and external) and T&D professionals often hear when they first begin working with executive teams:

- ❁ "We've been at this change initiative for about a year and it seems we haven't come very far. People are still questioning the vision," noted the leader of a financial services firm as his organization began a major restructuring.

- ❁ "Our organization doesn't lack for good ideas. We've got the best and brightest thinkers around. Our problem is we can't seem to implement those ideas," observed the top executive of a global chemical company.

- ❁ "We've moved fast to put the new organization in place. But now that people are in their new roles, they seem clueless as to what to do differently," worried the CEO of a large retail organization.

If the top executives of a company cannot agree on a common direction, then forget about rallying the 80,000 employees of that organization behind one. Indeed, employees who detect divisions or disagreements among an organization's top leaders usually stay committed to their immediate bosses and their beliefs, or they will opt to "sit tight" and see what happens next. Either way, the existence of fragmented constituencies (and multiple belief systems) inside organizations can result in confusion, chaos, turf battles, inertia, and, at worst, anarchy. Just try to create effective leadership programs in the middle of this chaos!

Why Is It So Tough to Form Top Leadership Teams?

Teaming at the top of an organization is often tough to accomplish. There are many reasons for this. For one thing, top executives often have strong control needs. By instinct, they rely more on their own wisdom and experience than on team approaches to solve problems. "[B]y the time most executives get to the top, they find it hard to allow their performance to depend on people who are neither their boss nor their subordinates," note Katzenbach and Smith (1994). This can easily keep a top team from coalescing around a shared purpose, and can prevent strong top team synergy from ever being realized.

Second, many senior executives are not temperamentally inclined to take on the "shirtsleeve" work that is required if they are going to be part of true team. The reason is that in their roles as senior executives they have typically managed staffs, been accustomed to delegating work to others, and relied on key subordinates for background materials, research, idea development, speeches, talking points, and even their "point of view" about many business and organizational topics.

Third, strong egos can easily get in the way of top executives taking the time—or exerting the energy—to "bond" with their fellow senior executives in true team settings. Because many top executives in organizations view their peers as potential rivals for the CEO job, forming a productive, top-level executive team becomes difficult, and creating strong and synergistic group dynamics can be problematic.

Finally, top executives have limited free time and may view top team meetings and assignments as activities to which they want to devote only the minimal amount of time required. Therefore, they may fail to personally involve themselves in top team activities, will send subordinates to key meetings, and may in many cases fail to inject themselves personally into the top team unity building process. This weak commitment can cause the group identity and dynamics of a top executive team to suffer from the very start. As Katzenbach (1997) aptly puts it, "Real teams need time to develop—shaping goals, brainstorming approaches to how to best work together. Most executives have little patience for the forming, storming, and norming that real teams need to go through" to get to high performance.

The Three *C*s of Change

Team unity can make or break your plans to develop leaders. Lack of unity often ends up clouding boardroom discussions with questions such as the following:

✦ Should we focus our efforts on improving what we are in the business of doing now, or should we redefine the business entirely?

✦ How much time do we have to make this transformation? Does it have to be accomplished in the short term (one to five years) or long term (five to 10 years)?

✦ How can we move in new directions, retrain, and re-deploy our existing talent base, or seek out those with new hot skills?

✦ How do we define our competition? Are they our current competitors or future companies that have yet to emerge?

✦ How do we cope with (let alone) exploit the power of e-business to enhance relationships with customers, and to change how we work?

In light of these challenges, how can a CEO create strong top team unity, and, more important for those responsible for creating LD programs, how do you create programs that address this critical component for organizational success? Our work in building top team unity to lead and manage change efforts was sparked from a systematic survey of nearly 1,000 global change agents working with top teams of global companies. We asked our change agents to think of truly exceptional leaders who had led and managed long-term change efforts and to describe the leadership characteristics embodied by these highly successful leaders. The survey responses were surprisingly similar and can be summarized as the three *C*s of change:

✦ They **CONNECT** people to their company's vision and mission

✦ They **CREATE** the conditions for new ways of thinking, working, and acting inside their organizations

✦ They **CHANNEL** their organization's energy to achieve new goals and objectives.

Step 1: They CONNECT People to the Company's Vision and Direction

Leaders who are effective team builders are obsessed with getting people connected to their company's vision and direction. They are genuinely interested in producing great change in their people, are strong and passionate in their beliefs about the future, and encourage people to try new things as a means to keep them energized. At the same time, leaders who are successful team builders do not act in a vacuum. Indeed, because they care both about their people and the future of their organizations, they tend to operate in a consultative manner, building consensus toward a vision in inclusive ways. Communicating a compelling vision relentlessly and getting buy in from people along the way are two of the tools such leaders use to stay personally connected to people and to ensure that employees stay personally connected to the organization's new or emerging goals.

Audrey Weil, senior vice president of America Online, is one such leader who operates this way. At the time that AOL acquired CompuServe, she worked assiduously to blend and harmonize two different organizational cultures and to engage CompuServe employees in the process of becoming part of a newly combined AOL-CompuServe organization. Not only did she cascade business goals throughout *all* levels of the organization, but at one point, she even read the personal goals and objectives of all 500 CompuServe employees to make sure they were aligned with those of the new, enlarged AOL organization (appendix E).

To facilitate these integration efforts, she provided regular opportunities for employees to voice concerns and offer feedback on integration activities. She also made it company policy to celebrate both individual and team successes as CompuServe employees took on new goals and were expected to work in new ways as part of a new, much larger "matrix" organization (Weil, 2000).

Take a look around and you will see many examples of companies that know how to CONNECT both externally and internally. Companies like Dell Computer, Sun MicroSystems, and USAA (a well-known insurance provider) are all leaders in the field of customer research and information gathering, regularly using market sampling approaches and feedback mechanisms to translate raw customer intelligence and information into data that is used to rapidly refine their business approaches and core best practices. They also work diligently to create internal organizational structures to ensure rapid information sharing and cross-functional communication.

Companies that connect are typically information rich; they know their customers, they hire or acquire their competitors, and they dedicate time to building relationships with their suppliers. The constant input of new information breeds energy for continuous change and organizational renewal.

Step 2: They CREATE the Context for New Ways of Thinking, Acting, and Working Inside the Organization

Leaders who are effective team builders work hard to create the context for new ways of thinking, acting, and working inside their organizations, a trait that change consultant Noel Tichy describes as "edge." This often begins with the leader questioning everything from established beliefs to entrenched business practices and engaging his or her top team in active dialogue, discussion, and debate about current and future strategic directions. Leaders who are strong team builders not only entertain new ideas, but they are relentless in pushing the envelope and encouraging out-of-the-box thinking. They encourage creativity and question the status quo because their goal is to forge new paths, new directions, and new opportunities for growth, and to do that they get their teams enmeshed in the grueling work of envisioning future business scenarios.

Lou Gerstner, CEO of IBM, is one leader who is very much a team builder in this sense. When he came to IBM he began immediately to shake things up, constantly asking people why they did things the way they did, and challenging them to find better, more efficient, and more customer-friendly ways to do business. Jack Welch of GE is another CEO who encourages creativity and risk taking, most notably by focusing on the importance of people adopting "boundaryless" behavior in doing their jobs, working across job titles, functions, and levels to "get the customer's work" done.

Today's economy is also replete with examples of companies that know how to CREATE. Some companies, including Intel, MicroSoft, and other high-technology firms, are known as creative seedbeds for new technologies, new customer approaches, and unique partnering arrangements between them and their customers. The cultures of such companies facilitate the transforming of new ideas into new business prototypes and value propositions. They are able to turn information (which is neutral) into knowledge and opportunities, through discussion, dialogue, and debate. The result is even greater energy, which provides the momentum for such companies to operate successfully in a world of growing competition and constantly shrinking product development cycles.

Step 3: They CHANNEL the Organization's Energy to Achieve New Goals and Objectives

Finally, leaders who are effective team builders are deft at executing goals and ensuring their sustained implementation over time. They know how to use individual team members as levers to drive change efforts, ensure completion of critical projects, overcome inertia and resistance, and achieve the organizational momentum to ensure that important initiatives neither fail nor get derailed. In so doing, they are able to "channel and amplify" initial team energy into a self-perpetuating cycle of change, no matter how hard the effort may initially be and regardless of the resistance that is first encountered.

Lee Griffin, former CEO of Premier Bank of Louisiana, is an excellent example of a leader who was able to channel the energy of his executive team to support transformation efforts. In the early 1990s, Premier Bank was one of the most profitable banks in the country, yet Griffin foresaw the need to radically redesign the bank's core business processes if it were to remain competitive over the long term. He galvanized members of his top executive team to take risks, to enter into heated and even fierce discussions with one another about the bank's future direction. As a result, tremendous organizational energy was released, which enabled Griffin and other team members to overcome internal resistance to change and fundamentally redesign how the bank provided customer services (Griffin, 1998).

Many companies today display a strong ability to CHANNEL their creative energy and output to achieve desired outcomes, for example, to create a strong brand identity. This is evident in such organizations as McDonalds, The Gap, GE, and Wal-Mart that have efficient structures and mechanisms to produce results most efficiently while minimizing loss.

Applying "Organizational Thermodynamics" to Leadership Initiatives

Connecting, creating, and channeling—all these "acts" provide the means to catalyze the available energy inside an organization, shape it, and direct it toward specific ends (for example, completion of a major business initiative or a large-gauge transformation effort). Stated differently, leadership is a dynamic force that has little to do with formally designated roles and everything to do with the ability of top leaders to create and channel organizational intent, to master, if you will, "the laws of organizational thermodynamics."

Nowadays, many performance interventions consultants become involved with have to do with helping top teams manage "energy flows" inside their organizations, usually to drive large-scale change projects. This process can be best understood in the terms of the three *C*s of change just described. Implicit in this model is the idea that the energy "creation and transfer" challenges of an organization will be different at different times but will always involve the commitment and participation of the top leadership team.

For example, at times it may be critical for an organization and its leaders to build connections if, for example, the company has lost touch with its external environment (changing customer requirements and so forth). At other times, a company may be connected to its environment but need to do creative work to make new kinds of breakthroughs—new ideas, approaches or technologies—that can be used as the basis of new competitive strength or marketplace position. In still other cases, an organization may be full of creative ideas but need help transforming (channeling) them into new solutions (new products and services). So, in these cases, channeling becomes the focus of necessary teamwork.

Nevertheless, the first and most important goal for any leadership team should be to CONNECT the organization to the outside environment. The quality of the organization's connections to the external environment becomes the critical determinant of its ability to then be adaptive (CREATE) and perform optimally (CHANNEL). All things being equal, an organization that is well connected to its environment has greater potential to create an adaptive response than one that is poorly connected.

As Burke and Trahant (2000) point out, connectedness is what ensures sustained organizational resilience and the ability of organizations to continuously change, grow, and renew themselves. But, creating such connections to the external environment cannot be performed by any one leader working alone. Instead, it takes many change agents in an organization who work together to connect, create, and channel energy into ensuring continuous organizational vitality.

Forging Top Team Unity: First Steps

So, where do you actually start in building top team unity around the concepts of connecting, creating, and channeling organizational energy? Specifically, what role should you, as a T&D professional, OD consultant, or executive coach, play in that process?

First, you must help members of your senior management team CON-NECT with each other, CREATE a preliminary team identity, and begin to CHANNEL their collective energies as a group. This is a necessary precursor and model for what then needs to be orchestrated elsewhere in the organization at other levels and in other areas. It begins by building team trust, articulating common goals, developing a common philosophy of doing business, and engaging in healthy, productive debate that leads to breakthrough solutions—solutions that everybody on a top team can live with even if none of the directions taken is any one individual's first choice.

At the beginning, you may have to spend time one-on-one with top team members to build the trust, credibility, and relationships needed to help them venture down the path of team discovery and decision making together. Having knowledge of individual team histories and member relationships is crucial at this stage. Not everyone on a leadership team enjoys the same level of credibility, trust, and respect from the organization, and not every leader respects and values every other. It is essential to explore these dynamics at the start of your work with the team, both in group settings and in one-on-one sessions with leaders.

If your company's senior leadership team is very fragmented to begin with (for instance, if they have had a long but difficult working history), help the team find common ground upon which to build (chapter 3). Often, in cases of team fragmentation, the perceptions team members have of one another (and of themselves) are of winners or losers. Relationships among team members may be strained, damaged, or even broken in some cases. Your role as a group facilitator is to get everyone on the team to realize that they, together, are *the* team leading the organization and that their individual success depends largely on their ability to work together collectively. It is critical to help your CEO leverage his or her influence to improve team atmosphere and group dynamics. Your coaching role will likely involve helping him or her understand the nature of the conflicts within the team and determine a coaching strategy for each member. If cooperation and respect still are not exhibited, that can become grounds for dismissing individual top team members.

If your top leadership team is newly formed, do some early work to help the team coalesce as a working group. One way to do this (even if there is only a single new team member on the team) is by holding informal activities outside of work. Icebreaker events, such as receptions, dinners, resort retreats, and so forth, can help bring the group together. New members can have a hard time working in a system that already has its relationships mapped out. They often feel outside the system, are sensitive to insider jokes and banter, and may need to be encouraged to enter into group discussions. Newcomers who are aggressive change agents, on the other hand, are at great risk of not being accepted by an established group, if the others perceive them to lack understanding about the system they are trying to change. When we work with senior leadership teams we often spend time getting new members up to speed about the dynamics of the team they are joining. We do this by sharing member histories with them and coaching them on the group's operating norms and culture.

As you begin working with your top leadership team, you must be not only a facilitator and one-on-one coach, you must also be a diagnostician, taking note of the group (and subgroup) dynamics at work within the confines of the team. Find out where team unity is already quite strong, as well as where team members are wide apart on issues. Assess where personality conflicts and style differences may be getting in the way of good communications or effective decision making, as well as where group functioning may be quite good. Finally, be alert to status differences among team members to determine how and where you must work to help repair relationships or generate mutual respect among team members.

Your powers of observation at this stage are critical to the subsequent courses of action you take with the group. To help you do the kind of group-process data gathering that is essential at this point, use assessment 8-1 to help you assess the present state of group dynamics within your organization's top team.

Consultative Issues to Consider

It will take you a bit of time to diagnose top team issues and dynamics and then map out a path to take in addressing them. However, this is time very well spent.

Connection Issues

If your organization's top leaders are challenged by connection issues, familiarize yourself with research organizations, survey firms, market research companies, and other outside vendors and services on which you can call, if necessary, for assistance. Such organizations can be helpful when it comes to tracking and analyzing environmental trends, demographic shifts, changes in the competitive landscape, and other facets that affect a company's overall

Assessment 8-1. Status of group dynamics within the top organizational team.

When it comes to CONNECTING:

1. How clearly do team members understand customer, competitor, and marketplace issues?

2. How clearly do members of the top team understand their organization's issues, concerns, strengths, and weaknesses?

3. How insulated is the leadership team from information that exists elsewhere in the organization, or is it closely in touch with what is happening at other levels?

4. How united are members of the leadership team in their views when it comes to understanding the company's present and future situation?

5. How well does the top leadership team understand the capability of the organization to make necessary changes?

When it comes to CREATING:

1. How much tolerance does the top leadership team have for those who challenge the status quo and question existing strategies, methods, and processes?

2. How passionate are senior leaders in their beliefs about the future and what will make for future success?

3. How does the leadership team handle failure? Is there a second chance granted for creative attempts that fail the first time around?

(continued next page)

Assessment 8-1. Status of group dynamics within the top organizational team. *(continued)*

4. How much does the leadership team invest in researching and developing initiatives, pilot testing ideas, and learning through clinical trials?

5. How does the leadership team make the most use of the connections among people to create a learning and growing organization?

6. How does the leadership team encourage and support diversity in the organization, not only diversity of ethnicity, race, gender, sexual orientation, and so forth, but diversity of thought, professional practice, and opinion?

When it comes to CHANNELING:

1. What kinds of structures are in place to test good ideas and evaluate their benefits?

2. What communication channels are most often used? Least used?

3. How does the current organization structure "fit or match up with" the future direction?

4. What kinds of feedback mechanisms are in place to monitor whether good, creative ideas make it to implementation?

5. How much time does the leadership team spend on implementation planning?

6. How diverse is the group of people involved in implementation planning and execution?

operating health, industry position, profitability, and competitiveness. Generating such objective data for a top team to use in decision making improves team productivity and performance enormously—especially when individual top team members (with strong though subjective opinions) are at loggerheads with one another, preventing the top team from coming to consensus about action steps and team goals.

Creativity Issues

To coax creative thinking out of your senior leadership team requires, above all else, expert facilitation skills on your part. You may have to challenge your group to think out of the box, to take personal risks, to think in new or even radical ways about the future of the organization and your business, and, most important, to take personal ownership for the ideas being discussed by the team.

In cases where creativity is stymied, it is often helpful to bring change agents in from other organizations to talk with team members about their experiences with corporate transformation. Field trips to observe practices in other organizations or even other countries can also open up peoples' perspectives and broaden the range of approaches that team members decide to take in tackling problems.

Consider using group survey tools such as the Kirton Adaptation Inventory (KAI), an excellent tool to apply to the visioning process and other group endeavors, to measure your senior leadership team's innovation quotient. Tools such as the Myers-Briggs Type Indicator assessment are also useful in helping team members understand their own thinking and decision-making styles and those of fellow team members.

Channeling Issues

As your top team moves forward to plan and implement major transformation initiatives or other business projects, identify individuals who can support your efforts in such areas as project management, systems implementation/administration, and process design. Having such staff on hand (or reliable outside contractors) can help ensure the success of complex, multiyear initiatives, for which rigorous project management, system tracking, monitoring, and evaluation of change efforts are required.

At the same time, do not overlook what might be the need for additional support and help in the areas of process facilitation and leadership coaching and development. The complexity of many change initiatives—the number of people involved, the number of meetings required, for example—can rapidly overwhelm a small internal team of organizational consultants. Therefore, you may need to supplement your internal team of strategists, organizational change experts, coaches, industry gurus, and technology experts with selected independent contractors or consultants from established professional service firms.

Recognize Who Your Client Really Is

When building top team unity, remember: There is no such thing as having a dedicated single client even if he or she happens to be the CEO of the company. Instead, to create what Harvard Business School professor John Kotter (1996) appropriately describes as a "guiding coalition" to drive change efforts, you will need to work with an entire organizational system of stakeholders, powerbrokers, process owners, and change champions at many levels on a going-forward basis. Monitoring and reappraising the interrelationships of individuals within this "constellation of organizational influence" will be key both to forging and retaining strong team unity and organizational momentum as business initiatives proceed. The job will require that you possess strong skills of observation, conflict management, and facilitation. You will also need to possess an astute political sense and the ability to continually "reframe" issues for discussion. This will be critical to smooth conflicts, guarantee clear communications, and preserve working harmony not just among top team members, but also among their lieutenants and proxies elsewhere in the organization.

Other Ways to Boost Top Team Unity

Given the potential roadblocks that can get in the way of high-performing top leadership teams, what can you, as a T&D professional, do to break the logjam? The following are specific things that will help create tighter team unity at the top of your organization, and more efficient, productive team dynamics as well:

> ✿ *Set rigorous timelines associated with concrete tasks and clear objectives.* Top team energy will be generated around completion of specific tasks, and this will help build momentum for the project to move

forward. One recent example of a top team rising to such a goal-oriented challenge occurred in 1998 as the Federal Aviation Administration was preparing to ensure that there would be no problems with the nation's air traffic control system when the calendar turned to the year 2000. The FAA Administrator Jane Garvey used the imperative of being "Y2K ready" as a powerful change driver to galvanize the senior members of her leadership team to ensure that the nation's skies would be safe and that no planes would drop out of the sky on January 1, 2000 (Garvey, 1999). Garvey and her senior leadership team had to oversee the repair or replacement of some 430 "mission-critical" systems that represented the very heart of America's air traffic control system. They also had to form strong working relationships with other players in the aviation industry, including airlines, aircraft manufacturers, trade groups, vendors, and even foreign countries whose own civil aviation Y2K efforts it did not control. Garvey aligned FAA's top managers behind achieving specific benchmark goals on a continuous basis right up to the end of 1999. The project proved to be an enormous success, ushering in the new millennium without a glitch.

✿ *Assign tasks to subgroups of the full team.* This enables individual top leaders to work together to complete substantive work assignments on their own or in small groups. Many senior management groups spend almost all their joint time as a full team reviewing the work of other people, but successful teams at the top "have broken out of this pattern by assigning specific tasks to one or more individuals and by expecting them to deliver essential work-products for integration by the entire team in subsequent working sessions," say Katzenbach and Smith (1994). "This causes members to do real work together beyond full-team meetings, allowing *team* involvement and accountability to grow outside the context of discuss and decide sessions."

✿ *Be sure the top team possesses a sufficiently diverse (and deep) skill set.* One reason many top teams do not function strongly as teams is that membership is based on hierarchical status in the organization, not skill sets. "When membership [for top teams] is selected across functional areas, sometimes representatives are chosen based on faulty criteria: who has time to fill the assignment, who needs something to do, or simply whose turn it might be. This does not guarantee members will have the best qualifications for the task at hand" (Essex & Kusy, 1999). Teams operate more efficiently and generate better quality work products when team membership is based on the skill mix required to complete a specifically mandated project rather than on a person's status within the organization.

❀ *Do an equal amount of work—this includes everyone, even the leader.* One way to ensure that top teams begin to function well is to require that individual members do equal amounts of work, put their own sweat equity into projects, and do not simply delegate everything to staff or less senior managers to complete. Katzenbach and Smith (1994) point out that in their experience working with one senior management team, the team "operated equipment, negotiated with suppliers, wrote advertising copy, constructed pricing models, and set up communications networks. As a result, the members of the team doing any particular piece of real work had personally invested in its lessons and outcomes, earning a higher regard and deeper trust from their teammates." There was no doubt that some work was delegated to others, they note, but "members did enough real work themselves . . . to engender the mutual respect and mutual accountability characteristic of team performance."

❀ *Break down hierarchical patterns of interaction.* Katzenbach and Smith (1994) suggest that to forge "organically" strong group dynamics among the members of a top management team, it is good to get people in tasks unrelated to their normal everyday position in the hierarchy. When people get involved this way, they leave job titles at the door, work cross-functionally, and create mutual accountability for the results that are achieved. When such work approaches are emphasized, say Katzenbach and Smith, individual contributors begin to think of the team's output, not in terms of what they have done by themselves, but in terms of what they have done in interaction with others. Action learning projects (chapters 5 and 6) provide one vehicle for achieving these "catalytic connections" of one person with others. So, too, do ice breakers and team-building exercises in which groups of executives take part in action scenarios or are forced to solve problems affecting their personal survival, security, or safety. "Such nonhierarchically oriented assignments provide fundamental building blocks for team work-products and team performance," say Katzenbach and Smith (1994).

❀ *Don't try to avoid conflict among members of a top leadership team.* Conflict can be an indicator of robust group dynamics and is, in fact, a necessary component in forging group consensus. A considerable body of research has demonstrated that conflict over issues is not only likely within top management teams but also valuable. Indeed, management teams whose members challenge one another's thinking develop a more complete understanding of the choices, create a richer range of options, and make better decisions (Eisenhardt, Kahway & Bourgeois, 1997). "Without healthy conflict, groups lose their effectiveness. Managers become superficially harmonious but privately act out their true positions." Notwithstanding, be sure that healthy competition does not turn personal or destructive. Consider using tools such as "Groupware" electronic meeting technology (appendix C) that enables members of a group to dialogue with one another, using laptops to record their feelings, opinions, and votes on significant (sometimes contentious) issues. Often, the use of such tools improves a group's discussion and decision-making process because it encourages less dominant personalities to speak up and voice their issues and concerns (electronically) and not be overshadowed by others who are more verbally dominant.

Applying the Three *C*s

This chapter has discussed the "thermodynamics" of energy flows inside organizations and why it is important that leaders be able to connect with employees and then create and channel organizational energy to achieve their business goals. A case study about A&P (appendix D) highlights how a 140-year-old grocery store chain has been using this approach over the last two years to create a new organization, connect leaders to rank-and-file employees, and channel organizational energies toward new and aggressive customer service and earnings goals. This case study provides an insightful look not just at how the methodology is being used at A&P, but how you might, in turn, use it in your organization, too.

Abundant supplies of organizational energy are very much needed in companies today, as they continually transform themselves in response to rapidly changing business conditions. Consequently, the leadership competency known as change management is perhaps the single most critical leadership requirement in organizations today, which is why it is the focus of chapter 9. Chapter 9 examines the components of effective change leadership and provides guidance on how you, as an HRD professional, OD consultant, or executive coach, can help your organization's leaders develop or enhance their leadership skills in this critical area.

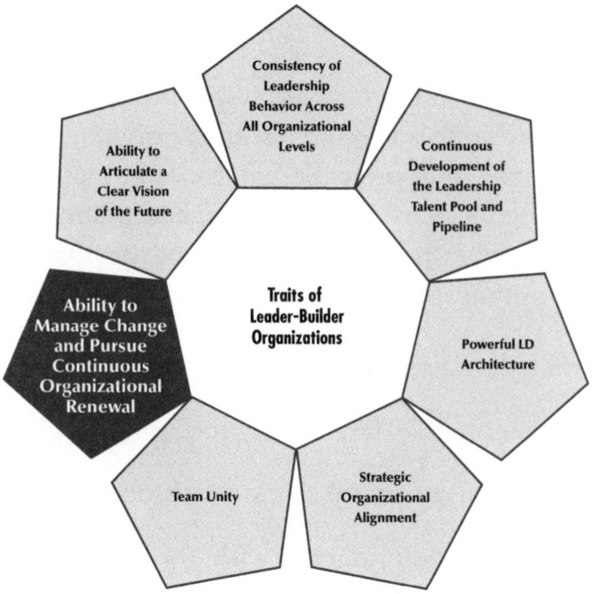
Consistency of Leadership Behavior Across All Organizational Levels
Continuous Development of the Leadership Talent Pool and Pipeline
Powerful LD Architecture
Strategic Organizational Alignment
Team Unity
Ability to Manage Change and Pursue Continuous Organizational Renewal
Ability to Articulate a Clear Vision of the Future
Traits of Leader-Builder Organizations

9

How to Initiate and Sustain Continuous Change

> The truth is that change is inherently messy. It is always complicated. It invariably involves a massive array of sharply conflicting demands. Despite the best-laid plans, things never happen in exactly the right order—and in fact, few things rarely turn out exactly right the first time around. Most important, the reality of change in the organizational trenches defies rigid academic models as well as superficial management fads.
>
> — David Nadler, *Champions of Change* (1998).

Being at the helm of a major change initiative is tough for leaders. If your leaders accept this fact readily and are prepared to do everything they can to make a change initiative succeed, then the prognosis for change is good. If, however, your leaders are inclined to challenge this fact, saying, "How difficult can this be?" then planning for and training your leaders in change initiatives could be problematic.

This chapter provides the information you need to understand change initiatives and prepare your leaders to lead these organizational realities successfully. The personal and professional leadership challenges associated with successful change leadership are not to be underestimated. Consider the following rather sobering statistics collected by Dick Smith of PricewaterhouseCoopers about business transformation initiatives:

- ✿ 80 percent of all major change initiatives fail

- ✿ 75 percent of those that fail are due to poor change leadership

- ✿ 70 percent of change initiatives start with poor leadership

- ✿ 100 percent of change initiatives with poor, long-term leadership fail.

This chapter is written for those who are about to lead a major change program and for those who must coach them through the process. By identifying and examining the behaviors, attitudes, and actions necessary for success, this chapter attempts to answer the questions most often raised by new change leaders.

Why Is Leading Change Different From Other Kinds of Leadership?

New change leaders often approach their role from any one of a number of perspectives:

- ✿ They have complete confidence in their abilities, knowledge of what is required, and familiarity with the process by which they will attain success.

- ✿ They have significant doubts and anxieties about their role, the skills required to do the job properly, and the steps that must be taken to attain success.

- ✿ They are resentful that they have been given significant extra duties on top of an already substantial workload and, therefore, have little or no commitment to either the change program or the reason for its creation.

The Gallery of Leadership Types

Some leaders (referred to here as "type A" leaders, who are accustomed to being in control) are often in for a shock when it comes to spearheading change initiatives. They find that the skills that made them successful earlier in their careers (the abilities to be hard-charging and domineering, for example) have little relevance or application when it comes to managing business transformation. Letting go of these skills as the primary method of leading while learning new skills and tools based mostly on collaboration and team-building is the main challenge faced by type A leaders in leading successful change. With appropriate support, however, type A leaders can make successful and highly effective transitions from being traditional, top-down CEOs to being flexible, empowering leaders, able to energize people, forge tight team unity, and move their organizations in new directions.

An excellent example of a leader who made such a transition in the mid-1990s is Errol Marshall, chairman of Shell South Africa. Long steeped in Shell culture and somewhat aristocratic in demeanor, Marshall recognized that to reverse his company's faltering business performance, he and his organization had to fundamentally reinvent how they did business. In essence, they had to roll up their sleeves, get rid of bureaucracy, become better attuned to customer needs, and move closer to a changing South African consumer marketplace. Within Shell South Africa, Marshall acted as the principal change agent to help the company give up what some had viewed as aloof and arrogant business practices. The story of how Errol Marshall adopted a new leadership style and transformed his company in the process is a wonderful study of human nature and of the capacity of both individuals and organizations to change.

"Type B" leaders (those who are well placed in an organization but who may lack large egos or strong reservoirs of experience in dealing with organization-wide change) face another kind of problem. Their personal challenge is to balance the need for humility with qualities that inspire and excite those whom they must lead. They are quite likely to embrace the learning required to become great change leaders but will need strong support networks within and without their organizations to keep their confidence levels high. Indeed, in the words of Harvard University professor John Kotter (1996), these leaders need strong "guiding coalitions" to help them drive and sustain change efforts.

Bill Weiss, former CEO of Ameritech, is a good example of a leader who fits this description. In 1991 he was preparing for retirement (and had in fact been encouraged to focus on that) when he decided to take charge of transforming Ameritech from a sleepy former Baby Bell company into a world-class telecommunications provider. The story of Weiss's "transformation" from Baby Bell CEO to world-class change agent is outlined in depth in Noel Tichy's 1997 book, *The Leadership Engine: How Winning Companies Build Leaders at Every Level.*

Next, there are "type C" leaders. Such leaders are often good at delivering Oscar-winning performances in support of why change is important (something they do exceptionally well in the presence of their superiors). They also exhibit a strong intellectual understanding of the requirements of the change leadership role.

Some type C leaders make exceptional change leaders largely because of the boundless self-confidence and personal energy they bring to the change process and because "what you see is what you get." Roger Enrico of PepsiCo is a wonderful example of a type C leader. He brings a high-energy, magnetic personality to his leadership of PepsiCo and to his coaching and mentoring of other leaders at all levels of the organization. Enrico's coaching of other PepsiCo leaders is in many respects his leadership signature. It is, in fact, one of the most compelling ways that he has spread the gospel of change at PepsiCo in recent years, generating higher corporate profits and greater leadership accountability, while fostering a strong and lean global organizational structure.

Other type C leaders, although they seem to evince large amounts of enthusiasm and support for change, are not in the same league with people like Enrico (or Jack Welch) for that matter. They may appear to be strong change agents in their organizations (especially when it comes to dealing with their board or the business press), but they lack a strong personal commitment to adopting new and different behaviors to be successful. Therein lies their problem.

The challenge for those organizations that appoint (or find themselves led by) this second variety of type C leader is to recognize their type and help them improve their commitment to change efforts. In the extreme, if this proves impossible to achieve, the only alternative is replacement if the change program is to succeed. The danger of keeping leaders who are leading or facilitating change when their behaviors and attitudes clearly do not reflect commitment to such efforts cannot be overemphasized. Keeping such leaders in place can put any change program very much in peril.

Lastly, there are "type D" leaders who often lack a strong personal commitment to the change efforts that they must lead. They face very serious challenges when it comes to leading change initiatives. For starters, they must focus on building their own personal commitment to change efforts before seriously engaging others in the process. Otherwise they can do far more damage to their organizations than good. Indeed, type D leaders need to reflect upon the previously cited statistics showing that more than 80 percent of all major change programs fail, primarily because of poor sponsorship! Though type D leaders can, with coaching, be converted into effective change agents, it may be wise for such leaders to depart an organization instead of taking on the responsibilities of business transformation.

Your Role in Developing Change Leaders

What can you, as an HRD professional, OD consultant, or executive coach to your company's top leadership team, do to identify and support strong change leaders? First, be sure that you understand the components of effective change leadership. These components change in complexity and difficulty over time. At the highest level, a top organizational leader must orchestrate many critical steps and do so in the right sequence to ensure that change initiatives have the greatest chance of success. This requires that a leader have a sophisticated understanding of the energy dynamics that operate inside his or her organization and harness them to achieve change objectives. The following sections list the steps that change leaders must take to ensure the success of change initiatives.

Create a Detailed Vision of the Future

For change efforts to succeed, an organization's top leader must create an image of the future that is not only challenging and compelling but also sufficiently detailed to allow everyone to understand the role he or she must play to achieve it. In the private sector, this is often done by creating a "burning platform" that suggests that an organization's very existence is at stake, unless people move quickly and boldly to change how they do their jobs. In other arenas (public sector agencies and organizations), it is not always possible for an organization's top leader to use the "burning platform" analogy, because the organization's future existence is not usually threatened. In such cases, the leader must make strong appeals to employee pride or to the need for the organization to change how it operates if it is to honor its organizational or institutional mandate.

Develop the Organization's Change Leadership Skills

Senior executives who have successfully transformed their companies from underperformers into profits and earnings superstars (GE's Jack Welch, Honeywell's Larry Bossidy, IBM's Lou Gerstner, and Disney's Michael Eisner, to name four) have several things in common. First, they are effective because they drive change through others, giving "arms and legs" to the change efforts they lead. Second, they identify the leadership behaviors that are critical to the organization's future and then cascade the importance of those traits down throughout all levels of the organization, reinforcing new work values, for example, or new organizational priorities.

Build Commitment

Successful change leaders build strong executive and employee commitment to their change efforts and, in so doing, ensure the momentum that such efforts need if they are to be sustained over time. Transforming employee commitment to a change into action is typically a graduated process of moving from "notion to motion." Typically, a top leader first enunciates a vision of the future and then sets about to overcome employee reluctance and resistance to change goals. He or she then engages employees in the mechanics of transforming how the organization operates (thereby fostering employee buy-in for solutions later implemented) and provides feedback mechanisms to employees to ensure that people's voices are heard at each step in the commitment-building process. Although potentially tedious, this lengthy process is often the only way to build solid support from the ground up for your change efforts, notes Sir Richard Evans, chairman of BAE Systems. For the past five years he has worked diligently to include successively larger circles of executives and managers in an intense discussion about BAE's own core business values. Those efforts, which Evans undertook at multiple leadership levels inside the organization, were prompted by the need for his firm to radically redesign how it operates, to become more operationally efficient, and, above all, to become more customer focused in how it designs and manufactures military and aerospace products.

Sustain New Leadership and Employee Behaviors

Today's most successful change leaders ensure that the systems, policies, and procedures necessary to support new ways of working (reward, recognition, evaluation, and promotion systems) are all effectively aligned to support new work habits, attitudes, and behaviors. In their book, *Business Climate Shifts: Profiles of Change Makers,* Warner Burke and Bill Trahant (2000) describe this as the process of creating a "climate of organizational alignment" to support a company's new business goals or operating mission.

Design a Systematic Change Plan

Pivotal to the success of any change effort is the ability of the top leader and his or her leadership team to put together a coherent change plan that identifies roles, sequences the strands of work that are involved, prioritizes events, manages the plan's rollout and management, and integrates change plans with the day-to-day operational goals of the business. Doing this typically takes far longer than any leader predicts at the outset.

Configure the Transition

"Configuring the transition" involves choosing—structurally and sequentially—how changes will actually take place. What organizational levers will be pulled, and in what sequence, to drive change efforts? Will change efforts commence with the introduction of new leaders in the organization, for example? Or, will change efforts be driven essentially by overhauling the organization's structure, management practices, and culture? What steps will make up the change plan, and what sequence will they take? Will there, for example, be a single, pilot program initially followed by widespread and simultaneous change projects? Or, will there be parallel change projects undertaken from the start, using learning loops, feedback mechanisms, and other devices to gain insights and adjust change approaches as the project proceeds?

Manage, Gauge, and Monitor the Transition

Once a transformation plan has been conceived and launched, its success will ride on the performance metrics, feedback mechanisms, and project benchmarks that a change leader puts in place, both to gauge and monitor success with change efforts over time and to change course, when appropriate. Having such mechanisms and structures in place is essential if change initiatives are to be effectively tracked, kept on course, and prevented from derailing as the result of organizational resistance or indifference.

At the outset, change leadership may seem to be difficult and unrewarding especially to a first-time change leader. However, as a leader gains both competence and confidence in using change leadership tools and techniques (detailed later in this chapter), he or she will begin to see how satisfying and rewarding being a change agent within an organization can be.

Is This Leader the Right Person to Lead This Project?

A key element of any successful change program is selecting the right people regardless of their level to lead efforts within their spheres. In your role as leadership coach, consultant, or trainer, you will need to advise your organization's top leaders on how best to cascade change leadership responsibilities within the organization. You must, in effect, help them build a community of leaders at all levels in the organization to ensure change efforts succeed. Before that can happen, you and they must fully understand the dynamics that the role of change leader entails. Figure 9-1 shows some of the costs and benefits associated with taking on the role of organizational change leader.

Even though an organization's top leader may focus a great deal of his or her time on "transformational" change issues to align the organization's top leadership team, mission, strategy, and culture to support and drive change goals, leaders elsewhere in the organization should focus on the "transactional" components—management practices, technology, systems, and employees' behaviors—required to actually move from notion to motion. Regardless of the domain in which they are working, however, change leaders must be credible, well-respected leaders within their organizations and have high levels of energy and commitment to making change efforts work. Having an intact power base upon which to build change efforts and plans is important as is a high degree of motivation to change the status quo.

What Are the Implications of Taking a Leadership Role?

It goes without saying that in accepting the role of change leader, a person's career will take a significant turn. A CEO close to retirement may suddenly be thrust (as was former Ameritech Bill Weiss) into the role of fundamental change catalyst. Similarly, a subject matter expert or middle-level manager, accustomed to working primarily within a small arena of the organization, may find that in accepting the role of change leader he or she is thrust onto the organizational stage of their firm as never before. As change leader, he or she must work with people across many organizational levels and functions and motivate people to change how they work rather than just delegating

Figure 9-1. The prices and benefits associated with change efforts.

Organizational		Sponsors	
Price	**Benefit**	**Price**	**Benefit**
Chaos	Resilience	Time	Caché
Attrition	Real change benefits	Energy	Career progression
Resources	Confidence	Career	Satisfaction
Management time and attention	Morale	Unpopularity	Personal growth
Management access	Motivation	Stress	Wealth
Business performance	Performance increases	New learning	Resilience increase
Delayed or cancelled initiatives	Effectiveness	Humility	Credibility
	Seized opportunities	Involvement	Opportunities
	Avoided losses		

work to them. The costs of taking on the role of change agent can be significant in terms of time, anxiety, personal learning required, conflict, broken friendships, and loneliness. Similarly, the benefits of taking on a change leadership assignment are equally numerous. Such an assignment can give a flagging career a real boost and can elevate a formerly obscure person to a role of great organizational prominence. It can provide someone with cutting-edge skills and experience in managing and motivating new kinds of employees, thus throwing the change leader into a higher career trajectory.

Who Is the Right Person to Lead the Effort?

Counter to popular belief, having the most senior-level leader in an organization lead a particular change effort is not always the best idea. Who, for example, would want the weight and prestige of the CEO's office getting involved in changing the type of business forms used in the organization? Or, for that matter, deciding on what kind of computing equipment was the best choice for everyone in the company? Instead, *the most appropriate person to lead a change effort is typically the lowest leader in the organization who can completely authorize and champion the initiative in the eyes of those being led.* This means the choice of change leader is based not necessarily on discretion but on proportionality and mathematics, on who is the lowest-level person in the organizational hierarchy with the scope of control or span of influence necessary to leverage change and sustain it. In the case of large-gauge change efforts, it may be critical to have the CEO or president lead change initiatives. But in other cases, the appropriate change leader could well be a divisional vice president, a key process owner, or even a department manager. It all depends on the scope and scale of the change efforts a company is planning.

How Much Time Is the Change Leadership Role Likely to Take?

This is a hard question to answer. Every change initiative is different, and each organization's priorities differ. In our consulting experience, most change leaders significantly underestimate the time they need to devote to change programs. In large-scale change, the role is so important and the time requirements so great that we advise CEOs to lead only one change program at any time. Leading more than one is likely to dilute the time available, probably to the point of failure, and cloud the priorities of the change program in the eyes of an organization's employees.

The amount of time a change leader should spend on a change initiative is not a matter of debate, it is more a matter of physics. Once the change is clear, the roles are understood, and all other aspects of the program have been defined, the time required from the leaders is fixed even if it not fully understood by all parties at that moment. Understanding how much time is needed is, therefore, critical for the leader of a change effort to appreciate— if success is to be ensured.

If A Leader Cannot Fulfill the Change Role, What are the Consequences?

Certainly high-caliber change leadership is undeniably vital to a change project, but it is not always possible for a change leader to take on the role. The consequences of the role not being fulfilled are usually considerable.

When the "correct" change leader, for whatever reason, feels he or she can not accept the role, one option is to pass it on to another member of the leadership team. This new change leader must be publicly vested with the power to make decisions previously residing with the former leader. The endorsement of the new change leader's role must be done very publicly and, for it to succeed, will often require the blessing, time, and resources of the "correct" leader to be sufficiently legitimate. Consequently, the costs of delegating change leadership at the highest levels of an organization entail considerable costs. A project whose "correct" change leader is not able to take on the role might therefore suffer from the following consequences: increased project complexity, delay, ambiguity, political maneuvering, poor employee morale, and skepticism as to the organization's commitment to making the change effort work.

Occasionally, a change leader takes on the transformational change role and then performs it in half-hearted fashion (a "type D"). This person's change leadership style is typified by lack of attention to the project, insufficient commitment of company resources to ensure the project's success, slow decision making, a lack of interest in resolving internal organizational conflicts, and discomfort in confronting senior managers who are hindering the program's success.

For a project with an inefficient change leader, when the incipient problems are allowed to fester, the project as a whole will be jeopardized. The preferred solution in this case is to do one of the following:

- ❖ reduce the scope of the change to the point at which sufficient change leadership does exist

- ❖ educate and develop stronger change leadership skills in leaders at all levels in the organization

- ❖ replace the change leader

- ❖ prepare for a failure of some kind in the project.

When a project has an effective change leader, the project team feels and acts empowered to move the project forward strongly. Resources are available, commitment grows, resistance is surfaced and dealt with, and others within the organization regard the project as an enviable and enjoyable initiative with which to be involved. In addition, the standing, credibility, and positive perception of the change leader, as viewed by the rest of the organization, increases.

Building a Supportive Coalition to Drive and Sustain Transformation

Look at any well-executed change program and you will find that there are numerous resources at the disposal of the most senior change leader. Indeed, many different organizational players are involved in giving sustenance and momentum to change efforts. Darryl Conner (1993) developed a taxonomy developed for his book *Managing at the Speed of Change: How Resilient*

Managers Succeed and Prosper Where Others Fail that shows the principal players who are always part of any successful change program. These include the following:

- ✿ *The change leader* is the individual who initiates, orchestrates, and confers legitimacy upon change activities on an enterprisewide basis. Change leaders also exist at other levels of the organization and constitute the leadership population that helps to amplify the top leader's change message and drive organizational change at the operational level. There are two types of change leadership. There are those leaders who actually spearhead or *initiate* change efforts and those that *sustain* them. The initiating change leader leads the overall change program and must have the power to legitimize all aspects of a transformation program without seeking permission. An initiating change leader typically has extreme discomfort with the organizational status quo. A sustaining change leader is someone who leads a subsection of the overall change program and whose own role is legitimized by the initiating change leader. A sustaining change leader must have the power to legitimize changes in his or her own area without seeking permission from others to do so.

- ✿ *Change agents* are people who actively deliver change messages and bring about change at an organizational or process level. Change agents typically do much of the practical work associated with putting a change program into operation. The role of change agent is legitimized by the change leader, both formally and informally, through written communications, for example, and through various informal channels and means. Change agents typically are people of influence or expertise whose daily jobs are at a line level within the organization.

- ✿ *Change advocates* are individuals who actively support change within the organization. Advocates are people within an organization who feel strongly that change should occur but who lack the organizational power to make it happen. The primary role of advocates is to find and then support change leaders who can legitimize the required change. Consultants often find themselves being asked to be change agents, but in most cases their roles can only be that of advocates.

🌸 *Change targets* are people within an organization whose roles will change as a result of the changes that are being planned and implemented. The consequence of this is that change leaders, agents, and advocates are themselves targets of change, even as they play implementation roles in bringing change about. This is a fact that the most senior change leaders within an organization cannot overlook.

The initiating change leader must cascade change leadership down through the organization to the point where change agents can carry out the initiating change leader's mandate and mission. This cascade is represented in figure 9-2.

At each stage of the cascade, targets are converted to change leaders. An example of this at the highest level would involve the initiating change leader creating a unified and coherent team of supporters who share and communicate a passion for the change, and who in turn create support beneath them and take on the sustaining change leader role themselves.

If the cascade process is imperfect, communications gaps and disconnects occur as shown in figure 9-3. To avoid these and other problems, we offer a few axioms associated with playing different change roles in a corporate transformation effort. We refer to them as the change management "get

Figure 9-2. How change leadership percolates throughout an organization stimulating sustainable change.

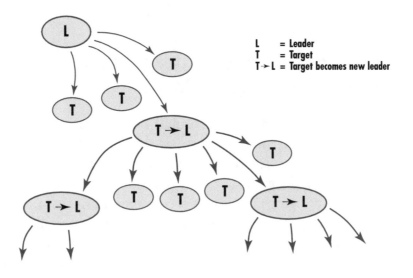

Figure 9-3. Some change messages fall short of the change target.

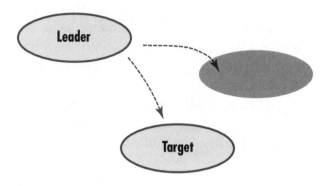

rights" that must be put in place, for transformation efforts to succeed (table 9-1). Otherwise, communications messages, commitment, and energy get sucked into this hole and absorb a disproportionate amount of the organization's energy.

Obviously some of these role axioms listed in table 9-1 are easier stated than followed, especially at lower levels in an organization. However, everyone in a change program, including change leaders and change agents, is him- or herself the focus of change efforts (in other words "targets") at some point in the process.

Because the behaviors that change leaders display are always noticed and mirrored by change targets, it is critically important that an organization's top leaders model the specific change behaviors that they want everyone else in the organization to display.

How Do Leaders Know if They Are Performing Their Roles Well?

If you are coaching your organization's leaders at various stages of the change process, you must be prepared if and when they ask, "How am I doing?" Change leadership is so critical to the vitality of all organizations today that it is probably best for change leaders to assume that most of the time they are not doing it quite right. That is why it is so important that they be open to continuous learning, that they facilitate communications up and down the organization, that they spend time with rank-and-file employees, that they mentor other leaders to help share the burden of change tasks, and that they always put themselves in the shoes of those they lead.

Table 9-1. Rules of engagement for the different players in a major change effort.

Change Leaders

- Only engage in changes that you can adequately support. Do not start change programs that you cannot appropriately lead.

- As a change leader, recognize that you will not only lead others but learn from them as well.

- Avoid falling into the trap of thinking that you or your top leadership team have all the answers to the challenges you face.

- Strive to create "a climate of internal alignment" to support and sustain change over time.

- Resist the temptation to delegate change work to others. The price to the change project will be high.

Change Agents

- Do not invest more personal energy in the change effort than your change leader does.

- Only engage in change initiatives that are properly led.

- Be clear in your own mind that change leaders own a change effort. This should be characterized by higher levels of energy, enthusiasm, and effort on their parts.

- Resist moves by change leaders to abdicate their responsibility for change efforts to you, especially when they dress it up as "employee empowerment." Recognize, however, that you, as a change agent, must become personally involved in change efforts in order to make a difference.

- Encourage your change leaders to lead well.

- Risk giving your organization's top leaders feedback that they may not want to hear.

Change Advocates

- You can do more to effect change by influencing others to play instrumental roles than by trying to playing an instrumental role yourself. Failure to recognize the limitations of your own power will cause you to waste time, energy, and effort.

- Ally yourself with respected change champions in your organization and support these individuals in every way you can.

- Remember that the primary role of an advocate is to find and support the most appropriate change leader.

(continued next page)

Table 9-1. Rules of engagement for the different players in a major change effort. (continued)

Change Target

- Become a willing supporter of your organization's change efforts and do not underestimate the degree to which your personal enthusiasm and commitment can make a big difference to the project's overall success.

- Be mindful of your own behaviors and whether they are contributing to the improvement of things or to maintenance of the status quo.

- Be aware of the ways you personally resist change, then ask: "Why do I act this way?" "What are my fears about what will happen if I do change?" By asking yourself such questions, you will eventually realize that you have nothing to fear from change and many things to gain. Moreover, you will be in a position to help other people overcome their own resistance to change.

- Invest your trust in leaders wisely, but do not withhold it out of spite, fear, ignorance, or vindictiveness.

- Be part of the solution, not part of the problem.

One characteristic of change leaders who are learning the change "role" is uncertainty about their current levels of performance. This is not unusual, and there are tools and techniques to help a change leader assess his or her own change leadership performance. It is particularly useful for change leaders to solicit feedback on their performance from those whom they are leading. It is critical that such individuals believe that it is "safe" to deliver such feedback, as it can provide the input necessary to significantly improve the change leadership performance of a CEO, front-line manager, or supervisor charged with implementing crucial aspects of a transformation initiative.

As a leader grows into the role of being a change leader, his or her behavior is likely to take on the qualities depicted in figure 9-4. This graphic is often used to illustrate the change of heart of organizational leaders, as they begin to embrace the realities of effective change leadership.

Figure 9-4. The nature of leadership learning about change.

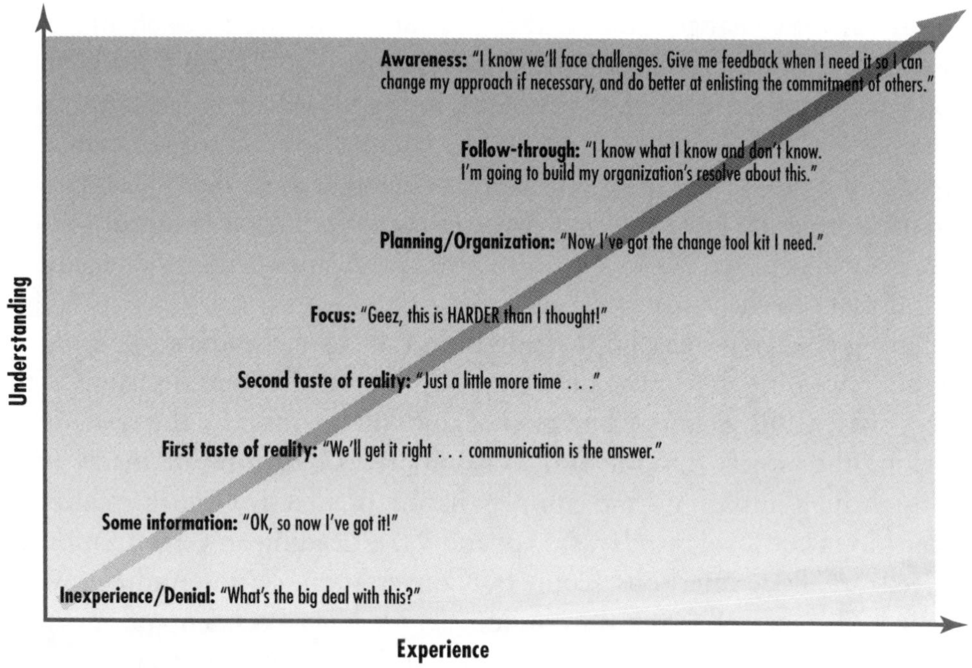

Awareness: "I know we'll face challenges. Give me feedback when I need it so I can change my approach if necessary, and do better at enlisting the commitment of others."

Follow-through: "I know what I know and don't know. I'm going to build my organization's resolve about this."

Planning/Organization: "Now I've got the change tool kit I need."

Focus: "Geez, this is HARDER than I thought!"

Second taste of reality: "Just a little more time . . ."

First taste of reality: "We'll get it right . . . communication is the answer."

Some information: "OK, so now I've got it!"

Inexperience/Denial: "What's the big deal with this?"

Understanding

Experience

How Long Will the Change Leader Need to Serve in This Capacity?

The time commitment for a change leader varies, but, as a rule of thumb, change leaders should become active well before the project actually starts and continue for some months after the project has officially been completed. Nevertheless, this is a generalization and many change leaders find their role needs to continue longer. Attempts to cut change leadership short or to hand the reins over to someone else prematurely can have an adverse effect on the project and jeopardize the sustainability of an initiative.

Sometimes it is impossible for the leadership of a change initiative to be continuous over the life of the entire project. People leave and move on in their careers, and others are asked to leave. When such contingencies are foreseen, you should take care to ensure the smoothest transition possible, with power being ceremoniously handed over as though it were a baton being relayed to another runner during a relay race.

The role of a change leader and the actions he or she takes change over the life cycle of most projects. At the outset, change leadership must be high profile, energetic, and relatively intrusive in the life of the organization and its employees. This helps to overcome any latent skepticism or reluctance to buy into the project. As things proceed, a change leader's role becomes one of repetition of key messages and involves many rounds of communication and personal appearances to spread the word and show senior management commitment to the project.

During change project implementation, the change leader's role is difficult but rewarding. He or she must make difficult and urgent decisions with speed, clarity, and accuracy. The pain of this will be offset by the rewards of watching the project leap forward after important decisions are made. (For an insightful glimpse into the complex nature of effective transformational leadership in companies today, see appendix E, "Leading an Organization at e-Speed: A PricewaterhouseCoopers Conversation With Audrey Weil, General Manager of CompuServe and Senior Vice President of America Online.") Additionally, at this stage of the project, change leaders are facilitating change in the ways that business processes work and critical units within the organization interact with one another. They do this by using their personal leadership presence to resolve internal political battles, facilitate conflicts, mediate questions about authority and responsibility, and generally monitor progress and empower other leaders to act on certain aspects of the transformation plan.

Toward the end of a project, when a tired change leader may be tempted to curtail his or her personal investment of time and energy, it will be important for you to encourage his or her continued involvement. It will be important to emphasize how only the top change leader is in a position to empower others in the organization to transform how they work and thus ensure the highest degree of attainment of change goals. It is sometimes hard for a change leader to believe at this stage of a project that anyone in the organization has not heard the change messages, but there will be some. Such people may be the last to hear the messages, but this in no way implies that they are not as important as others who heard the messages earlier. These people deserve and will expect change leadership to be just as strong for them as for others. It is at this stage of a project that tenacity and persistence will deliver the highest levels of personal and organizational satisfaction for the change leader. It is also at this stage when the final sustainability of the change will become ensured.

How Change Leaders Can Apply the "Laws of Organizational Thermodynamics"

To ensure that the change message percolates throughout the organization and to guarantee the sustainability of the change effort, change leaders must model clearly the qualities of change leadership that are essential not just to driving change efforts, but to building other change leaders in the organization. To do this, we think it is important that change leaders harness the "laws of organizational thermodynamics" described in chapter 8. The best change leaders embody the paradigm "CONNECT," "CREATE," and "CHANNEL" for generating and transferring energy throughout the organization. For example

CONNECTION

- Change leaders typically display strong personal leadership self-awareness and behaviors secure in the knowledge that they are the right person for the job.
- Change leaders understand the limitations of their own abilities and experiences and are able to enlist others to be part of their efforts and rely on others to be sounding boards and coaches.
- Change leaders display a great deal of openness to new ideas and approaches, even as they are leading others through times of change.
- Change leaders develop an understanding of change dynamics as a discipline and methodology and of the key players involved in successful change projects.
- Change leaders use a guiding framework and tool set to manage change in a consistent, metrics-driven way.
- Change leaders articulate a strong and convincing need to change to others but only after they themselves are convinced that the need for change is clear and compelling and that the overall price of implementation (in all currencies) is outweighed by the benefits to be derived from the effort.

- Change leaders build strong teams of highly committed, energetic, influential supporters to sustain their efforts at both the *transformational* and *transactional* levels.

CREATION

- Change leaders frame an inspiring vision of the future by ensuring that the change vision is holistic (containing technical, cultural, and behavioral components), that it embraces all organizational levels, and that it is a guide for decision-making resource allocation and strategic planning.

- Change leaders impart personal commitment, enthusiasm, and energy to change efforts. They inspire others to participate fully in the change by emphasizing others' roles in the change and by paying a price (personal, political, or organizational) for implementing the change.

CHANNELING

- Change leaders give high priority to the change effort; allocate sufficient resources to ensure its success; work with supporters to clarify the "price" to be paid for transformational activities in terms of the impacts on the organization, other projects, and everyday business operations; and publicly abandon or shelve low-priority activities and projects.

- Change leaders know that they are always in the public eye and model the best-practices behaviors that they expect of all leaders in the organization; they also solicit feedback on how well they model these best practices, taking corrective action as needed.

- Change leaders monitor performance and enable success by taking a flexible approach to change leadership, exercising direct supervision and oversight when necessary, and, at other times, stepping back and empowering others to "own" the solutions and approaches taken to address specific project challenges.

- Change leaders celebrate success with their team, especially in the early stages when securing "early wins" is critical to continued project momentum and employee morale.

The Impetus Behind Developing Change Leaders

Nowadays, the imperative of companies developing strong change management skills in their leaders cannot be overemphasized. The advent of the Internet and other disruptive technologies is quickly morphing the nature of business transactions and business relationships the world over. Leaders must become increasingly adept at organizational redesign, customer relationship management, e-commerce, rapid alliance development, outsourcing management, and many other things.

Thus, effective change leadership is quickly emerging as the single most critical leadership competency that leaders at all levels in organizations today need to possess. The urgency for developing this competency will only grow in the future. "Successful organizational change is becoming everyone's problem," note Katzenbach et al. (1995). "CEOs are held accountable for it. Customers require it. Shareholder performance demands it. [And] continued growth depends on it."

Part Three

Leadership Development:
The Road Ahead

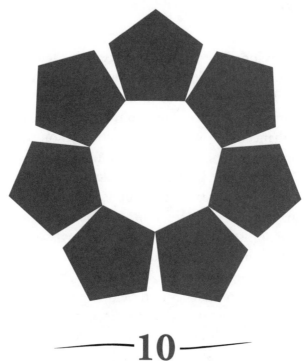

—10—

Emerging Trends in Leadership Development

[In the future] technology will play a growing role in how training (and learning) occurs in organizations. "Training will be much more granular. Everything will be specific and customized to a person's needs. That will greatly reduce the training scrap rate—the amount of nonrelevant information that participants are exposed to in a typical training class. At the same time, learning mechanisms will be everywhere. Instead of discrete classroom training, embedded training will be in workstations, cars, stores, telephones, and other devices."

— Jack Zenger, vice chairman, Provant, in "Where Technology and Training Meet" (Koonce, 1998).

Leadership development training has been on the radar screens of corporate executives for quite a while now and rightfully so. Companies need to be efficient, integrated "learning organisms" oriented toward continual information intake from the external business environment, rapid refinement and enhancement of core processes based on this intake, and the rapid growing and grooming of new populations of skilled leaders to sustain a company's competitiveness. To keep the leadership pipeline flowing, companies today are devoting a great deal of money, time, and human resources to turn their managers and executives into true leaders—*at all levels.*

Leadership development programs come in many shapes and sizes, from single-event training seminars to weeklong workshops to informal coaching of a company's emerging leaders by its more established ones. However, there are several modern approaches to developing leaders that are being driven today by long-standing industry trends and emerging technologies. Corporate universities, which feature top executives and managers as teachers and concentrate on conveying intense, company-specific content, continue to grow in popularity. At the same time, use of externally developed executive development programs that employ external instructors and subject matter and present material that is tailored to meet an organization's needs continues to grow as well. Finally, the rapidly developing world of Web-based learning is revolutionizing the nature and speed at which training and knowledge transfer occur in organizations and is, in many cases, bringing about the radical redesign of LD programs throughout the world.

How can you take greatest advantage of the most contemporary learning approaches and training technologies and employ them as part of your LD mix? This chapter discusses the plusses and minuses of these approaches and then offers you help with deciding how to use new technology approaches to developing leaders.

The Preferred Learning and Training Channels in Organizations Today

Of the many channels that currently exist to deliver LD training, the corporate university concept and externally developed executive development programs have emerged as preferred means of delivery in both large and small companies today. The corporate university, known as the "in-house" approach, either parallels a traditional university setting, boasting a large physical campus, or is more technically inclined, offering leadership courses via virtual means. The executive development program, or the "external" approach, consists of a LD curriculum (either customized or generic) that is developed by an academic or other private institution, which is then brought into an organization.

The Corporate University: What's All the Buzz About?

It seems that the corporate university has taken T&D to new heights, as shown by the growing number of conferences, journals, Websites, and other literature featuring the corporate university as the way to building a first-class workforce today. According to the 1999 *Corporate University Xchange Survey of Corporate University Directions,* for example, the number of corporate universities has increased substantially over the last 10 years from 400 in 1988 to more than 1,600 today, including 40 percent of *Fortune* 500 companies (Meister, 1999). If the current pace of growth holds steady, the number of corporate universities could exceed the number of traditional universities by the year 2010. What is the corporate university exactly? Why is it so successful? How can your organization create one to meet its own LD needs?

The concept of the corporate university emerged decades ago, when organizations recognized the need to establish a classroom setting to teach technical, on-the-job skills necessary to improve performance (Meister, 1998). The idea was that earning a certificate (or even a degree) would equip employees with the tools they needed to improve their on-the-job skills. Gradually, companies in all industries caught on and shifted from offering only technical courses to offering training in many disciplines, allowing their employees to choose courses that made the most sense for their particular career paths. Today, corporate universities offer educational programs, ranging from entry-level management to LD programs. Additionally, training has evolved from curriculum-based classroom courses to programs that heavily focus on the "process" by which people simultaneously work and learn. Hence the growth of action learning programs, which are extremely popular today in companies such as GE.

Corporate universities come in all shapes and sizes. Many, such as Motorola University, resemble the traditional university in that they feature large physical campuses in locations all over the globe. Although these universities boast traditional classroom settings, many offer nontraditional delivery methods and curricula, which differentiate them as innovative, cutting-edge educational providers. Others, like the Anheuser Busch Learning Center, are virtual universities and rely on a distance learning approach. They offer professional lectures via satellite networks, computer-based training (CBT) programs, home study materials, and Web-based training programs. Both physical and virtual corporate universities are beginning to attract those from outside their organizations, including customers and suppliers, which, as the number of corporate universities steadily increases, may threaten traditional universities in the view of some people.

Although the virtual university is indeed becoming the wave of the future, research indicates that it may be a little while before it becomes the primary vehicle for developing leaders at the senior and executive levels of the organization. Some may find this surprising; others may find this typical, validating the all-too-popular belief that those at the highest levels of companies are often the last to embrace technological breakthroughs.

The Many Benefits of Corporate Universities

As organizations grapple with how best to grow and groom future generations of leaders, the corporate university concept has clearly emerged as a favorite approach. A study conducted by the American Society for Training & Development (ASTD) found that 87 percent of companies surveyed had LD programs that were designed and delivered in-house (the corporate university approach) compared to 82 percent that had consultant-developed programs and 70 percent that offered university-based programs (Densford, 1996a). Why is this approach so popular for growing and grooming leaders? A company can derive several benefits by relying upon in-house resources to develop dynamic organizational leaders.

The Power of In-House Resources

In a corporate university setting, organizations can use their own resources as faculty. When senior leaders are called upon to be teachers, trainers, and workshop facilitators in classroom settings, they grow as a result of interacting with more junior level leaders, sharing their experiences, answering questions, and dealing with difficult or controversial business, management, and organizational issues. At the same time, junior-level leaders are the recipients of strong, first-person leadership learning and insights, gained not through reading or research, but through intense, personal interaction with top leaders often in informal, conversational settings.

Consider how it works at the Tennessee Valley Authority (TVA), for example. Today, TVA University is fully reaping the benefits of using its top managers as faculty members. Senior managers are required to go through a tough certification program to become instructors, the goal being for each instructor to deliver 150 hours of classroom instruction within a 12-month period (Meister, 1998). The intensity of TVA's instructor certification program and the actual LD training delivery represent a highly dynamic approach to developing leaders throughout the organization. Students benefit from interacting with live instructors whose leadership experience and current business responsibilities put them in a powerful position to transfer the latest techniques, knowledge, and know-how to the organization's new generation of leaders coming through the pipeline. Indeed, in such cases, instructors serve as excellent role models for the organization's junior-level managers and executives.

Even when employee or public confidence in a company's senior management may be lacking, there are still advantages to using management as faculty in corporate universities. If a company has come under fire for its business practices or is facing some kind of public scrutiny, senior leaders of an organization may be able to use the platform of training to rebound from public criticism, build employee morale and team unity, and use highly publicized business problems as a learning tool. This way, they can engage junior-level leaders in problem solving and action learning. Such situations, in fact, can create organizational esprit de corps to bind together different levels of leaders as they figure out how to address common problems or business issues.

The potential disadvantage to using in-house senior management to deliver training and lead executive development programs is that participants may not always buy into a particular leader's approaches and methods, especially if he or she is under fire elsewhere in the organization or by the press, consumer groups, or other entities.

Programs Reflect Business or Organizational Goals

Because the corporate university curriculum is developed in-house, it can be tied directly to a company's strategic priorities and objectives. Thus, leadership training classes, exercises, simulations, and curricula can all be designed with business projects and priorities in mind, giving emphasis to those leadership skill sets deemed critical to the company's future success.

In our consulting experience, the highest performing organizations today make a strong effort to align internal training initiatives and learning curricula with both the existing and emerging needs of their businesses. At a leading automobile manufacturer, for example, no training mission is specifically articulated. Instead, the training staff share the same business vision as everybody else in the company. Says one senior training manager, "We're not in the training business; we are in the automotive business" (Vander Linde, Horney & Koonce, 1997). The training staff works in tandem with line managers at all levels. When developing training goals and programs, staff members ask themselves these questions (Vander Linde, Horney & Koonce, 1997):

- ⚙ What is the company supposed to be doing?

- ⚙ What do people need to achieve that success?

- ⚙ How do we measure success?

- ⚙ What is the gap between what people need and what they have?

- ⚙ How do we close that gap in the best, fastest way possible?

Meanwhile, at a leading public sector agency, the activities of all employees are aligned in support of the agency's goals, to which end training's role is to eliminate deficiencies and give employees tools they need to ensure that the agency achieves its mission. Finally, at a leading retail store chain, training is used at multiple levels to create a strong "guest culture" for customers—a goal that is articulated frequently by the company's top leaders as critical to the chain's success (Vander Linde, Horney & Koonce, 1997).

Training can be aligned clearly with senior-management priorities and used to communicate and reinforce key organizational and business goals as articulated regularly and consistently by top management (Vander Linde, Horney & Koonce, 1997). Moreover, because such programs (courses, workshops, action learning projects, and so forth) are designed to be in alignment with corporate goals and objectives, their success rate in terms of "knowledge transfer" or "learning applied" can be measured against business objectives and outcomes. This is a huge benefit because many organizations today struggle to quantifiably realize and measure the benefit of their executive training programs.

Corporate Universities are Cost Effective

Corporate universities are usually more cost effective than outside LD programs. Although often expensive to establish, the long-term savings derived from having a corporate university can make it well worth the investment. Once programs are up and running, outside faculty do not need to be brought into the organization nor do conference facilities have to be rented. Because the design and delivery of the program is done in-house, there is also no need to update the program with the most recent off-the-shelf version. Rather, the program is updated continuously based on the growing and changing strategic needs of the organization.

The Intangible Benefits of Corporate Universities

Still another benefit of corporate universities is that they foster the creation of nurturing environments that promote friendships while promoting learning."[W]hen people in the same organization come together, a number of magical things happen. Important bonds are created, important links are established," says Jack Zenger, vice chairman of Provant and founder of Zenger Miller, one of the largest management training companies in the world. He predicts that there will be a big increase in the use of corporate universities in the future (Densford, 1997). Indeed, in-house LD programs often provide people with a sense of community that is otherwise missing from their day-to-day lives and careers in large and even small corporations.

Often, informal mentoring occurs as senior faculty members coach the future leaders of their organizations, share their insights and own learning, answer questions, offer advice, and at times spar with students over the best approaches to take in tackling business problems. This informal mentoring usually continues beyond the duration of the formal program, leading to long-time business friendships. In-house programs also foster relationships across lines of business and functional departments, well beyond the classroom walls. Indeed, participants who have been in corporate university programs often say that the benefit of meeting new colleagues and building working relationships is often a bigger benefit of attending such programs than the formal curriculum itself. "I found that the network of contacts and colleagues I established in the senior executive service [SES] candidacy program was at least as valuable as the course content," notes John Galligan, a director in the Financial Management Service of the U.S. Department of the Treasury about his experience at the Federal Executive Institute in Charlottesville, Virginia. (The FEI, the federal sector equivalent of a corporate university, offers a four-week curriculum of leadership courses, workshops, speakers, and even health/wellness sessions for fast-track public sector managers and executives in a campus setting in central Virginia.)

The only disadvantage of the in-house approach, say experts like Zenger, is the lack of sharing with peers of other organizations (Densford, 1997).

Up-to-the-Minute Learning

When thinking of the corporate university, most people tend to think of an actual physical campus setting, but, in doing so, it is important not to forget that the "corporate university" is a concept not a place or one-time event. In fact, the corporate university of the future will not be linked to any particular location but will operate on a virtual basis. One of the huge benefits of virtual learning, as epitomized by distance learning, Web-based, and intranet-based learning is that by virtue of the scale and speed with which such technologies disseminate information (everything from customer information and technical expertise to business goals and best practices) throughout an organization, it helps reinforce consistency in workforce competencies.

Many corporate universities are already starting to lean the virtual way, although not as quickly as programs that focus on technical or entry-level training. For example, Xerox uses CD-ROM technology to train technicians to repair copier and printer equipment. Such technology "enables technicians to practice equipment repair through computer simulation," says Lynn Edmonds, vice president of services revenue and business development for Xerox's Worldwide Customer Services Group. It is just one of the ways that "Xerox tries to rapidly distribute necessary learning, on a technical level, throughout the organization" (Edmonds, 2000). Meanwhile, Federal Express recently spent close to $70 million implementing an automated educational system (Fulmer, 1997). The system is designed to enhance learning and skill development among couriers and customer service agents through the use of interactive video disks (IVD). The IVD units are established in more than 700 locations, each containing a 20–25 disk curriculum updated monthly. Both initiatives clearly represent the trend of the future, although the actual training programs are not geared toward developing leadership among senior executives. In fact, according to a 1998 National Human Resources Development Executive Survey, "the use of certain electronic learning technologies has yet to become widespread for leadership training, perhaps reflecting the types of skills that such training tries to develop" (ASTD, 1998).

Best Practice Corporate Universities

The following two case studies represent best-in-class LD programs being implemented in corporate universities today. We have provided brief information on each program and detailed its critical success factors and benefits.

Disney University

Established in 1955, Disney University is one of the oldest corporate universities in existence. Founded by Walt Disney himself, it was intended to imbue Disney employees with the virtues, values, and vision that Disney saw as essential in helping them deliver what has become known the world over today as a "world-class customer satisfaction experience." Shortly after opening Disneyland in 1955, "Walt realized the need for an in-house training organization committed to his philosophies," notes Valerie Oberle, former director of Disney University. "He wanted to be sure that cast members, or employees, understood what their role was in creating Disney's product: guest happiness" (Densford, 1996b).

Today, every new employee at Disney theme parks—Disneyland, Walt Disney World, Disneyland Paris, and Tokyo Disneyland—spends time in a "Disney traditions" class where they are immersed in the history, philosophy, and concepts of quality guest service à la Disney, much of it done through the power of employee storytelling. People "begin to understand what their responsibility is in upholding the Disney reputation, regardless of their role, be it a new vice president or street sweeper," says Oberle (Densford, 1996b).

Over the years Disney University has shifted, like many corporate universities, from providing mostly technical on-the-job training for Disney cast members to offering training in a variety of disciplines and to people in all areas of the organization. It has also shifted from being primarily classroom-based in the training it provides to providing training on-site, giving people the opportunity to learn new things while actually doing their jobs.

For example, Disney often uses educational "SWAT" teams made up of subject matter experts both to develop and deliver training to other Disney cast members in the guest venues where they work. Such training is designed not just to impact people's job performance, but also the systems and processes that support people in doing their jobs. This paradigm shift began to occur after Disney realized that employees learned new things faster and more effectively when they had the chance to immediately translate new knowledge and information into new work behaviors and techniques on the job. Certainly the best place to do this is in the context of meeting the expectations and needs of theme park guests—Disney's ultimate customers. Creating such SWAT teams often requires that people in the training and HRD areas work closely with senior management, especially when it comes to earmarking line staff to be part of such training projects and when changes in fundamental line operations or processes are likely to result as part of developing new training packages.

Like its staff training, Disney's LD efforts are also designed to be intense, bonding, and transformational in nature. Today, Disney boasts a world-renowned LD training program, the foundation of which rests on 19 critical work behaviors that the company identified in 1994 as being critical to the company's mission of providing theme park guests with superlative "product quality" and "customer service." These leadership behaviors—intended to empower Disney staff and bring out the best in everybody—include such things as being enthusiastic, communicating honestly, setting challenging goals, listening intently to diverse opinions, and unleashing the full potential of each cast member by giving people developmental opportunities (Densford, 1996b).

Today, Disney provides an array of ongoing assessment tools and techniques to Disney managers to help sustain and reinforce critical behaviors in all employees. These resources include ongoing training classes, coaching, and mentoring. The company also requires that the company's senior leaders, everybody from vice presidents and directors on down, periodically swap their desk jobs to don costumes and greet the public, playing Disney characters at the company's various theme parks. Jayne Parker, former director of training and development at the Disney Institute, has described Disney's leadership program this way: "What [we did was] create a program where we tell people what is expected, give them a baseline, show them how they can improve, and then hold them accountable for changing" (Densford, 1996b).

Because Disney's leadership training program was developed in-house, it is a strategic effort, linked directly to Disney's overall goals and objectives. The program itself is designed from a Disney perspective, not a generic one, which is beneficial in that Disney is not simply molding its managers into leaders, but rather molding them into *Disney* leaders, giving Disney the edge it needs to stay competitive.

Over the years, Disney's emphasis on the critical behaviors and on training leaders at all levels has enabled it to achieve a remarkable degree of organizational vision, employee loyalty, team unity, and corporate profitability. The nature of training and LD efforts show as close a linkage to corporate strategy, core ideology, and business goals as we have seen anywhere, attributes that in many ways go all the way back to the company's founding by Walt Disney himself. As James Collins and Jerry Porras (1994) note in their book, *Built to Last: Successful Habits of Visionary Companies:* "Walt had a rage for order and control that he translated into tangible practices to maintain the essence of Disney. The personal grooming code, the recruiting and training processes, the fanatical attention to the tiniest details of physical layout, the concern with secrecy, the exacting rules about preserving the integrity and sanctity of each Disney character—these all trace their roots to Walt's quest to keep the Disney Company completely within the bounds of its core ideology."

General Electric's Crotonville Corporate University

GE spends millions of dollars each year to develop its people worldwide. Much of this training takes place at its Crotonville training facility in New York State's Hudson Valley. There, GE puts tremendous emphasis on developing its "global brains" (teaching its people to see things from a global perspective), nurturing its business and technical expertise, and infusing its LD efforts with an emphasis on leaders managing across both organizational and national boundaries (General Electric, 2000). One important distinction between GE's program and others is the emphasis it places on LD as an ongoing process throughout a manager's career rather than a series of training classes that may or may not be linked to a person's career path or current job assignment. "Crotonville's Core Leadership Development program is designed to intervene at the crucial moments of manager development, anticipating needs and providing appropriate tools" (General Electric, 2000).

Manager and leader development at GE comprise several components. Stage one consists of a three-day corporate entry leadership conference, which serves as a gateway to the company's culture, values, and business strategy for the more than 1,000 new hires who arrive at Crotonville each year (Tichy & Sherman, 1994). During this conference, there is heavy emphasis placed on learning the ins and outs of GE's businesses including the company's global business strategy.

In stage two, newly minted managers are introduced to GE's new manager development program where they learn how to manage the transition from working independently to leading teams of individuals. There is a great deal of emphasis placed on certain key skill areas (all deemed central to GE's global business strategy) including team leadership, Six Sigma, change acceleration, a process called "workout" (a technique for streamlining business operations and cutting costs based on both team and individual input), and e-business.

The third stage of GE's leadership training program resembles graduate school. In this program, future leaders are placed into their particular areas of expertise (marketing or human resources, for example) and thrust into study groups in which at least a third of the participants work in other specialty areas. The goal is to create an incubator environment in which professional attitudes and perspectives are shared openly among classroom participants so that everyone learns the value of alternative opinions and approaches to business problem solving (Smith, 1995).

To further nurture its future leaders, GE also developed its Impact Programme, which concentrates on training leaders in manufacturing and engineering processes. For this program, managers travel to visit competitor companies in foreign countries to study their business processes, as well as their approaches to HR management, quality, and IT development and implementation. Participants then bring the perspectives they develop on these trips back to their particular functional areas. The program provides an unprecedented opportunity for future GE managers to learn from their competitors and for competitors to learn from GE (Smith, 1995).

As managers progress up the GE career ladder, they become eligible to participate in stage four of GE's LD program. At this level, managers take part in three different programs over a five- to eight-year period, all of which are concerned with issues of global competitiveness. Managers spend time learning to manage multifunctional organizations, work collaboratively with others in executive team settings, and cooperate on completing intense, month-long projects intended to teach skills in high-level decision making and problem solving (Smith, 1995).

The very highest stage of GE's LD program, an executive development course, is intended only for the uppermost management. By invitation only, its goal is to give GE's most promising senior managers and executives hands-on interaction in small group settings with the company's top leaders where together they address unresolved corporate challenges and problems.

Leadership development efforts at GE serve as a powerful education and alignment tool to train, align, grow, and groom current and future leaders for future job and leadership assignments. For example, because GE wants to operate from a global perspective, its leadership program, at all stages, incorporates a global component, whether it involves traveling to visit a competitor in another country or solving business issues with global partners. Because it is developed in-house and offered via the university, GE's program is aligned with the company strategy and is meeting its goals.

GE's program is geared toward creating broad-gauge generalists. It encourages knowledge sharing among future leaders from all over the organization—across functional units, across countries. This enables participants to gain different perspectives and learn ways to solve business issues that take into account their overall corporate impact not just the impact to a manager's particular department or organization. This is key in building GE's future leaders. They learn early to approach business situations from an overall GE perspective, which may not necessarily be the perspective that they are used to, operating in their own individual divisions or areas.

Because GE's program brings together leaders from all over the organization, it encourages global thinking and "boundaryless behavior," both key tenets of Jack Welch's leadership approach at GE. Traveling to other companies' facilities, learning from their peers in other organizations, and working with cross-functional partners to solve business issues, enables program participants to absorb unique perspectives and innovative thinking based on a variety of backgrounds and experiences. All told, it makes for a rich mix of learning experiences on which GE's future leaders are then able to draw as they assume increasingly responsible positions and are called on to make increasingly critical business decisions. At the same time, GE benefits because of the new ideas, options, and business proposals and plans that often emerge from its business management program. Many of these ideas and proposals have been implemented in the company, leading to concrete results, including significant cost savings in some cases.

Another huge benefit of GE's ongoing leadership program is the bank of resources GE has developed. In terms of succession planning and ensuring future leadership within the organization, GE does not find itself scrambling as many of its competitors do, since its ongoing LD process seems to lend itself to the constant development and replenishment of a high quality talent pool.

Executive Development Programs

Another vehicle for developing future leaders is executive development programs. What are they? Offered by leading universities, consultants, and private organizations, executive development programs range from intense mini-MBA programs lasting several months to specialized seminars delivered in major cities to company-specific audiences. These offerings are usually pre-designed sessions offered periodically at provider sites and attended by a mixed group of participants from a variety of companies. In recent years, there has been an increase in the number of international participants in such programs, which, for example, constitute two-thirds of the students at Harvard's Advanced Management Program. In addition, the interest in customized programs is increasing, given the growing interest and priority many companies are placing on aligning their LD activities with corporate strategy.

Providers of executive development programs include prominent universities such as Harvard, the University of Michigan, the University of Virginia, Oxford University, the Wharton School at the University of Pennsylvania, the London Business School, Insead in France, and behavioral organizations such as Franklin Covey and the Center for Creative Leadership. These services are also offered by consulting firms and corporations that are recognized for their leadership success. New entrants to this market are organizations that have been successful in implementing leadership initiatives that offer sessions on their company's leadership management principles and philosophies. One example, the Disney Institute, offers a four-day seminar on "The Disney Approach to Leadership Excellence." There is an increasing trend toward partnering and alliances between executive development providers. With customized sessions, it is not unusual to find multiple providers working together.

One of the biggest appeals of executive development sessions is that they often involve famous authors, well-known professors, and admired business leaders who take part as featured speakers or even workshop presenters. Besides being audience draws, such speakers often bring fresh, invigorated insights to leadership topics, often using their own research as the basis for their opinions and ideas. Unlike in-house programs, externally run executive development programs also afford invaluable networking opportunities with other key corporate leaders. The diversity of ideas shared in such settings become catalysts for innovation.

Executive development programs such as those at the Center for Creative Leadership are often the byproducts of significant research. Providers are often recognized in the field of leadership, and course materials, activities, assessment instruments, and training tools are often the result of years of study and analysis. For example, the Center for Creative Leadership, a nonprofit organization focused on the understanding and practice of leadership, uses an assessment instrument that is completed by direct reports, peers, superiors, and, of course, the participants before the classes. The purpose is to determine leadership competency gaps in the participant. Then, during the actual learning experience, coaches provide participants with feedback to help them recognize leadership blind spots and to help them increase their leadership effectiveness.

Another benefit to executive development programs is the quality of the instruction. The facilitators and presenters who take part in such programs are often world-class presenters and facilitators with years of conflict resolution or group visioning work at the highest corporate levels behind them. Many are skilled enough to support flexible learning experiences and are thus able to move in the direction that is of most value to a given group of participants as opposed to sticking with a "rote" learning design.

Executive development programs can introduce a breath of fresh air into the learning experiences of executives and managers who may have been subjected to years of internally produced LD and training. Internal training, though sometimes exceptional, always runs the risk of being too narrowly focused, of being flavored with organizational bias, and sometimes stagnant with inertia when it comes to addressing new ideas and trends or introducing new techniques, practices, and processes into an organization. In externally developed executive development programs, rich interaction among professional peers of different organizations can deeply enrich peoples' learning experiences. Individuals have the chance to share career histories, compare and contrast business best practices, develop solutions to common problems, and build lasting professional friendships and networks.

In any case, when tailored to the needs of a given organization or a group of key individuals within a company, executive development programs can provide an important supplement to a corporate university curriculum of courses, workshops, and other activities. In some cases, they provide expertise, perspectives, resources, and learning opportunities not otherwise available to a company's senior leaders.

The Wharton School at the University of Pennsylvania

The Wharton School at the University of Pennsylvania (2000) is one of the most prestigious universities offering executive development programs today and also one of the most innovative. Its 11 departments and 19 research centers provide the foundation for some of the best known executive-level learning available anywhere. The course offerings touch on such areas as leadership, electronic commerce, mergers and acquisitions, financial markets, high-tech marketing, data mining, and global markets. A list of courses available from a recent edition of the executive development catalog includes executive team dynamics, leading organizational change, power through influence, and creating scenarios for successs.

Wharton's classroom-based programs (typically three to five days long) blend both traditional and nontraditional training methods including case studies, simulations, group presentations, videotapes, and action learning/research. Among the instructional tools used are real-time feedback from fellow participants and follow-up contact via the Internet.

Wharton has been a leader in introducing alternative delivery channels for executive/senior management learning. In 1998, it introduced Wharton Direct to meet the growing needs of executives and managers who desire high-quality business education but who are constrained from traveling away from work to attend campus-based programs. A distance learning approach that blends everything from lecturette and individual learning to collaborative learning and case studies, Wharton Direct features live, interactive programs broadcast from the school's Philadelphia campus to high-tech learning centers in more than 30 metropolitan areas. Management and technical professionals who plug into Wharton Direct programs are able to learn directly from Wharton faculty members and from one another using this live, interactive approach. Most programs are targeted at group learners who attend programs either at a Wharton distance learning site or at their own corporate learning centers. In late 1999, Wharton introduced a Web-only format of Wharton Direct, which uses streaming video to provide live and interactive Webcasts interspersed with lectures. All Webcasts are supported in both physical and virtual classes with a variety of online learning tools, self-assessment instruments, projects, and teaching assistants.

Supplementing Wharton's traditional and distance learning leadership programs is something called Knowledge@Wharton, a Website that features commentary, insight, and research for business people looking for information and solutions to contemporary business problems. Updated biweekly, Knowledge@Wharton is divided into 14 different areas that cover everything from finance and marketing to e-commerce and business ethics. A powerful search engine makes it possible for site visitors to quickly probe available literature on topics of interest or to research a variety of areas simultaneously to find in-depth information.

Besides offering a core set of courses to program participants, Wharton also customizes executive education programs for a wide range of companies including Bayer, Bell Atlantic, Merck, Morgan Stanley Dean Witter, and Toyota. Typically such programs are developed in tandem with industry or corporate partners and are tailored to have either a company or industry-specific focus. Programs are offered at Wharton and in many major cities throughout the world. (For more information about the school and its programs, go to www.wharton.upenn.edu.)

The Center for Creative Leadership

The Center for Creative Leadership (CCL) is a nonprofit training and research organization, headquartered in Greensboro, North Carolina, that provides a robust portfolio of open-enrollment leadership programs attended by some 25,000 participants each year. In addition, CCL offers organization-specific programs to approximately 200 client organizations each year, including many of the *Fortune* 100. Open enrollment programs include course offerings for executives, senior, experienced, and new managers, as well as HR managers.

The Center has a reputation for scholarship. Ongoing HR and OD research serves as a wellspring for development of new leadership programs produced each year, both as part of CCL's core curriculum, as well as the programs it produces for individual corporate and organizational clients. For example, many of the open-enrollment courses offered in the 2000 curriculum were pegged to simultaneous research being conducted by CCL in some of the cutting-edge areas of leadership, including the professional development issues and experiences of women and people of color. Thus, programs from the 2000 catalog carry names such as "The Women's Leadership Program," and "The African-American Leadership Program." Custom programs at CCL often emphasize such content areas as how to transform individual contributors into leaders, how to foster a creative climate in one's organization, how to transition to team-based work arrangements, how to undertake culture change, and how to make executive teams more effective.

The programs at CCL are known for being both robust and intense. In building custom programs, for example, CCL relies heavily on such tools as instrument-based feedback, real-time simulations and debriefings, coaching, group/process exercises, action learning, and other tools. Programs developed in tandem with client organizations typically involve front-end interviews and site visits to clients to determine appropriate course content/formats, and the mix of learning tools that will be included in programs. (For more information on CCL's programs, go to www.ccl.org.)

Leveraging Technology to Enhance Today's LD Programs

From Web-based instruction and distance learning to virtual reality and online peer communities, training and technology are converging in rapid and radical ways today. The convergence—speeded by the Internet and by the growth of company intranets and extranets—is having a revolutionary impact on the nature of leadership training and the skills that trainers will need to do their jobs in the 21st century.

The future of technology-based leadership training appears to have unlimited potential. Already technology is being employed on a massive scale to facilitate course customization, integrate just-in-time learning with daily work tasks, and deliver what was formerly classroom-based training to multiple sites simultaneously. All this can usually be accomplished for a fraction of the cost of traditional classroom-based training. Technology's power to influence training formats and learning models will only grow in the years ahead given likely breakthroughs in wireless technology, microchip speed, the power of new software applications, and broad band availability and access.

Distance Learning

Consider distance learning, which has exploded in popularity in recent years, enabling a trainer or group facilitator in one location to be linked to participants in multiple locations simultaneously, thus reducing travel expenses and other costs. "The ability of organizations to receive such training in a cost-effective way is increasing," says Jack Zenger, vice chairman of Provant, a Boston-based consulting and training company. "Consequently, even mission-critical people who can't travel for classroom-based training will be able to take part in the kinds of training opportunities that such technology enables" (Koonce, 1998).

Zenger says that, in the future, technology will play a growing role in how leadership training occurs in organizations. For example, because technology can make course customization easier and faster, the quality of training will improve. "Training will be much more granular. Everything will be specific and customized to a person's needs," he says. That will greatly reduce the training scrap rate—the amount of nonrelevant information that participants are exposed to in a typical training class. "At the same time," says Zenger, "learning mechanisms will be everywhere. Instead of discrete classroom training, embedded training will be in workstations, cars, stoves, telephones, and other devices" (Koonce, 1998).

Internet and Intranet-based Learning Approaches

Though distance learning is a channel that more and more companies are using to deliver leadership and other training to large numbers of people, the Internet and company intranets provide even richer learning alternatives. And the options keep expanding.

As companies learn to take advantage of the Web, Web-based learning and training experiences are blurring the distinction between work and learning in ways that traditional training never has. One reason: The Web enables people to have very intense interaction, sometimes more intense and more intimate than when they are face to face. So says Ann Boland, former chief operating officer of PBS The Business Channel. When people interact in virtual space, they do so without the distraction of appearances, personalities, or other personal characteristics that sometimes shade face-to-face communication. According to an article in *Technical Training,* Boland, one of several panelists at a discussion of training and technology at ASTD's 1998 annual meeting, says that when online discussions proceed well, they enhance brainstorming, goal setting, action planning, and project management (Koonce, 1998).

Training delivered via the Web offers many advantages, including the opportunity for many people to participate and collaborate on projects or joint assignments for continuous learning and knowledge sharing among peers. One example of this is taking place today at our firm, PricewaterhouseCoopers, which is currently introducing a new Web-based learning technology into its management consulting services group. The e.cademie[1] Website, which enables PwC consultants to share knowledge and expertise with one another in a virtual environment, is helping to facilitate increased and accelerated learning within the firm, thus closing knowledge gaps among consultants and blurring the distinction between learning and work.

The e.cademie system is an exciting approach to learning. It allows consultants to learn anytime, anywhere. It provides a suite of Internet-based courses to suit the needs of PwC consultants as part of an integrated learning program, which includes classroom-based and team-based learning.

---

[1] e.cademie is a registered trademark of PricewaterhouseCoopers.

PwC expects that 70 percent of its learning will move to the Internet over the next two years.

Many earlier generation approaches to self-paced learning have foundered, largely because learners have not been adequately supported. They have been expected to make do without adequate support or access to subject matter experts who can answer questions that arise. By contrast, e.cademie technology supports learning by providing a rich menu of collaborative online services including peer-to-peer email, peer-to-peer chat, telephone coaching, Web/email support, and help desk support to brainstorm solutions to learning problems. The e.cademie Website also monitors progress against agreed-upon learning goals and actively supports learners by providing coaching if they appear to be having difficulties.

"The goal with e.cademie is to capture key learnings and thought leadership developed during client projects and to quickly share that with other consultants within PwC," says Julia Collins, global partner responsible for the e.cademie site. "Imagine for example, that we had a transformation team working with a major European Bank in London or a process redesign group helping a major Asian manufacturer redesign its supply chain in Hong Kong. We can capture consultants' and clients' experiences from these projects within our knowledge management systems, then package it, integrate it into all the appropriate courses, put it online, and make it available to 200, 2,000, or even 20,000 PwC consultants working elsewhere in the world on similar assignments"(Collins, 2000).

One of the real beauties of the new e.cademie Website, says Collins, is that consultants will also be able to download Website information onto their laptops and take it with them when they are at client sites or in hotel rooms. Such learning technologies, she says, are helping to "elongate the learning process" so that people are provided with learning support whether they're at their desk, at a client site, or in a hotel room. It will also be accessible on a dial-up basis, so people who are traveling can maintain a continuous electronic link with peers or project team members.

Collins says the urgency of companies developing Web-based training and knowledge management applications like e.cademie will only grow in the future. "In an e-business world we can't wait three to six months for our training department to create a new training course based on new client knowledge," she says. "Instead, we must act at e-speed to leverage what we know. e.cademie provides the opportunity for us to create and enhance our learning material in real time and disseminate it across our global consultancy almost instantaneously."

The Challenges of Providing Web-based Leadership Training Within Corporations

The emergence of the Internet and the advance of technology hold tremendous promise for online leadership training and learning, but developing online training/learning programs poses unique challenges for instructional designers. Richard Koonce (1998) caught up with some innovators in the field of Web-based leadership training for an article in *Technical Training*.

"This is an evolving field of study for us," notes Peter Rothstein, director of distributed learning for Lotus Development Corporation, who says that his company uses teams of technologists, business process redesign experts, and OD consultants to create learning programs. "The speed of change is so fast in organizations today that to deal with skill gaps, we need to look at developing different training models. People want everything interwoven—the learning systems, the knowledge management systems, the content—in one seamless environment, and the question becomes this: How do we produce the learning nuggets that become part of learning experiences in classrooms and virtual learning communities?"

Rob Harris, director of Oracle University, agrees: "It's a question of chunking learning into smaller and smaller bits, what we call 'reusable content objects,'" he says. "These are important with Web-based learning because everything is being digitized, and learners want and need to assemble their own learning."

Then there is the issue of whether people will actually use the technology that's presented to them. John Humphrey of the Forum Corporation says that transferring something that has been classroom-based and putting it online can be a challenge. Formats and pacing, for example, are different online than in a classroom, he says. And technological flexibility is critical to people finding Web-based learning packages sufficiently user-friendly to access regularly. "Access to easily manipulated packages is key," says Humphrey, "and we're not there yet." Humphrey adds that companies need to commit themselves to the concept of technology-based training and be willing to do what it takes to make technology-based training work. "Many companies pride themselves on being on the technological cutting edge, but many are not," he says. Consequently, many companies will need to make capital investments to implement robust technology-based training programs within their organizations.

Technology Does Not Guarantee Quality

From the preceding discussion it seems that technology is well positioned to offer a wider variety of learning avenues (and venues) than traditional training ever could. And its potential to serve as an LD tool seems clear, not only as a pre- and post-event engagement device with training course participants but as a catalyst for creating online communities of leaders within organizations today. Such online communities will, in the future, serve as activity hubs to drive change within organizations, accelerate introduction of new work processes, diffuse conflicts, and most certainly facilitate better communication and coordination among leaders in different parts of an organization, as they work to achieve common goals.

But can technology really deliver everything it promises? Boland, for one, cautions that technology alone cannot guarantee that people will have unforgettable learning experiences at work. She cautions companies against pursuing the path of least resistance with technology, that is, implementing technology and hoping that it lives up to its full potential in helping to develop leaders, subject matter experts, or anybody else inside an organization. "We need to focus on how individuals learn, *then* use technology to provide a learning environment," she says. To Boland, that means creating "learner-centered environments" where people are able to optimize their own learning opportunities. "I'm not sure that left to its own devices, technology can do all that," she says. "There's a key role for trainers to play as mentors and facilitators of the learning process. We can't forget the high-touch component here" (Koonce, 1998).

Implications for the Training/HRD Professional

It is not necessary for you, as an OD consultant or T&D professional, to choose between implementing a corporate university or an executive leadership program, or between partnering with a university or a consulting firm, or between using lots of technology or no technology as part of your LD training and development architecture. The learning solutions presented in this chapter are not mutually exclusive. In designing a solution, in fact, many organizations use a combination. There are, however, a number of factors that are essential to your success, no matter what delivery method(s) you choose:

❖ First, understand your organization's needs.

❖ Two, ensure the program design addresses the identified needs.

❖ Three, use state-of-the-art delivery methods.

❖ Four, evaluate the impact of the program.

Step One: Understand Your Organization's Needs

In designing LD programs that are appropriate to your organization, ask yourself: What is it that we as an organization are trying to accomplish through LD? "The first step in articulating an executive resource strategy is to step back and take a big-picture view of the long- and short-term business requirements that determine the need for certain types of leadership competencies," notes Robert Barner (2000).

In other words, LD must be driven and derived from an understanding of your company's current or emerging strategy. Spend time developing an understanding of your organization's specific challenges and emergent priorities.

Step Two: Ensure the Program Design Addresses the Identified Needs

As part of your data-gathering, conduct a leadership assessment (chapter 2) or a competency assessment (chapter 5). This research drill-down is essential if you are to identify the specific leadership skill gaps as they exist in the organization or as they may emerge in the years to come. As part of this process, ask your organization's leaders to list major challenges they foresee, as well as unexpected changes (phase shifts) in marketplace dynamics, competitive relationships, technology, and so forth, that may affect the current or future balance of power between your company and its competitors.

Such challenges might also involve looming organizational changes (changes in work systems, processes, reporting relationships, customer requirements, or markets) that could potentially affect the nature of leadership skill sets. From this analysis, you will derive an understanding about

❖ the kinds of training you need to provide (the content)

❖ the audience(s) whom you need to serve

❖ what the most appropriate delivery vehicles are.

Step Three: Use State-of-the-Art Delivery Methods

Traditionally, case studies (made popular by Harvard) have been a mainstay in the delivery of LD programs and are still a popular learning method today. However, action learning approaches are today recognized by best-practice companies as a preferred technique (chapter 6). Because leaders work together to solve problems, they learn from each other. Action learning focuses on both the "hard" and "soft" skills required to make business decisions. And it focuses on the importance of taking action as the result of new information gathered or developed, not just analyzing problems.

Step Four: Evaluate the Impact of the Program

What is the return-on-investment from your training dollars? How do you assess whether existing (or future) programs in your organization are working? These are important questions to be able to answer in light of the growing leadership competency gaps and limited leadership ranks in many organizations today. In-house, corporate university approaches to LD sometimes provide their own metrics. For example, participant involvement and course evaluation can be pegged to completion of specific and successful real-world projects or demonstrated improvements in organizational performance (reduced cycle times, reduced expenses, and so forth). In other cases, however, you may need to develop a framework for assessing the success of LD programs by tracking increased levels of employee involvement, innovation, productivity, or process improvement back on the job.

What Does the Future Hold for Leadership Development?

Although the future of leadership training is hard to predict, it seems clear that the use of new technologies to support and enhance training is a trend you can count on. Similarly, the role of trainers and HRD experts will continue to evolve given the increasingly complex HR and performance issues companies must deal with in today's knowledge-based economy. These realities will thus afford T&D professionals with new career options and opportunities at every turn. Finally, the completion of the paradigm shift away from classroom and event-driven training toward just-in-time, real-world, and action learning at all leadership levels in organizations is inevitable. In his article, *The Evolving Paradigm of Leadership Development,* Robert Fulmer

Figure 10-1. The evolving paradigm of leadership development.

	Past	Transitional	Future
Participants	Listener	Student	Learner
Program Design	Event	Curriculum	Ongoing
Place	University Campus	Corporate Facility	Anywhere
Purpose	Knowledge	Wisdom	Action
Players	Specialists	Generalists	Partners
Presentations	Style	Content	Process/Outcome
Period	Past	Present	Future

Reprinted from *Organizational Dynamics:* 4. Fulmer, R., "The Evolving Paradigm of Leadership Development," (1997, Spring), with permission of Elsevier Science.

(1997) identifies seven shifts taking place within LD today. These shifts are determining the future direction of LD (figure 10-1).

Figure 10-1 reveals that there has been a fundamental shift in LD programs away from static, student-oriented, off-the-shelf training classes toward learning experiences that take a more team-oriented, results-driven, interactive approach. This shift in design has been driven both by the changing world of work and by shifting business priorities. In keeping with these shifts, what are the challenges for today's T&D professional? Clearly, if LD falls under your purview, you must be able to think ahead of the curve, anticipate your organization's future needs, plan the most appropriate channels and vehicles for LD programs and initiatives, and take a strategic approach to your everyday job. Chapter 11 provides details on how you can become an effective consultant and coach to your organization's senior leaders and, by so doing, help prepare your organization for the tectonic changes likely to rock the 21st century business environment.

—11—

From Traditional Trainer to Consultant and Coach

Outstanding coaches and mentors get inside the heads of the people they are helping. They sense how to give effective feedback. They know when to push for better performance and when to hold back. In the way they motivate their protégés, they demonstrate empathy in action.

— Daniel Goleman, *Working With Emotional Intelligence* (1998).

As the preceding chapters of this book make clear, there are many leadership challenges facing companies today, each of which is requiring that trainers and HRD professionals play increasingly complex, consultative roles inside their organizations. The whole purpose of this book is not only to describe these leadership challenges but to provide you with tools, techniques, and tips that will make you a more potent and effective consultant and facilitator in dealing with them.

We all realize that the roles of trainers and HRD professionals are being transformed today because of the tremendous changes taking place in business and organizations. Gone are the days when trainers simply presented "canned" presentations or training packages. Today, everything is customized, just-in-time, Web-based, or delivered in a distance environment. Consequently, many trainers and HRD professionals have moved away from being simply instructional designers and stand-up presenters, becoming instead subject matter experts, learning specialists, technologists, and internal consultants who are deeply ensconced in the line functions of their organizations and able to work at multiple levels inside their organizations.

Still, many learning professionals are not yet prepared to work with their leaders when it comes to addressing leadership challenges, nor are they equipped in terms of their own professional competencies and departmental resources to help their companies become leader-builder organizations. To meet these needs, your role as an HRD professional must increasingly become that of facilitator and coach. Being successful in these roles requires a rare blend of skills in the areas of consultative selling, LD expertise, training design, group facilitation, and individual coaching, as well as a strong organizational reputation for integrity and professional ability. All these skills will be required as you work with your organization's CEO and top leadership team to address leadership problems, and, in some cases, with individual leaders to address their own leadership issues—particularly as they relate to managing change.

So, what is the best way to get your hands around these challenges? The following sections list ways that you can help your organization become a leader-builder.

Step 1: Partner With Top Leadership

First, understand the importance of partnering with your organization's top leadership if you want to be viewed not as a "member of the training staff" but as a business consultant who can address the line-of-business needs of your organization. In chapter 10 we looked at the nature of GE's and Disney's leadership and employee development programs. In both companies (and in others like Ford and Motorola), trainers and HRD professionals are intimately involved with their companies' senior leaders in developing and designing leadership training programs that will meet the needs of the business.

At GE the impetus for this comes from the company's objective to develop global business skills ("global brains") in the company's current and future leadership cadres. To keep up the momentum, Jack Welch makes regular treks to Crotonville to personally deliver training and to facilitate workshops and seminars among GE managers and executives. Meanwhile, at Disney University, the HRD staff play a highly consultative role to senior management as well, working closely with line managers and subject matter specialists to develop training that is relevant not just to the operational sides of the business but also to the development of future Disney leaders. Suffice it to say, then, that to be viewed as an effective and knowledgeable resource on LD issues within your organization, you must develop a strong client orientation and set of attitudes that closely mirror the values and culture of your organization and its top leaders.

Step 2: Polish Your Professional Credentials

To be an effective facilitator and coach, especially at high levels in your organization today, requires that you have a grasp of the fundamentals of the business in which you work. Traditionally, trainers and HRD professionals have come out of such fields as human resources, OD, and education. To be viewed as a full partner by your company's top management means that you must have specific line experience in areas such as manufacturing, finance, sales, marketing, research and development, or quality.

As companies become more global, it is also important that you have international or cross-culture work experience, so that you are familiar with issues of cultural diversity and market globalization. And as companies become more concerned about measuring the benefits of training, it is important that you be conversant about the metrics of your business and their application to measurement of benefits of the LD and training programs you create and deliver.

Finally, as technology and training continue to converge, you must be comfortable with the many new kinds of training technology that are becoming commonplace in training architecture and infrastructure in companies. Distance learning and Web-based learning, for example, represent training's "brave new world" in this respect. But becoming familiar with how these tools are used requires discipline and learning on your part and, in some cases, will change the nature of training consultation and delivery.

Mini-MBA programs, professional certification courses, and Web-based virtual university programs all provide means by which HRD professionals can acquire formal credentials in any of the fields described here. Another way, of course, is by becoming intimately connected with the line functions of the company for which you work and finding ways to team or partner with line managers to develop and deliver LD programs that meet current or emerging needs.

Step 3: Educate Your Company's Leaders About LD Issues

Throughout this book, we have noted that as part of helping your organization deal with its leadership challenges, you will very likely need to surface issues and frame the debate about what is at stake for your organization in dealing with various leadership issues. What will be the consequences to corporate competitiveness if your company chooses not to take a deliberate approach to LD and succession planning, for example? What are the long-term consequences to the viability of your company if senior executives do not learn to do a better job of leading change or building top team unity?

Surprisingly, many senior company leaders still do not understand why it is important to put strong LD and succession plans in place, though more and more are being converted to the importance of such programs. So, take it upon yourself to articulate the reasons. Similarly, in many organizations there is still a reluctance to commit organizational resources, time, and leadership energy to growing and grooming new generations of leaders. Therefore, you may need to apprise your organization's leaders of the LD best practices in place at companies like General Electric, Fannie Mae, Dell, PepsiCo, and Intel that ensure that these companies remain highly competitive in today's turbulent business environment. Finally, when it comes to managing change, you may have to nudge your company's leaders to play visible and vigorous roles as change champions if they want your company's transformation efforts to succeed.

The Challenges of Coaching Change Leaders

Be aware that a good deal of your initial work with a CEO or other senior leaders around discussion of change initiatives and associated LD issues will involve emphasizing the importance of leadership resolve and change-leadership best practices. Many CEOs and senior business executives either are unaware that leading change efforts is different from other kinds of leadership, or they simply do not believe that it is different. Others just do not real-ize what kind of leadership commitment is necessary to ensure the success of a change effort. Colin Marshall, chairman of British Airways, is fond of saying that when he began culture transfor-mation efforts at British Airways in the 1980s, he believed it would take the company about five years to change itself from a tired, state-subsidized air carrier into a responsive, customer-friendly company. But as the five-year mark approached, he decided it would take more like 10 years. And as 10 years approached, he determined it would take much longer than that—a generation in fact (Burke & Trahant, 2000).

Marshall's experience is typical of other executives who go through a "journey to enlightenment" about leadership of change. During this time they develop both awareness of and commitment to the idea that bringing about large-gauge business change is a long-term process; one that requires considerable energy, time, and effort. They need to understand that leadership of change is not a "project" that they can delegate to subordinates, but is something with which they must be visibly and vigorously involved. Finally, they must understand that communicating with people clearly, consistently, and frequently throughout the course of a change initiative is critical to its success; that, in fact, it is the single most important thing they can do and that even then they probably will not communicate as much as they should.

As a T&D professional, do not underestimate the significant contribution you can make to enlightening leaders of your orga-nization about what is involved in leading successful change efforts. Nowadays many corporate leaders, especially at the most senior levels in companies, are often in desperate need of men-toring and coaching as they confront an ever-widening array of business challenges and problems. You can play a pivotal role in framing business discussions, suggesting tools to help your orga-nization's change leaders address organizational challenges and offering resources that address those challenges.

Step 4: Be a Resource on LD and Coaching Issues

It goes without saying that in today's business environment, you need to view your organization's top leaders, middle managers, process owners, and others as your clients. Seek opportunities to position the importance of LD with them and to position yourself as a coach/facilitator who helps the organization address its leadership challenges.

One thing you may want to do is broach your CEO or some other senior-level executive with the idea of your facilitation of a meeting at which LD needs and issues can be discussed in depth. This can be a very powerful way to position yourself not just as a professional resource to upper management but as an LD subject matter expert who can help design, develop, and deliver LD programs at various levels inside the organization.

In this meeting, which you should facilitate, explore with your company's leaders what the current and future leadership requirements of the organization are, perhaps by using looming changes in your organization or industry as the backdrop. What are the organization's emerging leadership challenges and issues? What needs to be done or has been done to address these issues? Get people to openly and provocatively share their views. You may want to use tools such as Groupware (appendix C) or some other kind of electronic meeting technology to record people's comments and help determine the first steps that need to be taken by the organization in dealing with these issues. It may be that this initial group dialogue will lead to strong consensus about the need to undertake a leadership assessment, for example, as described in chapters 1 and 2.

Your agenda for this kind of meeting should include the following:

- outlining the major leadership challenges the organization will face as it addresses changes taking place in its industry or as it prepares to undertake a major transformation effort

- highlighting important attributes of companies that do a good job of developing new populations of leaders

- discussing your company's specific leadership skill gaps and how they threaten the organization's future goals and even its organizational viability

- getting buy-in to do a leadership assessment to further identify the specific leadership challenges your organization faces

- describing ways that a deliberate, systematic approach to leadership coaching and development will help the company achieve short-term and strategic goals

- ✿ positioning the importance of evaluative tools (such as 360-degree assessments) as part of the leadership assessment process

- ✿ including discussion of the roles that those present in the room need to play to help move LD efforts forward

- ✿ assessing the current climate for the kinds of initiatives you and others are planning

- ✿ outlining your own role as potential coach to the CEO and executive team.

The visioning and process tools outlined in chapter 3 may prove especially useful to you as you facilitate early meetings with your organization's top leadership team to address pivotal leadership issues, identify current leadership strengths/weaknesses, and move forward to shape the future of the organization. You may also want to use the energy channeling ideas and techniques described in chapter 8 to build top team unity around the importance of addressing leadership issues at this point in your organization's life.

Step 5: Contract With Your Organization's CEO and Senior Leaders

As you work with your company's top leadership team, it will be critical to make a compelling business case for why LD is important to your company's future profitability and business success. Consider conducting cross-industry research and preparing an overview for senior leaders before asking for their support for a leadership assessment. Once you are in the contracting stage, suggest that you and they agree to specific outcomes that they want to achieve from the coaching and facilitation that will follow. Such outcomes may include the following:

- ✿ identifying or clarifying the organization's significant leadership challenges

- ✿ making a list of critical change leadership competencies that the organization needs in the short, medium, and long terms

- ✿ outlining the steps and timeframes in implementing an LD plan

- helping senior leaders become aware of their personal leadership strengths and weaknesses

- getting leaders to commit to development plans, programs, and projects

- orienting the CEO to the role he or she must play in helping drive organizational resolve and team unity around completion of specific leadership goals.

Step 6: Understand the Critical Role You Play

To this point, we have outlined a structure and process you can use to position yourself as a resource and leadership coach within your organization. But how do you convey credibility and convince others that you know what you are talking about?

As a coach you will serve as a catalyst for important discussions about change and leadership issues within your organization while you position yourself as a resource to your CEO and other leaders. At times you will work one-on-one with others at high levels in your organization. At other times, you are likely to be involved in facilitating conversations and even mediating conflicts among people who are part of management teams at either a senior or middle-management level. What is the best way to approach these tasks?

Being an effective facilitator/coach, especially at high levels in your organization, requires tact, understanding, empathy, rugged self-confidence, and flexibility, especially when dealing with people who have strong egos and competing agendas. Your ability to be yourself, to bring your professional point of view to the coaching/facilitation process, to set boundaries with others, and to establish expectations with people you coach are important to ensure the integrity and effectiveness of the coaching process.

Step 7: Know What YOU Have to Offer as a Coach

Most people who become coaches or facilitators for the first time experience at least a minor crisis of professional confidence. "What if people don't take me seriously?" they may wonder. Or worse, "Who am I to think that I can consult to people in the organization much higher and more powerful than me?"

Establishing your own identity and role as a coach (vis-à-vis your clients) requires knowing what you, as an individual, bring to the table whether you are coaching a single client, a group, a team, or dealing with multiple levels of leaders within your organization at the same time. There are times, for example, when you will need to suggest that individuals or groups move in new directions or consider new options, and you may find it useful to inject experiences from your own background into the discussions to help clients see the value of these ideas and choices. Alternatively, if you are working with an individual, you may find it beneficial to bring your professional experience from other companies with you to the coaching process perhaps to suggest how a major problem can be remedied or a critical issue can be addressed.

So what in fact, do you have to offer your clients as a coach? To answer that question, do a little inventory of your professional background, skills, and experience. When it comes to the coaching process, all these things represent "professional assets." In his book, *The Consultant's Calling: Bringing Who You Are to What You Do,* Geoffrey Bellman (1990) offers an initial list of these assets:

experience	friendship	support
eyes	vision	contacts
age	ears	authenticity
wisdom	information	perspective
accomplishment	time	objectivity
values	skill	equipment
products	style	compassion
expertise	guts	credibility
reputation	approval	personality
insight		

To this list, we would add stories, humor, confidentiality, concern, empathy, and creativity. Understanding what you have to offer as a coach will do a great deal to fortify your confidence in your ability to fulfill the role. Moreover, it will help build your clients' trust and willingness to risk in terms of what they are willing to divulge to you and what they are willing to accept from you.

Four Characteristics of Coaching Relationships That Work

- *The individual serving as a coach is well suited to the job and enjoys a high degree of respect in the organization.* To be an effective coach, particularly at senior levels, your clients must respect you, and you must be able to build rapport with them. Doing this requires sophisticated social and interpersonal skills, a knowledge of the company, its key executives, and the industry issues and pressures the company is currently confronting.

- *Both coach and client clearly understand the type of coaching the client needs.* Coaching takes many forms. It is possible that most of your coaching will take place with small to midsize groups of leaders at differing levels in your organization. Alternatively, you may be involved in one-on-one coaching. If others from your department or function will be working with you, be sure that people are appropriately placed, both for facilitator roles and for any one-on-one coaching of people. Only a very senior T&D person, for example, will have credibility with members of your organization's top leadership team. Less senior persons will be appropriate to use with other levels of leaders, especially as LD efforts are rolled out to other layers of the organization.

- *There is a clear scope and distinct boundaries to the coaching role.* Coaching can be defined in many ways. To help organizations develop leaders and manage change efforts, the coach's role consists primarily of helping individuals or groups where they can or should improve their change leadership skills. This involves observing individuals in action and providing objective feedback. It also means helping individuals obtain feedback from other parties and use it productively. Other roles you are likely to play as an executive coach include helping individuals set and own personal improvement targets, helping them develop individual development plans (IDPs) to achieve those targets, creating opportunities for people to practice desired skills, and helping individuals work through setbacks or issues that may be preventing them from performing to their fullest capability.

- *Measurable targets for the coaching process have been agreed upon.* As part of serving as a coach, be it for an individual or a team, you will have agreed to (contracted to) specific targets and outcomes that you will help individuals or groups achieve. This is part of setting appropriate boundaries for the coaching process and is critical to preserving your own role as an effective facilitator, coach, conflict mediator, and strategic stage-setter in executive venues.

Step 8: Engender Trust in Those Whom You Coach

What is the best way to coach individual leaders in your organization, either about the decisions they must make for others or their own issues of leadership effectiveness? Geoffrey Bellman (1990) offers some rich insights into the dynamics lying beneath the start of any new one-on-one coaching relationship. A client is aware that "a consulting intervention could benefit or cost him in ways far more important than money," says Bellman. Besides dollars, he or she will be spending time with you, putting faith in you, and taking your professional measure while you work together. "[The client risks] moving in directions as yet undefined based on information as yet uncollected. They are deeply invested in their own and the organization's success [and] are considering putting some portion of this potential success on the line with you, a consultant. They are considering giving you powers in their organization that they ordinarily reserve for themselves and a few trusted others. [Therefore,] they must ask themselves if this is a smart investment" (Bellman, 1990).

How do you as a coach or internal consultant ensure that your clients are comfortable and that they develop trust in you? In essence, it boils down to two things.

First, put yourself on the same wavelength as your clients. This involves showing empathy, concern, and practicing careful and discerning listening so that you begin to understand a client's personality, his or her needs, fears, operating constraints, and the political or organizational realities that he or she may be facing. Although it sounds simple enough, many consultants (both external and internal) wind up dealing with so many clients that after awhile they feel, "I've seen and heard it all." Such individuals often show carelessness or lack of engagement in dealing with new clients, something you want to avoid at all costs. Careful, discerning listening is the skill critical to building rapport with clients and engendering sustained trust with ongoing clients. You will find that the higher the level of the person you work with in the organization, the greater the need will be for you to exhibit empathy to the needs and situations of the individuals with whom you are working.

Second, keep your goals and those of your clients in mind at all times. The dynamics you experience and create with clients and groups will be different in every instance. Indeed, if you have already done a good deal of consulting and coaching you know that there is a unique "texture" to every single relationship you have with people, whether in a group setting or one on one. One of the rewards of coaching and consulting is to experience how rich this conversational texture can be (and at times to use it to your advantage), but you must not forget what your goals as a coach/consultant are. With groups you will be acting as a facilitator, subject matter expert, change agent, and even provocateur to stimulate discussions and help groups achieve their goals. With individuals you will be acting as a sounding board, a mirror, a coach, and even a mentor at times as people share openly and perhaps deeply about themselves with you.

Step 9: Use a Systematic Coaching Approach

As Figure 11-1 reveals, the executive coaching process has multiple goals. It can serve

- ❁ as a developmental vehicle for building overall leadership effectiveness

- ❁ as a training tool to help individual leaders develop new competencies (for example, in team building or change management)

- ❁ as an intervention tool to help "fast track" individuals deal with significant skill gaps or leadership blind spots

- ❁ as a channel to provide long-term developmental guidance/ performance feedback to individuals as part of a company's succession planning efforts.

What else is important to your success as a leadership coach? Certainly taking responsibility for your own career and professional development are central to your success, especially in a profession that is in as much transition

Figure 11-1. The effective coaching process.

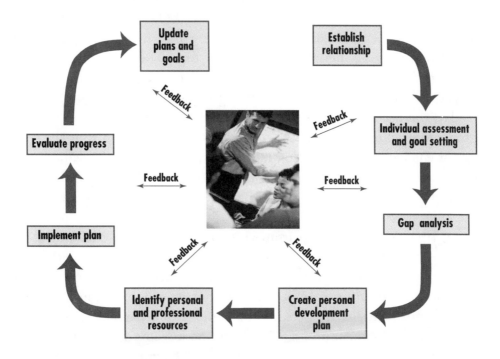

as training and HRD. Enhancing your skills and knowledge will ensure your "business fluency" with the issues your organization is facing. As chapter 10 revealed, new training technologies are rapidly and radically redefining the nature of training and the core skills needed to do it well. Ten years ago, trainers did not have to worry all that much about understanding modern communications technologies. Neither were they called on to be coaches to their company's senior executives. But nowadays both of these things are increasingly common, which is why it is important that you feel confident in your ability to be both a coach and consultant to your organization's leaders at many levels.

The Path to Becoming a Leader-Builder

As we have stressed throughout *Growing Leaders,* leadership in companies today is no longer a solo act if it ever was. The challenges facing companies today are too complex and the need for product quality and speed-to-market too great for companies to rely exclusively on "CEO wisdom" or on traditional leadership models that stifle creativity and discourage empowerment. "The old days when a Henry Ford, Alfred Sloan, or Tom Watson *learned for the organization* are gone," notes Peter Senge (1990). "In an increasingly dynamic, interdependent, and unpredictable world, it is simply no longer possible for anyone to 'figure it all out at the top.' The old model, 'the top thinks and the local acts,' must now give way to integrating thinking and acting at all levels. While the challenge is great, so is the potential payoff."

Today, the need for companies to develop leaders at all levels continues to grow more acute by the day. As companies struggle to confront the challenges of change—new technologies, emerging markets, globalization, and e-business—they must therefore become as aggressive about nurturing their leadership talent as they traditionally have been about developing products or pursuing new markets.

It has been our observation from years of working with clients that the companies and organizations that "learn how to learn" or, more specifically, learn how to learn faster are those that master the art of continuous change and organizational survival. To be sure, this notion of learning how to learn has been a cardinal tenet of personal improvement, self-renewal, and individual career development programs for years. So it seems only appropriate to apply it to how organizations and their leaders can similarly learn, improve, grow, and evolve.

What is the best way to translate this tenet into action? The best way to ensure that your organization survives and thrives in the century ahead is for its leaders to make an enterprisewide commitment not just to continuous learning but to the continual shrinking of its learning cycle. Additionally, your organization's learning focus should be not just on *adaptive* learning (which is about helping the organization cope with current problems or issues) but on *generative* learning, which is about helping organizations create, develop more learning capacity, and therefore become more capable (Senge, 1990).

We submit that many of the emerging trends in leadership and organizational learning described in chapter 10 are likely to facilitate both generative (intrinsically motivated) learning as well as adaptive (externally motivated) learning in organizations today. Still, pursuing either learning "mission" is likely to engender its own unique set of leadership challenges from time to time. For one thing, pushing people to learn faster and faster and to leverage their learning in continuously new and more effective ways will in time create pushback and resistance even among the most ardent and aligned of employees. People, including leaders, can experience learning fatigue as readily as they can experience work fatigue or battle fatigue.

In these moments it will be very important for you in your role as a facilitator and coach to keep in mind the importance that "creative tension" plays in helping to bring about organizational transformation—sometimes one or two people at a time. What is creative tension? Essentially it is a dynamic that you can embed in an organization's discussions about an LD issue that invites those involved to look at both where the organization currently is with regard to a certain matter (the present reality) and to compare that against where the organization wants to be and needs to go (the future state). The difference between the two results in a creative tension, which prompts both critical thinking and thoughtful reflection in people. The result is identification of next steps and the taking of appropriate action. Creative tension is more than a process tool or group facilitation device; it is more an induced state of organizational mind that needs to be established in an organization's visioning, LD, and strategic planning processes if an organization is to truly transform itself.

The principle of creative tension has long been recognized as a way to help individuals unblock their thinking and scrutinize their current "mental models." In your role as facilitator and coach, you will, of course, be helping your organization to do the same thing: to reconsider "old prejudices," engrained points of view, blocked thinking, traditional approaches to leadership and business, or other mental or intellectual "constructs" that block creativity, forestall action, or keep the organization from achieving its fullest potential. These challenges have been at the heart of our discussions in chapters 3 through 9.

What if your efforts to introduce creative tension in your organization spark conflict instead? At those times, remember what consultant and author Ronald Heifetz of Harvard identifies as the true work of leaders today: to arbitrate and mediate conflict. "The role of the leader nowadays is to help organizations face their problems and if necessary to lead people through conflict," he says. They must be able "to surface and orchestrate conflicts, they must have experimental mindsets, and they need to be risk-takers" (Taylor, 1999). This willingness to spark conflict takes real courage and requires a strong and proven structure to accomplish. In essence, this book has been about giving you the structure you need to broach and facilitate what can be very difficult conversations within your organization.

None of this is easy, of course. Growing people never is, whether you are doing it in a large, blue chip company or in a fledgling dot.com. But you bring much to the table for this job, not just your own knowledge and experience but also the ideas, tools, and techniques outlined in this book. Use both to raise your company's consciousness about LD issues, to optimize your effectiveness as a leadership consultant and coach, and to create the critical links between learning and LD that will ensure the vitality of your organization as it becomes a leader-builder.

Appendix A

Types of Leadership Development/Coaching Programs

Traditional LD programs normally are targeted at just the CEO and his or her top leadership team. Today, LCD programs, which include traditional approaches in some cases, encompass a wide variety of interventions, undertaken at both the *transformational* and *transactional* levels in organizations (figure A-1).

Programs aimed at the transformational level are designed to help leaders bring about large-gauge changes in culture, mission/vision, and strategy. Programs that companies undertake at a transactional (workplace) level typically focus on

- accelerating the introduction of new management practices

- bolstering work unit productivity

- facilitating process redesign/restructuring efforts

- improving communication

- speeding implementation of new systems, policies, and technology.

Today, LCD programs encompass a flexible blend of both types of efforts, depending on an organization's specific needs as determined in a leadership assessment (chapter 2).

Figure A-1. Types of leadership development/coaching programs.

Improved organizational performance →

Traditional Leadership Development
- Senior executive coaching
- Management coaching
- Strategic planning
- Informal succession planning
- Conflict resolution programs
- Communications programs

Mission and Vision Development
- Values clarification
- Articulation of the company's core "ideology"
- Senior team consensus-building
- Strategic goal setting
- Emphasis on development of team unity
- Development of a "teachable point of view" about the future
- Cascading of this "teachable point of view" to other leadership levels

Culture Change Programs
- Culture change planning
- Use of leaders-developing-leaders programs
- Strong articulation of the need to change and new shared values to support change
- Use of 360-degree and multirater evaluation instruments/feedback to shape/sustain new behaviors
- Emphasis on tangible process/performance improvement
- Effort to cascade change messages throughout organization

Organizational Redesign
- Development/implementation of new management practices
- Introduction of new systems/technology to support new ways of working
- Work unit team-building programs
- Process redesign projects
- Job redesign

Managing People Performance
- Introduction of new performance measurement and management systems
- Alignment of work behaviors and values
- Introduction of new reward and recognition systems
- Clear communication of work experiences
- Use of employee coaching/mentoring to enhance and sustain productivity improvements

Continuous Change Planning/Coordination
- Long-term scenario planning (2–10 years)
- Executive coaching
- Focus on building employee recommitment to changing goals
- Creation of a robust "climate of internal organizational alignment" to support and sustain organization renewal over time

Fulfill company core philosophy and business values ↑ (left vertical axis)

Build greater leadership capacity and enhance organizational resilience ↑ (right vertical axis)

External environmental factors ↑ (bottom axis)

Appendix B

Vision and Mission Statements of Five Unique Organizations

These five organizations have one trait in common: They are successful. Their success is due, in part, to their defined missions. Each has a different purpose, but their missions all enable them to be leaders in customer satisfaction, as well as product placement or service offering.

Ben & Jerry's is dedicated to the creation & demonstration of a new corporate concept of linked prosperity. Our mission consists of three interrelated parts.

- ❀ Product mission: To make, distribute and sell the finest quality all natural ice cream and related products in a wide variety of innovative flavors made from Vermont dairy products.

- ❀ Economic mission: To operate the Company on a sound financial basis of profitable growth, increasing value for our shareholders, and creating career opportunities and financial rewards for our employees.

✿ Social mission: To operate the Company in a way that actively recognizes the central role that business plays in the structure of society by initiating innovative ways to improve the quality of life of a broad community—local, national, and international.

Printed by permission of Ben & Jerry's.

To establish Starbucks as the premier purveyor of the finest coffee in the world while maintaining our uncompromising principles as we grow.

Printed by permission of Starbucks Coffee.

To provide every household and business across the United States with the ability to communicate and conduct business with each other and the world through prompt, reliable, secure, and economical services for the collection, transmission, and delivery of messages and merchandise.

Printed by permission of the United States Postal Service.

To build a global medium as central to people's lives as the telephone or television and even more valuable.

Printed by permission of America Online.

The objectives of Shell companies are to engage efficiently, responsibly and profitably in the oil, gas, chemicals and other selected businesses and to participate in the search for and development of other sources of energy. Shell companies seek a high standard of performance and aim to maintain a long-term position in their respective competitive environments.

Printed by permission of Shell Oil.

Appendix C

A Gallery of Process Tools

As discussed in chapter 3, process tools can be a highly effective way to move the visioning process along. We have found that several simple tools and techniques can help groups gain clarity and agreement about the direction in which they want to move.

Clarity Agreement Matrix

The first of these tools is a simple clarity agreement matrix (figure C-1), which is supported by polling techniques that can help facilitate a group's decision-making processes and ensure the integrity of group actions and decisions reached as the result of discussion.

As part of setting the tone for visioning workshops, it is critically important that you, as facilitator, moderate a discussion about the ground rules that will be used during the visioning process. How will the team make decisions? At which point will the team agree that consensus has been reached? How will you know when to move on to next steps? How can you be sure that the team has, in fact, reached closure and consensus about the directions in which it has decided to move? The clarity agreement matrix is an excellent tool to use to answer such questions, and ensure your own effectiveness as a facilitator. The following sections detail how the clarity agreement matrix works.

Figure C-1. Clarity agreement matrix.

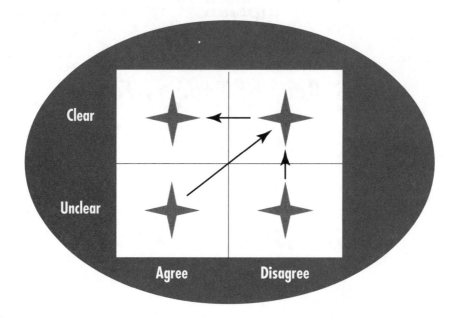

Step 1

When a leadership team is debating what the key values of the organization are, the matrix can be very helpful in ensuring that everyone in a group setting understands what a particular core value being discussed *means*. Is everyone in the room clear about what is meant by "customer responsiveness," for example, or "organizational agility"? Getting clarity around which values are most important to the organization (and how they are defined) is critical in the early stages of the visioning process, when many ideas about what constitute core values may emerge in discussion.

Step 2

Once an initial list of values has been generated, the group can then winnow and prioritize this list as it sees fit. Use a poll to determine the degree to which participants agree (or disagree) that any specific value is a core value of the organization's ideology that belongs on the final list. This stage of discussion may require time. So, don't rush it.

Step 3

Once a list of core values has been generated, you and your group are then ready to draft language about the organization's core ideology (based on the values you have just arrived at) and about where the company wants to be in the future. As the group plays with proposed language to describe both its ideology and its future goals, test the clarity of specific phrases and words in such statements, again using the clarity agreement matrix. Note which phrases and words that people like most and want to keep and discard the rest. Continue this stage of the facilitation as long as is necessary, or until conversation wanes.

Step 4

At the appropriate time, poll people again, this time to test their level of agreement as to what portions of "clarified" language they want to use as the basis of a final vision statement.

Vision work is an iterative, "storming and forming" process of eliciting people's ideas and opinions, testing key concepts for validity and relevance, and coming to agreement and consensus about the language that works best. In the early stages of the visioning process, you will use the clarity agreement matrix frequently to drive consensus, to prioritize values and ideas when appropriate, and, in some cases, to prolong discussions to achieve solid agreement and leadership alignment before the visioning process concludes. The goal, of course, throughout, is to thrash out a team consensus of what the organization's core ideology is and what its future direction needs to be.

Electronic Meeting Technology

Another process tool that is highly effective in driving groups towards clarity and consensus is electronic meeting systems technology (EMS). The menu of EMS tools includes the Groupware system, which is particularly useful as a meeting catalyst. It accelerates the storming and norming process, captures a verbatim record of peoples' comments, enables people to develop documents collaboratively, and records their responses to clarity and agreement polls that can then be rapidly discussed and processed if necessary by a group.

How do you use Groupware technology in a visioning or group facilitation session? Basically, you begin with laptop computers linked together in a classroom environment via a local area network. A typical Groupware session uses a large screen at the front of the room—an electronic flipchart—that displays participant responses.

Face-to-face discussion does take place, but participants also spend much of their meeting time using laptops to respond to questions, hold group discussions, and create joint work documents such as marketing plans and mission statements. The Groupware system also lets you organize participant input into bar graphs, charts, file folders, and hierarchical decision trees on participants' laptops and on a central display screen. Participants can either be located in one meeting room or geographically dispersed. Depending on the system configuration, any number of participants can take part in a Groupware session.

One reason that the Groupware system is such a powerful process tool is that it can elicit nuances of feeling and opinion from people who are reluctant to express their opinions when you facilitate a discussion and ask everyone in the room to contribute his or her ideas. What if people remain silent during such moments? You and the rest of the group may not be aware of or understand someone's lack of clarity about an issue, or why he or she does not agree with the others in the group on some topics. Addressing such issues is imperative, however, because as part of the visioning process one of your goals is to align people as tightly as possible behind statements of common purpose, shared vision, or organizational mission. Using the Groupware system or similar technology is invaluable in such cases, because it helps establish group unanimity and team unity (Clarke & Koonce, 1995).

Mind Mapping Technique and Concept Mapping

Still another tool we find useful in visioning workshops are "webbing" techniques such as "mind mapping", concept mapping, and so forth. As illustrated in figure C-2, these attempt to "map" the dialogue that a group may have about a particular issue or challenge. Rather than capture verbatim comments as they are broached, webbing techniques draw upon the associative power of the brain to recall large amounts of dialogue using short written phrases linked to other phrases.

For example, the diagram in figure C-2, created using Inspiration software (a product of Inspiration Software, Inc.) is a sample mind map image. It maps the dialogue of an organization as it explores how best to bring about big improvements in core process cycle times while improving

Figure C-2. Mind map example.

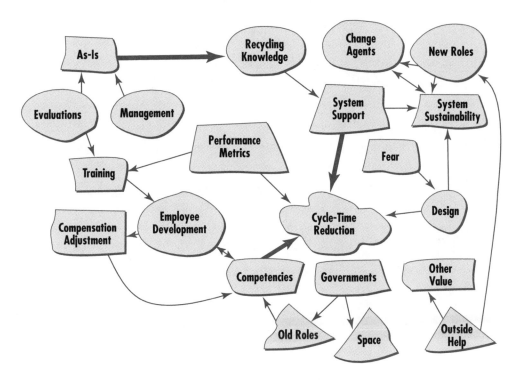

employee core competencies. Using visual representations that capture the gist of individual discussion points, this map helps the group see the inter-connectedness of various strains of thought, as well as "missing pieces" in their thinking. At the same time, participants find that by placing their individual ideas on a conference room wall, their thoughts quickly become "the property of the group," greatly improving the quality and richness of conversations that people have as a result.

Mind map images and concept maps help groups of all kinds get to a richer understanding of individual ideas, problems, and concepts. In turn, this helps create greater clarity of thinking as ideas are discussed by the group. Such maps also help people come to consensus more quickly about action steps and plans, because they foster rapid ownership of important ideas by a group as it strives toward its goals.

Appendix D

Case Study: The Rebirth of A&P

The Great Atlantic and Pacific Tea Company (A&P) is a $10 billion, 140-year-old food retailer that is working hard to undertake the most significant organizational transformation of its time. This is a huge challenge. The competitive landscape changes almost daily for A&P, with fewer big players competing for the loyalty of time-pressed shoppers who have many places to food shop, ranging from traditional grocery stores to "warehouse" stores, from high-end stores like Fresh Fields to Internet home delivery services. Moreover, A&P is competing from a disadvantaged position. Because many of its 800 stores are undersized and outdated, the company has experienced substandard performance for the past 10 years and has lots of organizational and strategic issues to resolve.

The time was ripe for change. In May 1998, Christian Haub took over as A&P's president and CEO and immediately engaged his top team in revolutionizing the company with a large-scale program of culture change, working in partnership with a multidisciplinary team of consultants from PricewaterhouseCoopers and more than 80,000 A&P employees nationwide.

Through mid-2001, the company is implementing a new strategic plan across its entire store base. The initial goal is to return the 140-year-old chain's business performance to at least industry average over the next year and a half and to return it to top quartile business performance within five years. A&P is expected to double sales in just a few years by focusing on store modernization, improved distribution and logistics, and improved category management practices (the "hard sides" of change). It also plans to emphasize people and customer service (the "soft" side of change).

To get there, A&P executives face major challenges when it comes to CONNECTING, CREATING, and CHANNELING organizational energy. As part of an energy diagnosis and intervention plan we undertook with the company from May to August 1998, we interviewed 32 top A&P executives and conducted focus groups and surveys with more than 700 employees across A&P's entire store base.

It did not take long to find the source of the company's failing financial performance. Employees talked of old, understaffed, outdated stores, of low employee morale, and a history of people being kept in the dark about the company's financial position, business direction, and competitive challenges. Negativity, apathy, absenteeism, and turnover were big problems as were outmoded recruiting, training, compensation, and performance appraisal systems. "We can no longer afford to view people simply as 'the biggest expense item on the company's profit-and-loss statement,'" noted CEO Haub when he learned of the diagnostic's findings. Instead, "We must see them as the important connection to customers, manufacturers, and to the communities in which our stores operate."

The Top Leadership Team Reestablished Connections

Based on the energy diagnostic, we determined that A&P first needed to recharge itself organizationally by connecting with best practices in the retail food industry and then by improving connections (communication) among members of A&P's top leadership team. Recharging the energy level in the company's top management team was, in our view, the "main switch" that had to be thrown for real transformational change to occur within A&P. Therefore, our intervention plans called for the CEO and 32 other executives to be included in this stakeholder group. Though bigger than most senior leadership teams, limiting the size of the group to just the seven most senior executives might have engendered employee resistance to the group's decisions downstream, something A&P could not afford as its change plans proceeded.

To connect team members with one another and with issues and best practices in the retail food industry, we helped Haub and his colleagues form seven critical issue teams (CITs) to research various problem areas and then report back to the entire leadership team with recommendations on how to address them. The idea behind these teams was for everybody to connect to a large amount of empirical information, which would help unite team members by encouraging informed discussion and debate about future directions. Out of these discussions, it was believed that a new, highly customer-focused business strategy could emerge. Every team member committed to the importance of taking part in these teams, which were organized as follows:

- ❂ *Consumer research.* Because A&P had fallen out of touch with consumer buying habits and trends, this team was charged with establishing a robust organizational process to collect and analyze consumer data that the company needed for long-term strategic planning.

- ❂ *Competitive assessment.* To ensure that A&P became more agile in responding to competitors and changing industry forces, this team was charged with creating a process to analyze economic, industry, and competitive trends and incorporating that data into the company's strategic planning efforts.

- ❂ *Operational assessment.* To build A&P's capacity for continuous improvement and organizational renewal, this team focused on developing benchmarking and best practices information related to process and organizational design, technology, and facilities planning.

- ❂ *Financial analysis.* This team developed a financial modeling framework and tools to use as part of strategic planning efforts. It was also charged with achieving consensus about a going-forward implementation scenario for transformation efforts.

- ❂ *Capital optimization.* This team was charged with identifying ways to realize costs savings on future capital expenditures, primarily through outsourcing and other contractual arrangements.

- ❂ *Retail concept format.* This team's charge was to assess and redefine the process and criteria that A&P would use to identify, select, and plan new retail concepts.

- ❂ *Merger/acquisition integration planning.* This team was charged with developing and documenting a process to integrate potential merger/acquisitions and to support pursuit of future strategic alliances that might be essential to ensuring nonorganic business growth.

The CITs met from September 1998 through April 1999 to pursue their objectives and function as real teams. This obviously required that they first move through the process of "forming and storming" as teams before they could actually perform team tasks. The process proved very effective. People left titles and positions at the door as teams did their work. This facilitated communications and interaction among groups of people who, in some cases, had never worked together before.

In a series of workshops that followed the end of the teams' period of work, each team shared with the others the big questions it had tried to answer (figure D-1) as well as the team's findings and insights.

These workshops coalesced leadership team thinking around the most pressing issues facing A&P and helped team members come up with a new business strategy and action steps to achieve it. For example, A&P executives

- identified specific competitive and consumer challenges facing the company on a going-forward basis, among them greater and fiercer competition, growing complexity of consumer demands, and continued tight business margins

- identified the main operating challenges faced by the chain with regard to business processes, technology, organizational design/ facilities, merchandising, customer service, pricing, advertising, and store formats

- developed multiple future industry scenarios to which the company might have to respond

- formulated the future vision for A&P: "To become the 'Supermarket of Choice'—the place where people choose to work, choose to shop and choose to invest"—and drafted a new mission statement to address the chain's challenges

- proposed strategies to overcome operating challenges and developed implementation steps to help move the company toward realizing its new vision.

Figure D-1. Questions addressed by A&P's strategic planning workshops.

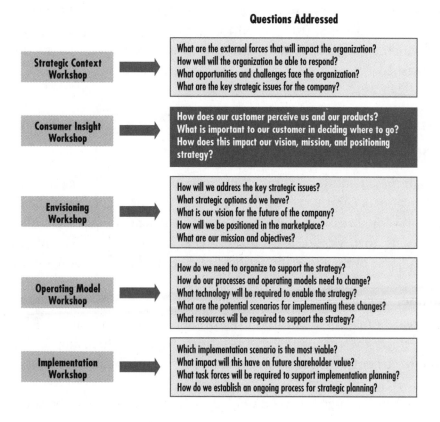

Questions Addressed

Strategic Context Workshop
What are the external forces that will impact the organization?
How well will the organization be able to respond?
What opportunities and challenges face the organization?
What are the key strategic issues for the company?

Consumer Insight Workshop
How does our customer perceive us and our products?
What is important to our customer in deciding where to go?
How does this impact our vision, mission, and positioning strategy?

Envisioning Workshop
How will we address the key strategic issues?
What strategic options do we have?
What is our vision for the future of the company?
How will we be positioned in the marketplace?
What are our mission and objectives?

Operating Model Workshop
How do we need to organize to support the strategy?
How do our processes and operating models need to change?
What technology will be required to enable the strategy?
What are the potential scenarios for implementing these changes?
What resources will be required to support the strategy?

Implementation Workshop
Which implementation scenario is the most viable?
What impact will this have on future shareholder value?
What task forces will be required to support implementation planning?
How do we establish an ongoing process for strategic planning?

Meanwhile, to rebuild connections with employees across the A&P organization, Haub and his team began a massive communications effort beginning in September 1998 to create a common vision of where the company was going and to communicate program specifics to employees on a consistent and frequent basis. This communications plan, the most extensive in the company's history, included

✿ top-level leadership meetings with employees to apprise them of progress with change efforts

✿ quarterly leadership conferences with the top 200 executives in the company to build team unity and enthusiasm around change goals

✿ creation of videos to communicate the importance of specific change efforts and themes to all employees

- the first-ever companywide employee attitude survey, designed to gauge how people felt about the company's change plans

- bi-monthly communication of milestones from the CEO to all A&P employees, using a toll-free, call-in message system through which employees could respond with questions or concerns if they wished.

Channeling Energy Across A&P via Long-Term Integrated Change Initiatives

Although these communication efforts were the most visible sign of changes beginning to occur in the company, A&P executives soon realized they needed to capitalize on the energy created in the workshops by channeling it into actions that would help make A&P become the "Supermarket of Choice." Some of these specific actions are described in the following sections.

Customer Service

To create a major turnaround in customers' perceptions about A&P customer service, the company's change efforts began by focusing on improving the treatment of customers and creating "the ultimate shopping experience" for A&P shoppers.

To that end, change teams fanned out to A&P stores across the country to

- conduct benchmarking studies of other companies and identify their best customer service practices

- undertake customer needs assessments at the store level

- create, pilot test, and implement customer service standards and performance measures across all 800 A&P stores.

Core Values/Leadership Development

At the same time, the company launched a drive to articulate common values that A&P leaders at all levels would now be expected to live by to support a stronger, more customer-friendly culture and a more supportive work environment for employees. A&P's 32 top leaders worked hard to articulate a first draft of these values in April 1998. Then, they cascaded discussion about them down into the organization, circulating them among a group of some 700 employees nationwide. Eventually, they became the basis for a new week-long LD program delivered to 2,000 leaders from across the company over a 10-month period beginning in January 1999. All A&P leaders from the executive team down to store managers went through the program, getting multirater feedback from bosses, peers, and direct reports on their practices of the core values, along with one-on-one leadership coaching from a PwC consulting team. In these sessions, managers learned firsthand how their own performance and behavior could contribute directly to the company's growth, how they would be evaluated in the new environment, and how they would be rewarded.

As A&P developed and launched this new LD program, PwC consultants worked closely with the CEO and his senior leadership team to mentor leaders at many levels in the A&P organization and get them to adopt new behaviors and management practices. This transfer of skills and knowledge is often critical in cascading change down a management line and in sustaining change efforts over time. In A&P's case, it has proven critical in helping to establish and reinforce new leadership values among the entire A&P leadership population. Coaching and mentoring are essential elements for fostering optimal individual and team performance in organizations today. But seldom are they as necessary as when an organization is trying to build strong top team unity and embark on a new business strategy.

As part of PwC's ongoing work with A&P, we have encouraged top leaders to closely monitor people's behaviors and to track team members' effective behaviors as well as ineffective ones. We also recommended that senior leaders hold regular sessions for coaching and feedback with more junior level leaders to ensure that new behaviors are being sustained and to help junior-level leaders create development plans, when necessary, to improve their day-to-day work performance. This is a highly effective way for any organization to channel organizational energy toward realizing real and long-lasting changes in people's behavior after much of the formal work of introducing change has been completed. Today, the coaching-mentoring model of management has begun to take firm root in the A&P organizational culture and is serving to help continue the company's transformation toward full achievement of its business and customer goals.

Business Process Reengineering/IT

No large-gauge transformation change effort can be truly successful unless there are also supporting systems, tools, and technology in place to support it. Legacy systems, aging technology, and incongruities across A&P's supply chain had all prevented the organization from getting the right products to customers in the fastest time. Therefore, out of the leadership workshops came several reengineering and IT objectives to help speed A&P's transformation efforts. These included recommended redesigns of critical business processes and assessments of what kinds of enabling new technology would be needed to support processes and procedures in the future. A&P moved quickly to act on these recommendations by identifying and planning several "quick hit" redesign projects and conducting an IT assessment to chart out upgrades that would be needed down the line as transformation efforts continued.

How Much Progress Has Been Made?

How much progress has A&P made to date both with its team building and organizational transformation efforts? Since initiating its transformation efforts in April 1998, A&P's top leadership team has made significant progress in getting people connected to the transformation ahead and in creating a long-term future direction. The hard work still ahead lies in channeling energy into very focused, integrated initiatives that the company will pursue over the long term.

The signs of progress are evident. A&P's sales momentum continues to grow each quarter, and financial performance thus far is coming close to the target. Store modernization is on schedule, and the focus is on store growth in core markets. A&P is also gaining public confidence in its ability to change, and this perception is resulting in higher sales performance and a higher stock price for A&P shareholders. "Our change program is gaining high visibility in the external business community and within the company," notes Haub. "People were skeptical at the beginning, but the actions are visibly and physically demonstrating that this change is for real."

Appendix E

Leading an Organization at e-Speed: A PricewaterhouseCoopers Conversation With Audrey Weil, General Manager of CompuServe and Senior Vice President of America Online

Few companies do as much to exemplify the spirit and reality of today's new economy and e-business world as America Online (now AOL Time Warner). From its founding in 1985, the Virginia-based company has grown from fledgling online start-up into the world's preeminent leader in interactive services, Web brands, Internet technologies, and e-business services. It is a company that continues to grow and evolve at what can only be described as dizzying "e-speed." This growth recently culminated in a much-touted business marriage with traditional media giant Time Warner.

Today AOL is a family of brands consisting of two worldwide Internet services, America Online and CompuServe (a former rival of AOL, which it bought in 1998) and several leading Internet brands including AOL Instant Messenger, Digital City, Netscape (and related Netscape services), and others. Under chairman and CEO Steve Case, AOL has emerged as the world's first $4.7 billion multibrand, new media company.

Within the AOL family of brands, CompuServe is a company with a unique Internet history. Founded in 1969 as a computer time-sharing service, Columbus-based CompuServe was the first online service to offer email and technical support to PC users. CompuServe broke new ground again in 1980 as the first online service to offer real-time online chat to users. But like many industry trailblazers, CompuServe had faltered financially by the time AOL bought it in 1998. At the time, Case believed that despite its relatively small cadre of online fans, it had the potential to become a much larger, more mainstream Internet service provider (ISP). That belief has proved true.

By using marketing rebates and aggressive advertising, CompuServe has enjoyed a remarkable resurgence in membership growth since becoming part of AOL. The company ended the December 1999 quarter with a net addition of 440,000 new members, according to CompuServe general manager and AOL senior vice president Audrey Weil. That momentum is giving CompuServe the edge it needs to compete in the so-called "value" ISP space against such feisty competitors as Microsoft, Prodigy, and Earthlink, says Weil. It is also helping position the company as a "customer solutions provider" to various industries, including the legal and insurance professions, airlines, and companies like Wal-Mart and AAA.

Weil became general manager of CompuServe in 1999 and since then has led the company to new records in usage (currently 2.2 million members worldwide). She has also added new content and commercial partners like Discover Brokerage, *The New York Times,* CBS Sportsline, CBS MarketWatch, CNET, First USA, and others.

Recently, our colleague Richard Koonce caught up with Weil at AOL's Virginia headquarters to talk with her about how she has engineered CompuServe's business turnaround. In Weil's words, "managing a company at e-speed" entails an artful blend of communication, motivation, leadership, and strategy. It also requires a deft ability to take risks, while motivating people to work grueling hours without burning themselves out. Here are excerpts from that interview:

PwC: When you took over the helm at CompuServe in 1999, the company wasn't doing very well. Then AOL acquired it and it began to grow. What were the challenges you faced at the beginning and what did you do to bring the company from behind to where it is today?

Weil: When AOL bought CompuServe, we did a lot of research to figure out what the CompuServe brand was about and found that people knew the CompuServe brand. It had had over 20 years of advertising. So there was an unaided awareness nationally that CompuServe was an Internet brand, even if people didn't know a lot about what it stood for. What it did stand for, in the beginning, was "business and serious." And in a small way, too, not enough for the mainstream consumer. So, we said, "Let's figure out how to [develop] a growth strategy because we're in the Internet business, we're on Internet time, and we've got to get this brand moving."

One of our first challenges was to get the strategy set. We came up with a strategy that emphasized growth. Then we had to figure out what to do about the infrastructure of the company because CompuServe had been for sale for a while and was suffering from underinvestment. One of the empowering things that we got by working with AOL was the ability to reinvest savings that we identified above our business plan back into our business. So, we had a nice situation of being able to scrimp and save as a division [of AOL] and reinvest in our future. Thus, we reinvested aggressively in changing out the old infrastructure and adopting best-of-breed AOL technologies for speed and access. We made it easier for people to get connected and to sign on to CompuServe. This was necessary because CompuServe had originally prided itself on being a little bit difficult to use. But because we wanted to go after a larger market space, we needed an easier service for people to connect to.

Another challenge we faced had to do with how to deal with what I call CompuServe "classic members." That is, people that were members of the original CompuServe service. We wanted to keep those features that had made them happy, but still grow the company for the future. So today we operate two different CompuServe services: a CompuServe Classic service and CompuServe 2000 in the new infrastructure. They have a common look and feel, and both use an all HTML approach. But with CompuServe Classic we left intact things like how the email operates. Classic CompuServe members we found are comfortable with that. And migrating people from one base to another, in terms of a platform, is very difficult.[1]

PwC: Adopting a new strategy obviously required that people begin to work differently. What was the culture of the "old" CompuServe like, and what did you decide the new company culture needed to be?

Weil: The new culture had to be an Internet-oriented culture, which is one of very rapid change and innovation. So we talked with our HR team about key behaviors that we needed in the management team going forward and in every employee. One of the key things we needed was flexibility. So today, when I hire people, I spend a lot of time thinking about how flexible they can be. Because once we identify a task, I need people to focus and move, but I also need them to be

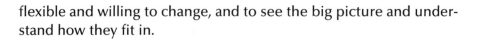

flexible and willing to change, and to see the big picture and understand how they fit in.

PwC: What other behaviors do you look for in new hires?

Weil: We also need people who understand the competitive landscape—
who can "think outside the building," as I put it, and who can con-
ceptualize about our industry and how it's developing. That's important because it's really easy at almost any company to get too
focused on what's right in front of you and not to think about what
you're trying to be.

PwC: When you came in, weren't there also some behaviors that you had
to eliminate? For example, CompuServe employees used to use a lot
of Microsoft Office technology on their desktops instead of
CompuServe technology, right? And you felt that had to change...

Weil: Oh yes. I noticed in the beginning, as I walked around the company,
that people's desktops were all Microsoft Office! They were using
Microsoft products all day long. And I said, "Our desktop *has* to be
our product. So, we're all going to change from using the Microsoft
mail system to using the CompuServe mail system." There was just a
huge uproar about that—major, major pains. But we moved, we
made the change, and now people look at CompuServe all day long;
they're in the service all day long, using it for all the things they need
to do on the Internet, and they're also living with our mail system.
And there's nothing like living with your own product to get you to
improve it because you know all the things that are issues with it, day
in and day out!

PwC: In the beginning, how did you align people's work behaviors to support the company's strategy and goals?

Weil: At first we did a lot of rethinking about our culture and said there
were key behaviors we needed to have in the organization. We said,
"Here's where we're going, here's the new mission, and we're going
to need everybody to move very rapidly from here to there." We set
out what I call "BHAGs"—big, hairy, audacious goals. We had a business plan but we also had a set of BHAGs that were above and
beyond the business plan. So people were really stretching and trying to move to the next level.

PwC: I'm fascinated that you talk about BHAGs, which, of course, Jim
Collins and Jerry Porras write about in their book, *Built to Last.* That

book looks at many long-time, blue chip companies and examines what has made them great, vision being a key thing. In CompuServe's case, you adapted the idea of BHAGs and applied them to transforming an Internet company. What kinds of BHAGs did you and your employees come up with early on?

Weil: Well, our number one metric is growing our member base. We had a business plan that was pretty modest for member base growth because we weren't sure how we were going to get there. So, we also put together a BHAG that was to get to a much higher number—"dramatically higher member growth"—and that was something we set out to do. We said, "Let's try to do this as a team" because I think people need to shoot for the stars, and that was something pretty new to the organization and pretty energizing.

We also focused on member retention. You know our business is pretty simple: We need to grow the membership, and we need to keep the members we get. And member retention is something that's very much a focus in Columbus because we're delivering a service every day. We can put up a link or a new page and find out immediately how many people are clicking on which parts of that page. We know immediately whether members like it or not. So we get great feedback, and we can turn that into immediate and constant improvement.

PwC: What other issues did you face when you came aboard CompuServe as general manager?

Weil: One of the other big issues in the transition was that we needed to build trust. We were new owners [in 1998]. I was new to the team. I inherited a lot of existing CompuServe management, and so we needed to rebuild their trust in the new management. So, we spent a lot of time focused on communications. Every four to six weeks we had a company meeting, all hands, where we said, "Now, here's the strategy. Here's what we promised. We were going to do these six things. Here's how we're progressing along these objectives, and here's how we're doing."

We tried to chop up the mission into small milestones and celebrate every piece of success along the way so that people felt good about where we were going. We needed to do that because there was a fair amount of "figuring it out," as we went along, and we needed to make it a very open process with employees. So, we'd say, "We're going to try these 10 things. They won't all work, but we're not going to try them in serial or we won't get there. We're going to try them in parallel. It may be a little confusing at first because it'll look like we're trying a lot of strategies, but really we're going to test everything and then continue on with the ones that worked."

We tried some things that didn't work. CompuServe had a long history of selling premium services, premium databases. So we said, "Well, maybe there's some money there. Let's see what we can do." We put a team together, focused on it for three months, but it really just didn't make any progress at all. So we cut that and moved on to the next thing. It was important for people to see and to understand that we were trying things, experimenting, but also to see progress and to understand what we were doing.

Finally, we celebrated individual team members and what their accomplishments were because we needed a lot of teamwork, and we needed people to focus and deliver and to work overtime. We were looking for people to go that extra mile.

PwC: As you created the new CompuServe culture and aligned the organization to support it, how did you reach out and incorporate levels of leaders beyond you and your immediate leadership team?

Weil: Below the executive level of the company, we did a number of things. First, we cascaded goals. I put together the company goals, and then we cascaded them to the vice presidents who were running the individual divisions. Initially, I *also* read the goals of every person in the company (500 employees) because I wanted to make sure that each person had a mission at 8 o'clock every Monday morning, and knew what they were going to do. Today, we review our goals every 90 days and measure our progress against those goals on a continuous basis.

The other thing we did was to leverage the infrastructure back at AOL, as I mentioned earlier, and that's one of the big reasons for our success as a division and for that of other AOL organizations. We've been able to leverage technology [and other] good knowledge from AOL and build on the skills we have out in Columbus. That's been important because the transition demanded that our employees learn a new set of skills. Being part of a matrix organization (like AOL) is very different from anything they'd done before.

PwC: One of the skills you've noted that CompuServe needs to possess — and that its people need to have — is the ability to stay closely connected with customers. You said earlier that as an Internet company,

CompuServe has unique ways to get immediate feedback from customers. Talk about other ways you stay in touch with customers, and why this is so important to CompuServe's (and AOL's) future.

Weil: We use classical research, as well as unique Internet research, to figure out what our members want and how to target our products appropriately. We do unaided brand awareness just to figure out where our brand is at any given time. We do a lot of phone surveys, and we do online research; we will do online polls and surveys to find out what members think. We actually do some online focus groups, talk to members directly. We do a lot of usability testing too, where we bring in members and ask them to do things with our products.

All that research is important because we can get so close to the product that we may think it's always easy to use, but the next 10 million people who are coming on the Internet really can't tell the difference between a computer mouse and a TV remote. So, we've got to make sure we continue to communicate with the next generation of consumers *all* the time.

PwC: You've described many of the challenges of leading a company through rapid change—especially in the era of e-business. What in your mind are the challenges that lie ahead for you personally as a change leader and also for AOL/CompuServe?

Weil: Well, being on Internet time is a challenge for any company. Thus, I have learned that, for us, "communication is core." I think when people hear a new message, for example, it takes awhile for them to *hear* it, to *understand* it, to *absorb* it, and then to *act* on it. Without careful communication and multilevel communication, therefore, messages may not get across to people. There is a way to communicate through cascading and a way to communicate directly, and you have to have a mix of both in order to be really successful. One thing that has helped us [with the transformation process] is electronic mail and instant messaging. They enhance your ability to communicate with people rapidly and do things simultaneously to many levels at once. Instant messaging is probably the best innovation, the best application I've seen AOL come up with since I've worked here. The rapid flow of information inside this company means that we are moving—changing—all the time. It's very exciting, but it also feels a lot like you're riding down the highway on a motorcycle with your hair on fire all of the time. Employees need to understand that that's the environment we're in, and we're always going to be in that kind of rapidly changing environment. So, one of my leadership challenges is to make sure people don't burn out. You never get everything done on your to-do list. So, you've always got to be reprioritizing to keep on top of things. Because at the end of the day, we're in a marathon, not a sprint.

---

[1] AOL made a conscious decision when it acquired CompuServe not to sunset any of the client versions of the product that long-standing CompuServe members had been using for years. However, the company has utilized AOL's dial-up network, technologies, email system, and instant messaging in the latest client version, CompuServe 2000.

References

AlliedSignal. 1997. Annual Report.

American Society for Training & Development. (1998). *National HRD Executive Survey: Leadership Development, 1998 First Quarter Survey Report.* Alexandria: Author.

Anonymous. (1998, July 29). "A Question of the Right Mindset." *Financial Times.*

Anonymous. (1999, November 3). "Black Marks and Spencer." *The Economist,* 66.

Argyris, C. (1962). *Interpersonal Competence and Organizational Effectiveness.* Homewood, IL: Irwin-Dorsey.

Barborek, S., and J. Brown. (1999, August). "Skillful Inventory." *Bank Marketing,* 16.

Barner, R. (2000, March). "Five Steps to Leadership Competencies." *Training & Development,* 48.

Bauman, R., (1998, November 23). Interview by R. Koonce. London: PricewaterhouseCoopers.

Bellman, G.M. (1990). *The Consultant's Calling: Bringing Who You Are to What You Do.* San Francisco: Jossey-Bass.

Benimadhu, P. (1999, June). "Whither Leadership." *The INSIDEDGE (Conference Board of Canada),* 3(4), 6.

Bentz, V.J. (1990). "Contextual Issues in Predicting High-Level Leadership Performance: Contextual Richness as a Criterion Consideration in Personality Research With Executives." In *Measures of Leadership,* K.E. Clark & M.B. Clark, editors. West Orange, NJ: Leadership Library of America.

Blakeslee, J. (1999, July). "Implementing the Six Sigma Solution." *Quality Progress,* 77–84.

Bolman, L., and T. Deal. (1991). *Reframing Organizations: Artistry, Choice and Leadership.* San Francisco: Jossey-Bass.

Bray, W.B. and A. Howard. (1983). "The AT&T Longitudinal Studies of Managers." In *Longitudinal Studies of Adult Psychological Development,* K.W. Schaie, editor. New York, OR: Guilford.

Brown, E. (1999, March 1). "America's Most Admired Companies." *Fortune,* 139.

Burke, W.W., and W. Trahant with R. Koonce. (2000). *Business Climate Shifts: Profiles of Change Makers.* Woburn, MA: Butterworth-Heinemann.

Byrne, J.A. (1998, June 8). "A Close-Up Look at How America's No. 1 Manager Runs GE." *BusinessWeek.*

Catalyst. (2000, January 6). "2000 Catalyst Award Winners Focus on Corporate Culture Change." www.catalystwomen.org.

Charan, R., and G. Colvin. (1999, June 21). "Why CEOs Fail." *Fortune, 139*(12), 68.

Clarke, J., and R. Koonce. (1995, November). "Meetings Go High-Tech." *Training & Development,* 32.

Cohen, E., and N. Tichy. (1998, July). "The Teaching Organization." *Training & Development,* 26–33.

Collins, J. (2000). Personal communication.

Collins, J., and J. Porras. (1996, September–October). "Building Your Company's Vision." *Harvard Business Review,* 68–69.

Collins, J., and J. Porras. (1997). *Built to Last: Successful Habits of Visionary Companies* New York: HarperBusiness.

Conger, J.A. (1992). *Learning to Lead.* San Francisco: Jossey-Bass.

Conner, D. (1993). *Managing at the Speed of Change: How Resilient Managers Succeed and Prosper Where Others Fail.* New York: Villiard Books.

Cooper, B.K., and S. Ayman. (1997). *Executive EQ: Emotional Intelligence in Leadership and Organizations.* New York: Perigee.

Covey, S.R. (1990). *Principle-Centered Leadership.* New York: Simon & Schuster.

Dauphinais, G.W., G. Means, and C. Price. (2000). *Wisdom of the CEO: 29 Global Leaders Tackle Today's Most Pressing Business Challenges.* New York: John Wiley & Sons.

Deci, E.L., and R.M. Ryan. (1985). *Intrinsic Motivation and Self-Determination in Human Behavior.* New York: Plenum.

Densford, L. (1996a, November–December). "Companies Are Revamping Management Development." *The Corporate University Review,* 10–11.

Densford, L. (1996b, May–June). "At Disney, Education Underpins Excellence." *The Corporate University Review,* 14–21.

Densford, L. (1997, March–April). "Jack Zenger, One of Training's Strongest Voices, Says the Best Days Are Yet to Come." *The Corporate University Review,* 14, 15, 51.

Diversity/Careers in Engineering & Information Technology. (2000a, August–September). "EDS Reinvents Its Diversity Programs." www.diversity-careers.com.

Diversity/Careers in Engineering & Information Technology. (2000b, August–September). "Hoffmann La Roche Wants People With a Passion." www.diversitycareers.com.

Drucker Foundation. (1996). *The Leader of the Future.* San Francisco: Jossey-Bass.

Edmonds, L. (2000, September 15). Interview by R. Koonce. Vienna, VA: PricewaterhouseCoopers.

Eisenhart, K.M., J.L. Kahway, and L.J. Bourgeois III. (1997, July–August). "How Management Teams have a Good Fight." *Harvard Business Review,* 77–85.

Essex, L., and M. Kusy. (1999). *Fast Forward Leadership.* Harlow, United Kingdom: Financial Times/Prentice-Hall.

Fulmer, R. (1997, Spring). "The Evolving Paradigm of Leadership Development." *Organizational Dynamics,* 4.

Garvey, J. (1999, February 5). Interview by R. Koonce. Washington, DC: PricewaterhouseCoopers.

General Electric. (2000). "GE Crotonville: Leadership Development Center." www.ge.com.

General Electric. 1997. Annual Report.

General Electric. 1998. Annual Report.

Goleman, D. (1998). *Working With Emotional Intelligence.* New York: Bantam.

Griffin, L. (1998, December 7). Interview by R. Koonce. Baton Rouge, LA: PricewaterhouseCoopers.

Grossman, R. (February 1, 1999). "Heirs Unapparent." *HR Magazine,* 36.

Gubman, E.L. (1998). *The Talent Solution.* New York: McGraw-Hill.

Hamel, G. and C.K. Prahalad. (1994). *Competing for the Future: Breakthrough Strategies for Seizing Control of Your Industry and Creating The Markets of Tomorrow.* Cambridge, MA: Harvard Business School Press.

Harry, M.J. (1988). *The Nature of Six Sigma Quality.* Rolling Meadows, IL: Motorola University Press.

Heller, R. (February 1, 1999). *Management Today,* 23.

Hogan, R.H., G.J. Curphy, and J. Hogan. (1994). "What We Know about Leadership: Effectiveness and Personality." *American Psychologist, 49,* 493–504.

Hunter, D., and B. Schmitt. (1999, October 6). "Six Sigma, Benefits and Approaches." *Chemical Week.*

Katzenbach, J., and D. Smith. (1994). *The Wisdom of Teams: Creating the High-Performance Organization.* New York: HarperBusiness.

Katzenbach, J., RCL Team, F. Beckett, and C. Gagnon. (1995). *Real Change Leaders: How You Can Create Growth and High Performance at Your Company.* New York: Random House.

Katzenbach, J.R. (1997, November–December). "The Myth of the Top Management Team." *Harvard Business Review.*

Kelman, H.C. (1974). "Further Thoughts on the Processes of Compliance, Identification, and Internalization." In *Perspectives on Social Power,* J.T. Tedeschi, editor. Washington, DC: American Psychological Association.

Kiernan, M. (1996). *The Eleven Commandments of 21st Century Management.* Englewood Cliffs NJ: Prentice Hall.

Koonce, R. (1996, October). "Fostering Better Communications at Work." *Training & Development,* 14.

Koonce, R. (1998, November–December). "Where Technology and Training Meet," *Technical Training,* 10.

Kotter, J.P. (1996). *Leading Change.* Boston: Harvard Business Press.

Kuczmarski, S.S., and T.D. Kuczmarski. (1995). *Values-based Leadership: Rebuilding Employee Commitment, Performance, and Productivity.* Paramus, NJ: Prentice-Hall.

Lao-Tzu. (no year). In *Tao De Ching: A New English Version,* (1988). S. Mitchel, translator. New York: Harper & Row.

Levine, R., C. Locke, D. Searls, and D. Weinberger. (2000). *The Cluetrain Manifesto: The End of Business as Usual.* Cambridge, MA: Perseus Publishing.

Maraniss, D. (1999). *When Pride Still Mattered: A Life of Vince Lombardi.* New York: Simon & Schuster

Marquardt, M.J., and R. Revans. (1999). *Action Learning in Action: Transforming Problems and People for World-Class Organizational Learning.* Palo Alto, CA: Davies-Black Publishing.

Marshall, E. (1998, December 12). Interview by R. Koonce. London: PricewaterhouseCoopers.

McDonald, M. (1998, September 23). Interview by R Koonce. The Hague: PricewaterhouseCoopers.

McLean, B. (1999, November 8). "Merging at Internet Speed." *Fortune,* 164.

Meister, J. (1998). *Corporate Universities, Lessons in Building a World-Class Work Force.* New York: McGraw-Hill.

Meister, J. (1999). "Executive Summary: Survey of Corporate University Future Directions." *The Corporate University Xchange of Corporate University Directions,* 10–20.

Moeller, M., and V. Murphy. (1999, November 29). "Outta Here at Microsoft: The Software Giant Is Losing Key Talent to the Internet. *BusinessWeek.*

Nadler, D., with M. Nadler. (1998). *Champions of Change.* San Francisco: Jossey-Bass.

O'Toole, J. (1995). *Leading Change.* San Francisco: Jossey-Bass.

O'Toole, J. (1999). *Leadership A to Z.* San Francisco: Jossey-Bass.

Peters, T., and R. Waterman. (1982). *In Search of Excellence.* New York: Warner Books.

Poses, F. (1999, January 19). Interview by R. Koonce. Morristown, NJ: PricewaterhouseCoopers.

Ramelli, D. (1999, January 19). Interview by R. Koonce. Morristown, NJ: PricewaterhouseCoopers.

Rhinesmith, S. (1996). *A Manager's Guide to Globalization.* Chicago: Irwin Publishing.

Senge, Peter M. (1990, Fall). "The Leader's New Work: Building Learning Organizations." *Sloan Management Review, 32,*(1).

Smith, E. (1995, November–December 1995). "At GE, Management Development Is a Continuous Process." *The Corporate University Review, 1.*

Taylor, W. (1999, June). "The Leader of the Future." *Fast Company.*

Thomson, T. (1999, Summer). "The Dynamics of Introducing Performance Metrics Into an Organization." *National Productivity Review,* 51–55.

Tichy, N., and S. Sherman. (1994). *Control Your Destiny or Someone Else Will.* New York: HarperBusiness.

Tichy, N., with E. Cohen. (1997). *The Leadership Engine: How Winning Companies Build Leaders at Every Level.* New York: HarperBusiness.

Vander Linde, K., N. Horney, and R. Koonce. (1997, August). "Seven Ways to Make Your Training Department One of the Finest," *Training & Development,* 20.

Weil, A. (2000, February 8). Interview by R. Koonce. Dulles, VA: PricewaterhouseCoopers.

Wetlaufer, S. (1999, March–April). "Driving Change: An Interview With Ford Motor Company's Jacques Nasser." *Harvard Business Review.*

Wharton School of the University of Pennsylvania. (2000). Executive Development Program. www.wharton.upenn.edu.

Zalesnik, A. (1977). "Managers and Leaders: Are they Different?" *Harvard Business Review, 15,* 67–84.

Additional Resources

Bennis, W. (1989, April). "Why Leaders Can't Lead." *Training & Development*.

Burke, W.W., and G.H. Litwin. (2000). "A Causal Model of Organizational Performance and Change." In *Business Climate Shifts: Profiles of Change Makers*, by W.W. Burke and W. Trahant with R. Koonce. Woburn, MA: Butterworth-Heinemann.

Cherniss, C., and M. Adler. (2000). *Promoting Emotional Intelligence in Organizations*. Alexandria, VA: American Society for Training & Development.

Cohen, E., and N. Tichy. (1997, May). "How Leaders Develop Leaders." *Training & Development*.

Harry, M., and R. Schroeder. (2000). *Six Sigma: The Breakthrough Management Strategy Revolutionizing the World's Top Corporations*. New York: Doubleday.

Koonce, R. (1994). *Career Power: 12 Habits to Get You From Where You Are to Where You Want to Be*. New York: AMACOM.

Koonce, R. (1998, February). "How to Prevent Professional Obsolescence." *Training & Development*.

Koonce, R. (1999, January–February) "Standup Trainer to Standout Facilitator; How to Make the Transition." *Technical Training*.

Slater, D. (1999, November 15). "Alignment Check." *CIO Magazine*.

Sood, S. (1997, October). "Sears, Roebuck and Co." *Stanford University Graduate School of Business Magazine*.

Sull, D. (1990, July–August). "Why Good Companies Go Bad." *Harvard Business Review*.

Acknowledgments

Like leadership, writing a book is "never a solo act." It always depends on the goodwill, creativity, and expertise of many people working together as a team to create a finished work that is more than the sum of its parts. When you are writing a book such as *Growing Leaders,* that is especially true, because handbooks like this are invariably a compendium of different people's experiences woven together into a single narrative.

The subject of leadership is a rich and evolving field of study; change practitioners, consultants, and their clients learn more each day. Therefore, we first thank the PwC clients whose leadership stories we were permitted to share in this book, including those of British Airways, SmithKline Beecham, BAE Systems, Shell South Africa, the Federal Aviation Administration, General Electric, Honeywell, Bank One of Louisiana, Royal Dutch Shell, and A&P.

Second, we recognize and thank our PwC colleagues and friends, many of whom played a significant part in this book's creation by sharing their ideas, client experiences, and writing talents at various times in the manuscript development process. In particular we gratefully acknowledge the following contributors:

- ❀ Gregg Gullickson, whose insightful contributions to chapter 3: "What to Do When Your Company Suffers from Poor Vision," derived from his enormous experience working with organizations as they have struggled with this issue. This chapter reflects his deep knowledge of the visioning process and all that is involved.

- ❀ Aaron Desmet, who plumbed the depth of his experience in the area of 360-degree assessments for chapter 4: "How to Create

Positive, Consistent Leadership Behaviors in Your Organization." This chapter contains much of the critical instrumentation we think can help you create more effective leaders in your organization.

❁ Tim Phillips, a London-based colleague, whose rich experience working with organizations as they have dealt with leadership development and succession planning challenges proved essential to the development of chapter 5: "How to Develop Your Company's Talent Pool and Pipeline." Chapter 5 is essential to any organization trying to identify its emerging leadership requirements as well as leadership skill gaps that currently may be hindering its business performance.

❁ Suzanne Maxwell shared her insights about how organizations can create strong leadership competencies. We are indebted to Suzanne for the material in chapter 6: "How to Create a Powerful Development Architecture." This chapter provides a detailed overview of different learning approaches your organization can use to design powerful leadership development programs for current and future leaders.

❁ Dick Smith, Tim Voight, and Jerry Blakeslee contributed the fruits of their hard work for chapter 7: "Creating Strong Organizational Alignment in Your Organization." Helping organizations deal with alignment issues is particularly tough, and Dick, Tim, and Jerry brought a rich knowledge and understanding of Six Sigma, performance management, and other alignment tools to the development of this critical chapter.

❁ Celeste A. Coruzzi, Ph.D., and Diane Hamilton contributed the breakthrough ideas for chapter 8: "Building Top Leadership Team Unity." This chapter offers a unique view of how you and your organization can forge strong top leadership team unity by harnessing the principles of "organizational thermodynamics" to create strong leadership focus.

❁ Wayne Lewis, a London-based colleague, injected humor and hard work into chapter 9: "How to Initiate and Sustain Continuous Change." As one who has worked with senior leaders on the front lines of change for years, Wayne brings to his daily consulting work a deep knowledge not only of organizational dynamics but also of human nature, both of which are clearly evident in Chapter 9.

✿ Yvette Robinson and Amy Blumhof provided rich narratives of their ideas about the future of leadership development in chapter 10: "Emerging Trends in Leadership Development." They provide an important overview of the new approaches to leadership development—from high tech to high touch—that your organization may want to consider implementing as part of addressing leadership skill gaps or other leadership effectiveness issues.

✿ Karen Vander Linde, a PwC partner and member of the board of directors of ASTD, drew from her wealth of experience facilitating leadership development programs worldwide, most notably for Amtrak. Her insightful ideas about the emerging role of leadership coaches in organizations today make chapter 11: "From Traditional Trainer to Consultant and Coach" rich reading indeed.

We are also indebted to Christian Haub, president and CEO of the Great Atlantic and Pacific Company (A&P) and other executives of the 140-year grocery store chain, who permitted us to share how A&P is systematically rebuilding its top leadership team using these principles (appendix D). We express our gratitude to Audrey Weil, senior vice president of America Online and her colleagues Kathy Bushkin and Anne Bentley for providing us with a compelling case study for appendix E, the story of how AOL has successfully integrated CompuServe (its former Internet rival) into the AOL "family of brands."

Bill Trahant and Julia Collins (both of PricewaterhouseCoopers) and Warner Burke, Ph.D., of Teachers College, Columbia University, made significant contributions of thought leadership to this book's development, most notably in chapters 3 and 9.

There are still other PwC colleagues, consultants, and staff whose behind-the-scenes roles were essential to producing *Growing Leaders*. David Cosloy, a consultant in PwC's Arlington, Virginia, office, was of invaluable professional assistance to us in conducting research, refining the manuscript, developing material for the chapter sidebars, reworking chapter drafts, creating chapter graphics, and working with chapter contributors. Also deserving of mention are Carole Cimitile for her contributions to chapter 2 and to the creative designers in PwC's Arlington, Virginia, graphics department including Scott Upright for his work on book images, Matt Jacobs for his work on the book's cover design, and Shelly Neil for her coordination support. Other PwC staff we wish to thank include Dawn Edmiston, Shirley Cauffman, Robin Masinter, and Bertha Ballard.

Still others we wish to acknowledge for their contributions to this book include Christopher Nickerson, Michael Bazigos, Martin Costa, Steve Towers, Matthew Costagliola, Michael Simpson, Andrew Simpson, Ricardo James, Doug Eldridge, Cindy Karasick, Richard Davis, William Wiseman, Kim Albataew, Christa Hart, Kari LePage, Shantha Farris, Amy Federman, Liora Brener, Peter Lustiber, Jay Owen, Patricia Hastings, Michelle Renbaum, Michael Mead, Kerry Baker, Justin Bakule, Drew Riegler, John Roegiers, Dave Pelto, Garry Birkhofer, Lynn Gonsor Anvari, Mark Lorenz, David Krause, Jon Madorsky, Ed Shumaker, Cynthia Anderson, Carey Epstein, and Rachel Finlay.

Finally, we gratefully acknowledge the significant work of our colleague and collaborator Richard Koonce who sculpted this book into its final form. Rick was responsible for the book's overall organization and format and for blending the voices of many into one. The author (or co-author) of two previous books, *Business Climate Shifts: Profiles of Change Makers* (Butterworth-Heinemann, 2000) and *CAREER POWER!* (AMACOM, 1994), Rick is a former public radio commentator and a member of the editorial board of ASTD's publication *Training & Development*. His consulting background and journalistic expertise proved essential in making this book the accessible and reader-friendly handbook to leadership development that it is today.

The Authors

About the Authors

Stephen L. Yearout

Steve Yearout is a partner with PwC in Arlington, Virginia. He is a key member of the firm's global organization and change strategy practice and leads the development and refinement of the firm's methodologies, thought leadership activities, and strategic business alliances for managing complex organizational change.

In the course of a 28-year career, 15 of which have been in consulting, Steve has managed or participated in a wide range of engagements involving organizational analysis and assessment, process improvement, process redesign, benchmarking and best practices, and leadership development. He has worked across numerous industry sectors, including government, consumer and industrial products, financial services, insurance, health care, utilities, and energy industries. His clients have included the U.S. Air Force, Pratt & Whitney Aircraft, Carrier Corporation, Kraft USA, Blue Cross and Blue Shield of Ohio, Armco, Pennsylvania Power and Light Company, Prudential, Public Services Electric and Gas, Delmarva Power, Sundstrand Aerospace, Deere & Company, GE Capital, Royal Dutch/ Shell, and Harris Corp.

A member of the Malcolm Baldrige National Quality Awards Board of Examiners, Steve serves as the director of PwC's Center for Advanced

Studies in Transformational Change in conjunction with Noel Tichy of the University of Michigan. Steve is a graduate of Miami University where he earned a bachelor's degree of science in systems analysis. He earned a master's degree of business administration at Xavier University. He can be reached at steve.yearout@us.pwcglobal.com.

Gerry Miles

Gerry Miles has more than 25 years' experience in change and human resource management and was formerly a director in PwC's London-based organization and change strategy practice. As an expert in helping companies develop their leadership capabilities, he regularly works with top corporate and organizational teams and has coached many senior executives on how to effectively plan, implement, and lead successful change programs.

Gerry has consulted to many blue chip companies over the years in a range of industry sectors including aerospace, manufacturing, retail, telecommunications, aviation, consumer goods, financial services, and energy. His most recent clients include Barclay's Bank, British Aerospace (now BAE Systems), British Airways, Cable & Wireless, and Marks & Spencer. During that time, he has developed a special interest and expertise in helping to foster creativity and innovation in client-consultant teams.

Before joining PwC, Gerry spent 14 years with British Petroleum, working in the areas of recruitment, employee development, employee relations, compensation and benefits, and general administration. He holds a bachelor's degree of arts in business studies and is a fellow of the U.K.-based Institute of Personnel & Development. He is a regular contributor to PwC books on change management and organizational transformation. Gerry can be contacted at g.miles@totalise.co.uk.

Richard Koonce

Richard Koonce is an accomplished interviewer, radio commentator, author, and business consultant who is the author or co-author of two previous books, *Business Climate Shifts: Profiles of Change Makers* (with W. Warner Burke and William Trahant) and *Career Power! 12 Winning Habits to Get You From Where You Are to Where You Want to Be.* A former broadcast journalist and contributing commentator to Public Radio's "Marketplace" Program, Rick has interviewed many business and public figures over the years, ranging from CEOs and celebrities to authors and U.S. presidents.

Besides his work as a writer and interviewer, Rick is also a consultant to PwC and a nationally known expert on job and workplace trends. He has been interviewed on job and workplace issues by *The Wall Street Journal, The New York Times, Money* magazine, *U.S. News and World Report, USA Today,* ABCNEWS radio, the *The Washington Post, Glamour,* and *Working Woman,* among others. He can be contacted at RHKOONCE@aol.com.